Holland and the Dutch Republic
in the Seventeenth Century

HOLLAND
and the
DUTCH REPUBLIC
in the
Seventeenth Century

The Politics of Particularism

J. L. PRICE

CLARENDON PRESS · OXFORD

Oxford University Press, Walton Street, Oxford OX2 6DP

Oxford New York

Athens Auckland Bangkok Bombay
Calcutta Cape Town Dar es Salaam Delhi
Florence Hong Kong Istanbul Karachi
Kuala Lumpur Madras Madrid Melbourne
Mexico City Nairobi Paris Singapore
Taipei Tokyo Toronto

and associated companies in
Berlin Ibadan

Oxford is a trade mark of Oxford University Press

Published in the United States
by Oxford University Press Inc., New York

© J. L. Price 1994

First published 1994

British Library Cataloguing in Publication Data

Data available

ISBN 0–19–820383–7

Library of Congress Cataloging in Publication Data
Price, J. L.
Holland and the Dutch Republic in the seventeenth century: the
politics of particularism / J. L. Price.
p. cm.
Includes bibliographical references and index.
1. Holland (Netherlands: Province)—History. 2. Holland
(Netherlands: Province)—Politics and government. 3. Netherlands
History—Wars of Independence, 1556–1648. 4. Netherlands—Politics
and government—15563112–4
ISBN 0–19–873113–21648. 5. Netherlands—Politics and
government—1648–1795. I. Title.
DJ401.H6P75 1994
949.2'3—dc 20 93–27130
ISBN 0–19–820383–7

3 5 7 9 10 8 6 4

Printed in Great Britain
on acid-free paper by
Ipswich Book Co. Ltd, Suffolk

PREFACE

In a study of this kind, the author is necessarily dependent to a great extent on the work of previous scholars, and this debt is only partly acknowledged in the references and bibliography. One scholar in this field has stood out in recent decades, and I should like to take this opportunity to make clear my awareness of how much I have learnt over the years from the late Professor D. J. Roorda despite, or perhaps even because of, the fact that we were often in, I hope, amicable disagreement.

I should like to thank the members of the Dutch History seminar at the Institute of Historical Research and of the History seminar at the University of Hull for the comments and encouragement they gave in response to earlier versions of sections of this book. In particular, I wish to express my gratitude for the help and advice of Professor Jonathan Israel, and to my friend and colleague Louis Billington who read the whole of a draft version of this work, and advised me on its intelligibility for those not quite as immersed in Dutch history as myself.

J. L. Price

September 1992

CONTENTS

Introduction

The economic and political importance of the Dutch Republic in seventeenth-century Europe is evident, but while the Dutch economy has received considerable attention in recent years the same cannot be said for its political system. This is perhaps hardly surprising as, while the Dutch economy had an enormous impact on Europe, and indeed the world, at this time, and inspired almost universal admiration and envy, their political system was regarded by foreign contemporaries as something of a shambles and it has not fared much better at the hands of later historians. It is also notable that, while there has been a welter of modern studies on various aspects of absolutism, the republican polities of early modern Europe have suffered relative neglect, and this is certainly true of the Dutch state. There is no adequate treatment of the political process in the Republic in English at all, and even in Dutch the only modern general study, though excellent, is brief[1] and the standard text remains that of Fruin, a classic, but firmly rooted in the nineteenth century and with a number of other serious drawbacks.[2] Moreover, both these works are largely concerned with the formal political system, being essentially examples of traditional constitutional history, and this method has very serious limitations as far as the Dutch seventeenth century is concerned. A rather different approach is needed to understand how Dutch politics actually worked.

The present study approaches the task of re-interpreting the politics of the Republic in the years of its greatness in three main ways. First, and conventionally, the centre of attention is the province of Holland as by far the most important member of the Union, but its role in the government of the Republic and particularly the practical problems which arose in its relations with the other provinces are also seen as central issues. Secondly, and less

[1] S. J. Fockema Andreae, *De Nederlandse staat onder de Republiek* (Amsterdam, 1961).
[2] R. Fruin, *Geschiedenis der staatsinstellingen in Nederland*, ed. H. T. Colenbrander (The Hague, 1901).

usually, the political process is looked at from the ground up, which seems more appropriate to such a decentralized system than a conventional top-down approach. Thirdly, attention is focused not on the formal and constitutional aspects of the system, but on how it worked in practice, which was often quite a different matter. The structure of the book reflects these aims: starting with the roots of political power in the towns of Holland, then turning to the way decisions were made, and the influences affecting political action, at the provincial level in Holland, and finally dealing with the part this province played in the politics of the Union as a whole.

This is primarily a study of Holland, its politics, and its relations with the central government of the Republic, and so the internal politics of the other provinces, and the relationships between these provinces individually and Holland, have had to be, regretfully, neglected. If such an approach brings down on the author the charge of Hollandocentrism, so be it. Holland had a unique role in the Republic, being by far the wealthiest and most populous province, and an understanding of its internal politics and the way in which it acted in the Republic as a whole are among the most important issues confronting the historian of this state. Equally, however, if the historian needs to know about Holland in order to comprehend the Republic, Holland's actions can only be properly understood when taken in the context of its relations with the other provinces and with the princes of Orange. The tendency to conflate the province with the Republic, and to forget that there were six other provinces, so evident in both contemporary and later linguistic usage, also leads to serious misunderstandings.

Starting with the towns is not a stylistic device but a consequence of the nature of political authority in this state: the far-reaching particularism of this polity can be best regarded not as a result of the devolution of powers from the centre or top to the local level, but rather as a reflection of the fact that the basic location of such authority was at the local level, with only certain and strictly limited powers being granted to provincial and central government. While it makes sense in more conventional polities to start at the top, with monarch and central government, and work down, it makes much more sense in the Dutch system of this period to start at the bottom and work up. This approach also helps to make it clear that particularism was not just a matter of provincial autonomy *vis-à-vis* central government, but that provincial government in Holland, as in the other provinces, was itself the projection of a more fundamental level of political authority at the level of the towns.

The way in which a political system works is only partly described by its formal or constitutional aspects, and this is particularly true for the Dutch Republic. Indeed, it is only a slight exaggeration to say that the official Dutch system was literally unworkable, and that what really ran the state was an informal system, or rather systems, which underlay and to some extent subverted the formal constitution. The Republic could be governed through the power of the States of Holland or by the authority of the prince of Orange, but neither case can be adequately explained in terms of constitutional law. Moreover, just as conventional constitutional history alone cannot provide a proper understanding of past politics, neither can political history in its narrow sense. So this study tries to place seventeenth-century Dutch politics in its context, and to show the way in which it was fundamentally affected by the economic, social, and cultural conditions of the time. Such an approach is particularly enlightening in the case of the towns of Holland, and an understanding of what was happening at this level is vital, it is argued, for the interpretation of politics in the Republic as a whole.

The central argument of this study is that this political system worked remarkably well in practice—certainly by contemporary standards—and that it did so not despite its extreme decentralization of effective power but because of it. Those aspects of the Dutch political system most historians have seen as its chief weaknesses should be better seen as its strength, as they reflected contemporary realities. Primary political loyalty was to the town or local area—as it was probably throughout Europe—and the sense of common identity as subjects of the same state, let alone members of the same nation, was relatively weak. The Dutch political system worked with this grain rather than against it, and although this created problems of leadership and central direction, it was also a source of fundamental stability.

The seventeenth century, for the purposes of this study, extends from the late 1580s—the appointment of Oldenbarnevelt as *Advocaat van den Lande* and the final departure of the earl of

Leicester from the Netherlands—to, rather more conventionally, the death of Willem III. The justification for the starting point is that it was only after the failure of Leicester that the Advocate, by working with what was to hand rather than pursuing an ideal, was able to turn the Republic into a workable state. The Republic as it existed in the seventeenth century was to a large extent the creation of the first years of Oldenbarnevelt's leadership of the Republic. The final date is less easy to justify, as there is no distinct caesura in Dutch political life in the early eighteenth century, but it seems clear that significant developments began to take place during the long second stadhouderless period, and so it seemed sensible to stop before this time of possibly fundamental change.

Although partly based on my own research, a study of this nature has necessarily to rely to a very large extent on the existing secondary literature and printed sources, and consequently there are large—and sometimes alarming—gaps in the evidence. Ideally, perhaps, much more research should have been done before starting to write, but one has to stop somewhere. What follows is a provisional sketch towards an interpretation and cannot hope to be definitive. If I say that my chief aim is to stimulate others to challenge my interpretations and suggestions, then on this occasion at least this modest claim, while not entirely true, is far from being a mere conventional formulation.

I

Town Politics in the Province of Holland

The political dominance of the towns within Holland was a consequence of the Revolt of the Netherlands, but was established on the basis of a position which was already strong. Indeed, to a significant extent it was the strength of the towns which made the success of the Revolt possible, though not certain. The importance of the role played by the towns of Holland in the Revolt has to some extent been obscured by uncertainty among historians as to what the Revolt was and when it began. The traditional date of 1568 for the beginning of the Eighty Years War between the Spanish and the Dutch has lost much of its significance as a result of the emphasis in modern studies on earlier events, especially the opposition of both the higher and the lesser nobility to the policies of the Spanish government in the Netherlands in the early 1560s. However, this is the revolt of the Netherlands that failed, and failed repeatedly: the opposition movement led by the nobility crashed to ignominious defeat in the aftermath of the iconoclastic riots of 1566; the invasions organized by Willem of Orange in 1568 also failed; and the similar military incursions of 1572 were beaten off by the Spanish army without too much trouble. Later, the collapse of the fragile unity created in 1576 by the Pacification of Ghent, and the effective division between north and south in the Netherlands in 1579, can, in retrospect, be seen as the final defeat of this particular version of the Revolt.

The Dutch Revolt that succeeded, on the other hand, began in the towns of Holland and Zeeland in the summer months of 1572. The beginnings were not very propitious: Amsterdam remained in Spanish hands and the defeat of the rebel armies in the south and north-east of the Netherlands left these few towns isolated and exposed to the full force of Spanish military pressure. Haarlem was lost to the Spanish army, but Alkmaar resisted successfully, Leiden survived an epic siege, and the rebel towns held out until relieved by the temporary collapse of the Spanish position in 1576. The Pacification of Ghent of this year gave the rebels a much-needed respite, and also the opportunity to consolidate their position. By the time the Pacification collapsed in 1579, both Haarlem and, most importantly, Amsterdam had been brought over to the side of the rebels. Holland was now united and in a position to form the political and economic nucleus of a new state; this secondary revolt was to triumph where the grand revolt had failed.

The towns of the county of Holland had been at the centre of

this revolt right from the start, and in its course they established a
grip on the political system of their province which they were
never to release during the history of the Dutch Republic. This
dominance did not come from nowhere, however, but had its roots
in the importance of the towns in the life of Holland long before
the Revolt began. Already by the beginning of the sixteenth century Holland was one of the most urbanized areas of Europe, but,
in contrast to Flanders and Brabant in particular, the towns of
Holland were individually modest in size and economic importance, and none of them could compare with the achievements of,
successively, Bruges, Ghent, and Antwerp. The strength which the
Holland towns possessed came through collective action, not individual influence, and this circumstance gave an incentive to co-
operation which may have had a decisive effect on the way in
which the political system of the county came to work.

The political institutions of the towns themselves took on their
more or less definitive forms quite late, being created or confirmed
by charters from the Burgundian and Habsburg rulers in the
fifteenth and early sixteenth century, along lines which varied
locally but within a broadly similar pattern. Again in contrast to
Flanders and Brabant, and even to some other areas of the northern Netherlands, burgher or guild participation in government
seems always to have been weak or non-existent in Holland; the
only limitations on the power of the oligarchy in the towns came
from the influence, especially over appointments to office, of the
sovereign. In this system, the magistrates (burgemeesters and
schepenen, changing yearly or every other year) and the councils (*raad*
or *vroedschap,* whose members held their seats for life) which grew
up to support them were chosen from and by a restricted urban
élite. The rulers of the county on the whole supported the oligarchic system, as long as they could exercise sufficient control
over it. One consequence of the early establishment of oligarchy
was that the town militias—the *schutterijen,* originally organized in
guilds,[1] which were recruited from the middle strata of society—
took on some of the function of representing popular opinion,
although they were at the same time the chief weapon in the hands
of the magistrates against civil disorder. This pseudo-representative
role for the militias could still have considerable resonance in the

[1] Th. Reintges, *Ursprung und Wesen der spätmittelalterlichen Schützengilden*
(Bonn, 1963).

seventeenth century. In essence, the governmental institutions in place in the towns of Holland at the beginning of the sixteenth century continued unchanged through the Revolt and the establishment of the Republic. The new tasks and responsibilities which resulted from these changes were undertaken at the level of the town by the old political system.

At the level of the county, there is convincing evidence that the States of Holland—consisting of the representatives of the six leading towns plus the nobility—were growing in both political importance and in the scope of their administrative activities in the decades before the Revolt.[2] In particular, the financial pressure on the Habsburg governors of the Netherlands induced them to allow the States of Holland to develop their own fiscal system, both for the collection of taxes and for their expenditure. One reason why the States were able to perform at least adequately as their own masters during the Revolt was that they had been running their own affairs to a considerable extent for some time before the break with Spain. This success had its drawbacks, however: as was the case in the towns, the States of Holland could rely largely on existing structures to deal with their new tasks. It never proved necessary to introduce significant changes to cope with the new demands on government. That the existing system did so well in handling the problems and emergencies of the Revolt is remarkable, but that the governmental structure that thus emerged and was to run Holland throughout the Republican period was less than ideally suited to the task is hardly surprising.

The experience of limited self-government before the Revolt put the States in the position to be able to take over control of politics in Holland in the disturbed years after 1572, their only rival being Willem of Orange as *stadhouder* (governor) of the province. The States increased their membership in the first years after the Revolt, admitting twelve more towns, and this both strengthened their urban base and weakened the position of the nobility. What emerged by the end of the century was a system which not only allowed Holland a great measure of autonomy, if not sovereignty, within the Dutch Republic, but gave the towns of this province a considerable degree of independence also. The changes and

[2] J. D. Tracy, *Holland under Habsburg Rule, 1506–1566: The Formation of a Body Politic* (Berkeley, Calif., 1990); see also his *A Financial Revolution in the Habsburg Netherlands: 'Renten' and 'Renteniers' in the County of Holland, 1515–1566* (Berkeley, Calif., 1985).

adaptations that were necessary and possible took place in the decade or so after 1572; subsequently no further change was possible, at least formally.

The office of stadhouder also developed in the course of the Revolt out of an existing post. Originally the provincial governors appointed by the absentee sovereign (when the county of Holland became part of successive agglomerations of territories), the stadhouders retained functions and powers from that period both during the Revolt and in the Republican period. Willem of Orange was recognized by the rebel States of Holland as stadhouder in the summer of 1572, and the fiction of continued loyalty to Philip II was maintained for a number of years after this. The importance of the leadership which Willem provided was rewarded by the continued acceptance of his exercise of the traditional powers of his office, and by the time of his death the stadhoudership in this form seems to have been recognized as a necessary and right part of the political system, despite the fact that the sovereign whom the stadhouder represented had been repudiated. Even the rights of appointment to urban magistracies (from short-lists submitted to him) were retained by Willem and his successors, though such powers seemed like an exercise of a sovereignty which they neither possessed nor represented any longer. The stadhoudership is a notable example of an institution which was available at the beginning of the Revolt, was found useful during the first traumatic years of opposition to Spain, and thus found a (in this case, nearly) permanent place in the constitution of the new state.

The political system of Holland as it emerged from the Revolt was essentially the pre-Revolt system with the outside influence of the sovereign removed. Within this system enormous power accrued to the towns, or at least to those which had maintained or achieved representation in the States in this period. The nobility had been swamped by the increase in the number of the towns in the States, and there was only the somewhat anomalous figure of the stadhouder to present any sort of challenge to the authority of the towns: it was to be some years after the death of Willem before the true potential of this office revealed itself again.

1. The Urban Setting

Throughout the seventeenth century, the towns represented in the States of Holland were the fundamental source of political power in the province, as they were throughout the history of the Dutch Republic from the first days of the Revolt to the French invasion in 1795. These eighteen—the *stemhebbende* or voting—towns were the dominant element in the representative body, the States (*Staten*), which controlled the government of Holland. The nobility (*ridderschap*) also had a voice in the States and was regarded in theory as representing not only its own interests, but those of both the countryside in general and of the towns which were not members of the States in their own right. However, the nobles together constituted only one member of the States with only a single vote and thus were in political terms clearly less powerful than the voting towns, each with a separate vote, which collectively mustered eighteen.[1] The unrepresented towns and the countryside were governed by their own local institutions, and enjoyed a considerable amount of autonomy in local affairs, but they had no influence on the political life of the province outside their own areas. On the contrary, the countryside in particular was subject both to the influence of local nobles and to an increasing amount of encroachment by the towns.[2]

Thus, the politics of the province of Holland is largely the politics of the voting towns: they controlled the States of Holland and, through the States, the province as a whole. The political supremacy of these towns and only these towns means that the nature and composition of their governments becomes of particular

[1] Socially, however, the nobles probably retained rather more prestige and, possibly, influence than this formal weakness in political terms might suggest: see H. F. K. van Nierop, *Van ridders tot regenten: De Hollandse adel in de zestiende en de eerste helft van de zeventiende eeuw* (Dieren, 1984), 232–3.
[2] One of the most important ways in which this took place was through the purchase by the voting towns, most notably Amsterdam and Rotterdam, of rights of jurisdiction (*hoge-* and *ambachtsheerlijkheden*) in their surrounding areas, thus giving them effective control over the personnel of local government and so to a great extent of political life in these areas of the countryside.

importance for an understanding of the political life of the province. The town governments controlled the States primarily through their control of the delegations which they sent to its meetings. These town delegations were spokesmen for their principals and very definitely not plenipotentiaries: the close control maintained over them was symbolized by and exercised through the principle of *ruggespraak*, whereby these delegations were forbidden to take decisions on their own initiative, but had to obey to the letter the instructions they had been given by their principals in the towns. This meant that, if any new matter arose in the assembly of the States, the delegates had to refer back to their towns for new instructions. Thus it can be argued that in a very real sense sovereignty lay not so much with the States of Holland themselves, but in effect with the governments of the voting towns collectively; although the towns were not individually sovereign, their governments together were. This basic fact of Dutch political life gives the politics of the towns, or more precisely of the voting towns, of Holland its peculiar importance.

Urban self-government was a powerful tradition in Holland, as in the Netherlands as a whole; the towns' political institutions may have been set up and regulated by charters from the sovereign in the first instance, but by the sixteenth century at least they had come to be regarded as fundamental rights. Such charters were seen as recognition by the sovereign of existing privileges rather than as conferring new and conditional rights. A wide range of causes has been put forward to explain the Revolt of the Netherlands, but one matter can hardly be denied a fundamental importance: the defence of privileges, which in most instances meant local, and particularly urban, rights. Similarly, whatever else may be disputed, it is abundantly clear that one of the major consequences of the success of the Revolt was the preservation, indeed political canonization, of the powers and privileges of local, and again particularly urban, government. The idea of the new state which emerged from the Revolt was inextricably bound up with the defence and preservation of traditional privileges; this was the essence of the 'Freedom' the Dutch had fought for and which was so treasured in the seventeenth century. This was a defensive and negative form of liberty: freedom from encroachment by superior and particularly monarchical or princely power; and what was to be preserved in this way was a set of existing rights and privileges—the only principle involved was an absolute loyalty to the existing system. A large degree of autonomy for the towns was a fundamental part of this system of privileges. In Holland, more than in any other province except perhaps Zeeland, only the power of the stadhouder could challenge that of the towns (see Part 2, Chapter 2). The powers and privileges of the towns were consistently supported by the States because this body was effectively controlled by the votes of the town delegations. Thus, although the States of Holland were the supreme political authority in the province, in practice they acted as the expression of urban power. Even towns which found themselves politically isolated on any particular occasion were to a very large degree protected from coercion by the majority, as no town wanted to set a precedent which might be used against itself on some future occasion—no town could be certain that it might not some day be in a vulnerable minority.

Unfortunately, the logic of the system thus constituted and confirmed in the course of the Revolt, and firmly established by the first decades of the seventeenth century, severely hindered not only any centralizing or rationalizing tendencies in government, but also made any change at all in any formal sense almost impossible. For the justification of the existing system was just that: it was the existing way of doing things, and thus sanctified by tradition. In this regard the Dutch Republic was entirely typical of early modern Europe in its attitudes to political rights and systems of government. What was right was what was prescribed by immemorial antiquity. The more or less official interpretation of the nature of the Revolt of the Netherlands, which was firmly established by the first years of the seventeenth century through the writings of Grotius in particular,[3] traced the origins of the Dutch political system as far back as the Batavians, a Germanic tribe thought to have lived in the northern Netherlands at the time of the Roman empire. This argument took the form of a—very largely mythical—historical account which asserted that the rights and privileges of the states, nobles, and towns of the Netherlands had remained essentially unchanged and unbroken since the time of the Batavian revolt against Rome, and that the powers wielded in particular by

[3] Grotius' *De antiquitate reipublicae Batavicae* (1610) was written in Latin in order to reach an international audience, and gave the interpretation of the Revolt which was convenient for *politique* regents.

the counts of Holland and Zeeland had only been delegated to them and had not been exercised by them as of right. According to this interpretation of Dutch history, the attempt by Philip II to undermine the existing system of political rights and privileges by strengthening the powers of the government at Brussels had both caused and justified the Revolt. This version of the Revolt allowed the Dutch to argue that in fact it was Philip who had been the revolutionary, attempting to subvert the Dutch constitution and impose his own arbitrary authority on the Netherlands; the Dutch, acting through the States of the various provinces, had resisted in order to preserve the ancient and legitimate ways.

So, although the Revolt in fact created a new state, and the absence of a ruler above the States brought a radically new situation in which the old institutions had to operate, in theory and spirit the system remained traditional and conservative. After a period of rapid, practical readjustments of the way in which the existing institutions worked—between 1572 and about the end of the sixteenth century—the new system stabilized (by the eighteenth century 'ossified' might seem the more appropriate term) and there was no way in which change could be acceptable, except as reform in the conservative sense of correcting corruptions or deformations and returning to the supposed pristine perfection of the system at the time of its institution. Ideologically, traditionalism prevented any change or reform in accordance with abstract principles, because at every level of the political system what was done was justified by precedent not by reference to what was felt to be right or just—or, rather, the only acceptable definition of what was right or just was provided by precedent. In practical politics, also, there was no person or body with the power or motivation to enforce fundamental constitutional change. Although the stadhouders have appeared to many historians as a potential force for salutary reform, in the end it seems that even they could not escape from this ideological and practical straitjacket.[4]

Before the Revolt, six towns had been regularly represented in the States of Holland: the 'great' towns of Dordrecht, Haarlem, Delft, Leiden, Amsterdam, and Gouda. In the course of the Revolt twelve

---

[4] See H. H. Rowen, *The Princes of Orange: The Stadholders in the Dutch Republic* (Cambridge, 1988), chs. 9–11 for the inability of the eighteenth-century stadhouders to embrace fundamental reform.

more towns gained permanent representation in the States: Rotterdam (which came to be considered as the seventh of the 'great' towns), Gorinchem, Schiedam, Schoonhoven, Brielle, Alkmaar, Hoorn, Enkhuizen, Edam, Monnickendam, Medemblik, and Purmerend. For a brief period during the early, critical years of the Revolt new towns were able to gain places in the States—a representation which might not have seemed an unmixed blessing in those dangerous times—but quite quickly the system froze again and towns which had failed to establish themselves among the voting towns during this brief period of opportunity and uncertainty were forever excluded from the charmed circle.[5]

All the towns represented in the States of Holland had the same, single vote (or voice, *stem*) and thus had, formally, equal power and influence, despite their great disparity in population and wealth. Apart from this formal political sense, the towns were indeed very unequal in both size and wealth. At one extreme was Amsterdam, an economic power of European if not world proportions, with a population rising from *c*.100,000 at the beginning of the seventeenth century to about 200,000 at the end. Next came a group of largish towns: by around 1675, Leiden had reached a population of *c*.65,000, Rotterdam *c*.45,000, and Haarlem *c*.37,000; Delft and Dordrecht were in the region of 20,000–25,000; Enkhuizen, Gouda, and Hoorn 15,000–20,000; Alkmaar between 10,000 and 15,000; Schiedam, Edam, and Gorinchem in the region of 5,000–10,000; and Brielle, Schoonhoven, Monnickendam, Medemblik, and Purmerend under 5,000.[6]

However, different population sizes at any one point in the century are only one aspect of the very varied demographic history of the towns of Holland during this period; also important is the differential dynamism of the various towns during the century. The general and fairly rapid growth of the population in both town and countryside during the sixteenth century was followed by a much more uneven pattern in the following century. If we take as a starting point the fairly reliable figures which are available for all the towns for 1622, the magnitude of the differences in development

[5] J. W. Koopmans, *De Staten van Holland en de Opstand* (The Hague, 1990), 26–36.
[6] D. P. Blok *et al.*, *Algemene Geschiedenis der Nederlanden*, v (Haarlem, 1980), 137.

The population of the voting towns in 1622

Dordrecht	18,270	Schoonhoven	2,891
Haarlem	39,455	Brielle	3,632
Delft	22,769	Alkmaar	12,417
Leiden	44,745	Hoorn	14,139
Amsterdam	104,932	Enkhuizen	20,967
Gouda	14,627	Edam	5,647
Rotterdam	19,532	Monnickendam	3,990
Gorinchem	5,913	Medemblik	3,983
Schiedam	5,997	Purmerend	2,556

Source: A. M. van der Woude, *Het Noorderkwartier* (Wageningen, 1972), 114.

between the towns during the rest of the century begins to become apparent.

The point to stress here is that it seems that even at this fairly early point in the century of Dutch economic ascendancy, most of the towns of Holland had either already reached, or were very close to, their maximum *ancien régime* population. Over the following half-century, Dordrecht's population probably rose slightly, but Haarlem's may well have fallen, and Enkhuizen was already beginning its long and, by the eighteenth century, startling decline. In contrast, the largest towns, excepting only Haarlem, were still growing fast. Leiden increased its population by about 50 per cent in this half-century, but Amsterdam doubled and Rotterdam more than doubled in size.

The broad demographic pattern seems to be that the general, rapid growth of the sixteenth century—in which the population of Holland as a whole more than doubled between 1514 and 1622—slowed down in the countryside and small towns in the first half of the seventeenth century, but continued in a handful of large towns. After the mid-century, growth ceased in most of the province, and the population was possibly already starting to fall in the countryside of North Holland and some of the smaller towns. However, in Amsterdam, Rotterdam, and Leiden growth continued until about 1675, after which the first two experienced almost a century of stagnation rather than significant decline, while Leiden suffered a disastrous fall in its population. So for much of the seventeenth century the demographic history of the towns of Holland showed almost as much dissimilarity as did their absolute sizes. Both sets of circumstances affected the domestic politics of the towns in important ways, as well as the relations between the voting towns.

The very different economic and demographic experiences of the towns of Holland must be taken into account when attempting to understand the politics of the province. The seventeenth-century economic history of Enkhuizen, which faced permanently difficult times after the second decade of the century, contrasts sharply with that of Rotterdam, which more than doubled its size after this point. One of the tasks of the historian of the politics of this period is to try to assess the political effects of these economic and social differences.

One important town has been ignored so far, because of its peculiar status, but it deserves a mention at least at this point although it will not figure largely in the remainder of this study. The Hague was already a town of almost 16,000 in 1622, and had passed 20,000 by 1675, and it continued to grow even after this time. Although it was thus a sizeable town at the beginning of the century, and a major one by the end, it was not represented in the States of Holland, and played no part as a town in the politics of the province. It had tried to gain a seat in the States in 1581, but this was already a little late for such a change, and, moreover, as the seat of both the States General and the States of Holland—not to mention what there were of institutions of central government in the Dutch Republic—it was apparently felt that the town should remain politically on the sidelines.[7] Perhaps it was believed that if the town had a voice in the States then its government would inevitably come under the influence of powerful interests at the centre of the political life of the province.

Also excluded from consideration in this study of the politics of the towns of Holland, as it was from the formal political life of the province, is the Zaanstreek, despite its size and economic importance. This area, though an important industrial region with a population in 1622 of around 20,000 rising by mid-century to about 24,000, and with a distinctly urban character socially and economically, was legally only an agglomeration of villages. Therefore the affairs of the largest concentration of population outside the half-dozen biggest towns had to be dealt with by the

[7] Cf. M. 't Hart, 'Cities and Statemaking in the Dutch Republic 1580–1680', *Theory and Society*, 18 (1989), 668–9.

ordinary political institutions of the Holland countryside, and the area was naturally unrepresented in the States of Holland. This exclusion from participation in the government of the province, together with the fragmentation of authority in the area arising from its lack of urban institutions, might help to explain the serious nature of the rioting which occurred there from time to time during the seventeenth century.[8]

[8] R. M. Dekker, *Holland in beroering: Oproeren in de 17de en 18de eeuw* (Baarn, 1982), 31–2, 87–8, 139.

2. The Town Governments of Holland

As the previous chapter has indicated, while some sizeable concentrations of population were not represented in the States of Holland, the voting towns did include a number which were relatively small, being dwarfed in size and wealth by some of the other towns in the province, Amsterdam, Rotterdam, and Leiden in particular. Yet politically each of the voting towns was equal, in theory at least, having one vote in the States of Holland irrespective of size or wealth. The bigger towns had no special rights or privileges,[1] and precedence among the members of the States as marked by order of voting and similar procedural matters remained as established by tradition; thus, for example, Dordrecht continued to be recognized as the senior town, as precedent prescribed, despite its economic decline relative not only to the giant Amsterdam, but to Leiden, Rotterdam, and Haarlem as well. It is true that in practical politics the bigger towns were able to exercise more influence than the smaller; nevertheless, these latter had a share in power and have to be taken into consideration in any discussion of the way that politics worked in Holland. The smaller towns as well as the more prominent are included in the following account of the structure of urban government in the province.

A comparative approach is made possible by the fact that, despite their great differences in size, the systems of government within the eighteen voting towns were sufficiently similar to make a relatively brief general discussion possible, though it cannot do justice to the rich variety of local institutions and practices. All of the town governments had more or less the same components, but the way in which these worked, and in particular the location of final political power within the governments, varied considerably from town to town. The main elements of government were the

---

[1] The seven senior towns had the privilege of attaching their seals to the acts of the States, and had certain advantages in the matter of appeals from the decisions of their local courts.

schout (or *baljuw*, *officier*), the representative of the sovereign and chief police official; the burgemeesters, responsible for the day-to-day administration of the town; the *schepenen*, the local court of law; and the *vroedschap* (or *raad*), concerned with general policy. Also the *schout*, burgemeesters, and *schepenen* together formed a body (often called the *gerecht*) to issue local ordinances and deal with relatively minor administrative matters.

Each town had a council (*vroedschap*, *raad*, *veertigen*, etc.) varying in size from fourteen to forty members, all sitting for life and filling vacancies by co-optation. In a number of towns this latter right was limited by the power which the stadhouder had to appoint new members to supply such vacancies from a nomination of three men submitted to him by the existing *vroedschap*. The councils in Leiden and Gouda, for example, had forty members; in Amsterdam thirty-six; in Haarlem thirty-two; in Rotterdam, Alkmaar, and Gorinchem twenty-four; and in Purmerend, Brielle, and Hoorn twenty. It is perhaps as much a consequence of the mentality of the oligarchy as of economic stagnation or decline that a number of towns actually reduced the size of their councils in the course of the seventeenth century. The justification usually given for such reductions in the size of the local oligarchy was a lack of suitably qualified candidates for membership of the *raad*, but as no such complaints appear to have been voiced in the previous century when all these towns were significantly smaller than they were in the seventeenth century, it seems more likely that what was happening was a closing of the ranks of these local regent groups rather than a simple response to unfavourable economic or demographic conditions. The towns concerned were chiefly the smaller ones (Medemblik, Purmerend, Brielle, Gorinchem, Schoonhoven), but also included medium-sized but far from booming towns (Alkmaar, Gouda).

In some towns, such as Leiden and Gouda, there had originally been two bodies, a *veertigraad* with the main if not exclusive function of nominating the burgemeesters and *schepenen*, and a *vroedschap* consisting of sitting and former members of the *gerecht* (i.e. former burgemeesters and *schepenen*), but in the course of time the membership of the two bodies had merged, for the obvious reason that the *veertigraad* tended to nominate its own members as burgemeester and *schepen*. Certainly by the seventeenth century the distinction had disappeared, and the terms *vroedschap* and *veertigraad* were used interchangeably in these towns.

The actual power of these councils varied greatly. In some towns they were dominant, in others subordinated in practice to a smaller body within the government. In Rotterdam the *vroedschap* was the most powerful part of the government of the town, controlling general policy, the activities of the burgemeesters, and the instructions of the town's delegates to the States of Holland. This situation was not necessarily considered to be a good thing by contemporaries: when he was offered the post of *pensionaris* of Rotterdam, Pieter de Groot commented sourly to De Witt on the unattractiveness of this office in a town 'where the least regent is a sovereign and the youngest member of the vroedschap has as much to say as a burgemeester of Amsterdam'.[2] Clearly, De Groot preferred a situation such as he had experienced in Amsterdam, where the *raad* had very little say and the *oudraad*, composed of sitting and former burgemeesters and *schepenen*, was more important, but real power lay with the burgemeesters and ex-burgemeesters. In a number of other towns real power also lay with the burgemeesters; this seems, for example, to have been the case in practice in Leiden, though this was not always as obvious as in Amsterdam. There was certainly a marked tendency, unmistakable by the eighteenth century but probably beginning much earlier, for real power to come into the hands of an inner group within the oligarchy consisting of burgemeesters and former burgemeesters, another example being the 'consulars' in Gouda.

Even in Rotterdam there were rumours in 1672 that decisions were being taken by a small group rather than by the *vroedschap* as a whole,[3] but this does not seem to infer a formal shift in the structure of government: rather, it seems to reflect the feeling of some of the regents that they were being excluded from power. The reference may simply indicate the activity of the dominant faction (or party), or it may reflect the facts of life of any committee system—the feeling, usually justified, of many members that the decisions are really being made elsewhere.

The frequency of meetings of the *vroedschap* seems to have varied greatly from time to time and from place to place, from several

---

[2] J. Melles, *Ministers aan de Maas: Geschiedenis van de Rotterdamse pensionarissen met een inleiding over het stedelijk pensionariaat 1508–1795* (Rotterdam and The Hague, 1962), 123: 'daar de minste heer een soeverein is en de jongste van de vroedschap zoveel te zeggen heeft als een burgemeester van Amsterdam'.
[3] D. J. Roorda, *Partij en factie* (Groningen, 1961), 53.

times a week to a few meetings a month. It would be reasonable, though not necessarily correct, to infer that the greater the real power of the *vroedschap* the more often it met. In principle at least, the *vroedschappen* of the voting towns of Holland dealt with the most obviously political of matters: they debated the issues which were to arise in the States of Holland and drew up the instructions for the delegates to that body. Before each meeting of the States the voting towns were sent the 'poincten van beschrijvinge', i.e. a list of the matters which were to be discussed in the forthcoming session of the States. These subjects would then be discussed in the *vroedschap*, decisions taken or positions determined, and the appointed delegates told more or less precisely how they were to act in the States. How this actually worked in each individual town is unclear, except that there were almost certainly considerable differences in practice. For example, it is reasonably clear that the burgemeesters of Amsterdam were able at times to exclude the *raad* from decisions about what the town's delegation was to say, and from comment on what they had said, in the States. This situation could have important political consequences. For example, during discussions in the States of Holland in 1670 over the terms on which the young prince of Orange was to be allowed a place on the Council of State, a compromise solution put forward by De Witt was rejected by the burgemeesters without allowing the *raad* any say in the matter.[4] In Rotterdam, in contrast, the *vroedschap* was firmly in control of what the town's delegation said in the States. In 1667, when there was serious disagreement within the Rotterdam delegation to the States about how they should vote in the complicated discussions surrounding the passing of the Eternal Edict (which was, in effect, intended to prevent the young prince of Orange from ever becoming both captain-general and stadhouder of any of the provinces), it was the *vroedschap* that acted decisively. It reprimanded two of the four delegates and another member was sent to The Hague to ensure that the council's instructions were carried out to the letter.[5]

The *vroedschappen* were also normally responsible for general policy matters within the town, notably with regard to the eco-

---

[4] H. Bontemantel, *De regeeringe van Amsterdam, soo in 't civiele als crimineel en militaire (1653–1672)*, ed. G. W. Kernkamp (The Hague, 1897), i. 107–9

[5] J. L. Price, 'The Rotterdam Patriciate, 1650–1672', Ph.D. thesis (London, 1969), 125.

nomic concerns which had such a high priority for most town governments in the seventeenth century. All decisions were taken collegially, that is, the *raad* was assumed to have reached a common opinion, and to be acting as a single body. Dissident minorities were expected to go along loyally with the majority, somewhat on the lines of English cabinet government. Indeed, considerable effort was made to maintain an appearance of solidarity, and not only *vis-à-vis* the outside world. In Rotterdam the minutes of the meetings of the *vroedschap* normally simply recorded what had been agreed, but occasionally the formula 'met eenparigheid van stemmen' (unanimously) was added. Contrary to what might have been expected, this form of words seems to have been employed when there had been serious disagreement in the council, and was used to emphasize the collegial nature of the final decision. Votes were never (or very rarely) entered in the records of council meetings, and information on divisions of opinion usually comes through leaks or other informal routes. Except in circumstances of abnormal political conflict, the principle of confidentiality was maintained. Secrecy excluded all outsiders from matters which were regarded as the business of the regents alone. The rest of the citizens had no right to know what their rulers were up to, and the regents regarded any comment from outside their own ranks, let alone any attempt to interfere with their running of affairs, with the deepest indignation and resentment. Their attitude was that the citizens would be told what they needed to know and for the rest they should leave matters to those, the 'vroetscap en rijckheit', who were qualified to deal with them.

Politically a very significant part of the powers of the councils was the appointment to a whole range of offices within the towns, as well as to bodies outside them. Normally, it was the *vroedschap* which made the nominations for burgemeester and *schepen*, though in most towns the final choice was made by the stadhouder from a short-list (*dubbeltal*) of twice the number of names as there were vacancies. In Amsterdam the choice of burgemeesters was free from this important degree of outside interference into local politics, and only the nomination for *schepenen* had to be submitted to the stadhouder. Of course, during the first stadhouderless period (1650–72) all the voting towns were able to shrug off this curious remnant of the count's authority in Holland. In a number of towns, other bodies made or influenced these vital nominations. In

Hoorn the choice of burgemeesters and the nomination of *schepe-nen* was made by nine *keurmannen*, chosen by lot from a group of prominent citizens (the *boongangers*) appointed for life by the regents. In practice, however, this system seems to have represented very little challenge to the domination of the oligarchy, because of the degree of pressure and influence which the regents could and invariably did bring to bear on the *boongangers*.[6] In Dordrecht representatives of the guilds had a say in the choice of burge-meesters, but they normally went along with the nominations of the presiding burgemeester.[7]

These important elections were always liable to cause divisions within the oligarchies. To limit such conflict, and perhaps to pre-serve the fiction that the most deserving men were chosen for the posts, Rotterdam had devised a system whereby five *boonheren* were chosen by lot from the *vroedschap*.[8] These *boonheren* then proceeded immediately (thus in theory preventing corrupt practices from developing) to make the nominations. The final choice was then made by the stadhouder from the short-list they had drawn up or, during the stadhouderless periods, by lot again. This system does seem to have prevented one party or faction from dominating the burgemeesters' chamber, but as final power rested with the *vroedschap* rather than with the burgemeesters in this town this result was perhaps more tolerable to the dominant group than it might have been in many of the other towns.

The *vroedschap* also controlled the most important of the local administrative posts: the town treasurers, *weesmeesters*, *kerk-meesters*, tax collectors, etc. These posts were usually reserved for members of the *raad*. More specifically political appointments were also made by the councils from their own members: the delegates of the town to the States of Holland and the town's representative on the *gecommitteerde raden* (see Part 2, Chapter 1). Each town also had the right, according to a strict rota, to nominate a mem-ber of the provincial delegation to the States General; again, this nomination was made by the *vroedschap* and was, of course, restricted to its members.

[6] L. Kooijmans, *Onder regenten: De elite in een Hollandse stad, Hoorn 1700–1780* (Dieren, 1985), 38.

[7] Roorda, *Partij en factie*, 47.

[8] They were called *boonheren* as they were chosen by the 'drawing of white and black beans'.

This control over the appointment to a whole range of profitable and influential posts was, not surprisingly, the cause of a great deal of competition, rivalry, and conflict within the town councils. In the course of the century attempts were made to minimize such conflict by restricting competition for desirable positions: at least this was the ostensible—and possibly even the true—reason for the introduction of the 'contracts of correspondence' and similar agreements. These were probably only formalized versions of the way in which dominant parties or factions in the councils had controlled such appointments and reserved the most desirable positions for their own group throughout the century. In any case, written agreements regulating appointment to offices, often far into the future, survive from the last decades of the seventeenth century. It seems clear that, by the eighteenth century, these agreements worked in such a way as to exclude from offices of profit and power a large minority of each council, with the dominant majority maintaining its solidarity by distributing the prizes strictly according to seniority. To what extent such practices were already present in the Holland towns in the earlier years of the seventeenth century, perhaps in less well developed forms, is not clear. A tentative suggestion might be that they only became common after 1672, as one way in which the parties which achieved power in that year stabilized their control over local politics. This certainly seems to have been the case in Rotterdam, and such developments may well have been deliberately encouraged by Willem III in the hope of gaining more reliable support for his foreign policy in the States of Holland. On the other hand, it may well be that what was new in the last third of the century was only the formal, written agreement not the political practice of restricting access to desirable offices.

The 'contracts of correspondence' have often been seen as a prime example of the lack of public spirit among the regents, and the essentially self-serving nature of the regent regime. Indeed, the first major historian of the system suppressed the names of the regents involved in the contracts he described, presumably to protect their descendants—himself, as it happens, included—from the shame he felt was involved.[9] It may be more pertinent and useful to see such contracts as reflecting changes in the nature of town

---

[9] J. de Witte van Citters, *Contracten van correspondentie* (The Hague, 1873).

politics, particularly in response to the transformation of the social and economic environment. Two developments seem to have been involved: the leaching out of party politics from local government, and the generally increased reliance of regents on the profits of office as they moved away from trading or manufacturing activities in the later seventeenth and early eighteenth century. At least such is the picture strongly suggested by recent studies of the regent groups in three eighteenth-century towns.[10] However, it may well be a mistake to read back this eighteenth-century evidence to the previous century as both the political and the economic situation were significantly different. As far as the seventeenth century is concerned, there are reasons for believing both that party conflict within the urban oligarchies was much more important than it appears to have been in the eighteenth century, and that the direct involvement of regents in trade and manufacture was greater and their dependence on the profits of office less than in the following century. In particular, it seems unlikely that such strict rota-systems could have been applied to posts of political importance at a time of serious and continuing political conflict. Ability, however measured, seems likely to have been more influential than seniority, otherwise—in a system where members of the *vroedschap* held office for life—the result would have been rule by the senile, which does not appear to have been entirely the case.

The most important position within the town governments was that of burgemeester. Each town usually had four burgemeesters, each holding office for one or two years, and then being ineligible for the office for a similar period. They were responsible for the day-to-day running of the affairs of the town, and for the conduct of its relations with the central authorities of the province. The office had considerable prestige and, as we have seen, often considerable power. One indication of the prestige attached to the office is that men who had once held the post were subsequently addressed by the title for the rest of their lives. However, the real political power of the burgemeesters varied greatly from town to town: in some towns they were very powerful and constituted,

---

[10] Cf. J. J. de Jong, *Met goed fatsoen: De elite in een Hollandse stad, Gouda 1700–1780* (Dieren, 1985); M. Prak, *Gezeten burgers: De elite in een Hollandse stad, Leiden 1700–1780* (Dieren, 1985); and Kooijmans, *Onder regenten*—at least in my assessment of the evidence presented in these works, no such conclusions are drawn by the authors themselves.

along with former burgemeesters (the *consulare heeren*), the real rulers; while in others they were little more than executors, in important matters, of the will of the *vroedschap*. One aspect of the burgemeester's office which could have quite considerable importance was the patronage it controlled: a whole range of minor posts was in the gift of the burgemeesters, and control of such patronage was an important part of the local prestige of a regent family. To avoid conflict between the burgemeesters, it was normal for each in turn to have the gift of posts falling vacant during a specific period of the year.

Together with the *schout* and *schepenen*, the burgemeesters also constituted the magistracy or *gerecht*. This body, originally the government of the town before the emergence and rise to power of the *vroedschap*, was responsible for by-laws and local ordinances (*keuren en ordonnantiën*), and for the appointment to a host of minor offices, such as to the boards of governors of the town's hospitals, orphanages, and the like. Many modern commentators have continued to see the *gerecht* as the real government of the towns. Although formally true, this can be seriously misleading: the *gerecht* was certainly the executive body for local government in the narrow sense, but the real decisions were normally taken elsewhere but carried out through and by the *magistraat*. Whether the dominant element in a town was the *vroedschap* or an *oudraad*, the *gerecht* was in practice subordinate to a more powerful component of urban government. In general both *schout* and *schepenen* had declined in political importance with the rise of the *vroedschap*, and in some towns the *schepenen* were not necessarily members of the local oligarchy in any full sense.

The *schepenen*, usually seven, nine, or eleven in number, normally held office for two years; about half of the *schepenbank* was replaced annually to give a balance between change and continuity. They constituted the town's court of civil and criminal law, their decisions in important matters being subject to appeal to the provincial courts (*Hof van Holland* and *Hoge Raad*: see Part 2, Chapter 3), and as part of the *gerecht* they also had significant administrative functions. The *schepenen* are in general a curiously uncertain body as far as their relationship to the oligarchies of the Holland towns is concerned. The post was a subordinate one, and the duties attached to it were onerous, but in some towns it was a vital step on the road to real power—as in Amsterdam, where it gave access to the *oudraad* and superiority over the ordinary *raden* of the town. In other towns only regents became *schepenen*, and here the office functioned as something like an apprenticeship in government for junior members of the *vroedschap*; while in some towns the *schepenen* represented a sort of half-way house between ordinary citizen and regent. In Hoorn, a period of service as *schepen* was normal before entry into the *vroedschap*, but in Rotterdam a considerable proportion of the *schepenen* never became members of the *raad*—here it was the highest office to which non-regents could aspire.

The *schout* or *baljuw* (commonly known as the *officier*) was originally the representative of the count's authority within the town and head of local government, but by the seventeenth century the office, though still important, had become less politically powerful. The *schout* was a combination of police chief and public prosecutor: he was responsible for the maintenance of order and the apprehension of criminals (helped by his non-too-numerous subordinates), and prosecuted cases before the local *schepenbank*. Because of the historical origins of the post, the *schout* in most towns was appointed by the stadhouder (or, during the stadhouderless periods, the States) from a nomination presented by the *vroedschap*. In a few towns, such as Rotterdam, the appointment was wholly in the hands of the *vroedschap*, as it had been bought from the States in the early years of the Revolt. Length of service varied from place to place: in some towns it was for a fixed period of years, in others it was indefinite and could in practice be for life. The *schout* usually came from the regent élite, but the post was generally held to be incompatible with membership of the *vroedschap*, though this rule was not universally adhered to and was contested from time to time.

The *schout* was in a somewhat paradoxical position, and in a way that was far from atypical of the Republic's institutions as a whole, as he was formally the representative in his town of the central authorities of the province, but was (usually) chosen from the local regent group and was in practice tied by family and other interests much more closely to the local oligarchy than to the government of the province. He received, and was supposed to obey, instructions from the States and the *gecommitteerde raden* (see Part 2, Chapter 1), but he was usually more likely to follow the wishes of his local government in the case of any clash of interests. On the other hand, the *schout* could be the tool of central authority in a town, and this was not unknown under Willem III. A notorious example was the *baljuw* Van Zuylen van Nievelt in Rotterdam, an outsider brought in by the stadhouder in the 1670s and rapidly rising to power—and wealth—as a political boss acting in the prince's interest. Partly because of the dictatorial manner in which he ran the politics of the town, and partly in reaction to the unscrupulous way in which ‘he used his powers as *baljuw* to squeeze money out of his fellow citizens—including, it was alleged, blackmail—resentment against him broke out in 1690 in large-scale rioting, during which his house was destroyed by the fire of cannon taken from the local arsenal.[11] He was briefly ousted from power, but returned through the firm support of Willem III, who was more concerned to enforce his authority in the town than to uphold a high standard of morality in public affairs. In a far less extreme case, Lodewijk Huygens was sustained as *schout* of Gouda despite long-running disagreements with the majority of the local regents, though here Willem III's support can be explained as a reward for the long service to the house of Orange of Lodewijk's father, Constantijn, rather than as a way of controlling the oligarchy of Gouda.

As might be gathered from such cases, the position of *schout* could be a lucrative one, though much depended on the moral standards of the incumbent. The chief sources of income were a fixed proportion of all fines imposed by the local court, and so-called ‘composition’ payments made directly to the *schout* to avoid prosecution. These latter payments could be quite legitimate, but were open to exploitation by the unscrupulous.

In the course of the seventeenth century, the *pensionaris* became an increasingly important figure, although formally—as the title indicates—his was no more than a salaried post. The *pensionaris* acted as legal adviser to the town government, and was usually the town's spokesman in the States of Holland; this strategic position enabled many pensionaries to build up considerable local power, and some were able to make it the jumping-off point for important political careers. Their regular attendance at the meetings of the States also allowed some pensionaries to play a significant part in

[11] G. Mees Azn., *Het Rotterdamsche oproer van 1690* (Amsterdam, 1869); R. M. Dekker, ‘Het Kostermanoproer in 1690, complot of spontane beweging?’, *Rotterdamse Jaarboekje* 1981: 192–207.

provincial politics. The post was sometimes held by members of local regent families, but it was perhaps as often given to complete outsiders as a way of limiting the power of the office and insulating it as far as possible from local rivalries. The pensionary was usually, however, subordinate to the regents of his town, or if he was not it was because he had been an influential member of the regent group before his appointment and had become pensionary because he was powerful and not vice versa.

Some individuals were able to use the post as a stepping-stone to much higher things. The best example of this is Oldenbarnevelt, who was able to use his position as pensionary of Rotterdam as a springboard to leadership of the Republic, despite having no regent connections and being born outside Holland (in Utrecht). In the seventeenth century, Fagel and Cats were also able to reach the position of *raadpensionaris* (or grand pensionary: see Part 2, Chapter 1) from the office of town pensionary. Johan de Witt is perhaps a less telling example as he came from a powerful Dordrecht regent family in any case, and so was not without influence in his own right, quite apart from his period of service as pensionary of his home town—though this certainly gave him the opportunity to show his paces when the *raadpensionaris*, the elderly Pauw, was absent.[12] These were exceptions, however, and it was more usual for the holders of the office of town pensionary to be as much jurists as politicians, not only by training but in their ambitions, and they looked to crown their careers by an appointment as councillor in one of the provincial courts, the *Hof van Holland* or *Hoge Raad*.

Each town also had a number of secretaries serving the *vroedschap*, the *schepenen*, the *weeskamer*, and performing other tasks. By the middle of the century the larger towns would have two or three. Although these were originally purely subordinate administrative positions, they tended in the course of the century to take on greater political significance; not perhaps because of the power or income which they provided, but rather because they came to be regarded as training for office and reserved for the sons of the more powerful regent families. A post as secretary could give experience and occupation to a young regent while he waited for the

---

[12] The pensionary of the senior town of the province, Dordrecht, automatically became acting *raadpensionaris* in the case of absence or incapacity of the incumbent.

opportunity to move on to better things. Such a waiting period was often unavoidable, especially for those with a father or brother already on the council and thus blocking their entry. So the post of secretary became an important stage in the career structure of the Holland regent, especially for those families which had retreated from active participation in trade or manufacture to concentrate on politics and administration.

There were a number of other positions in the gift of the local councils, the most important being to the admiralties and the great trading companies. Most towns had some influence over the appointment of members to one or more of the four admiralties in Holland and Zeeland. Rotterdam, for example, nominated members for the boards of both the Maas and the Zeeland admiralties. (Those nominated were always members of the *vroedschap*.) Rather more curious was the right which towns containing chambers of the East and/or West India Companies had to appoint their local directors. These appointments were made from a short-list presented by the chief shareholders, and, surprisingly enough, the regents did not restrict these important and lucrative posts to their own numbers, but also chose leading merchants who were not members of the regent élite.[13] Some of these, however, may have owed their appointment to family connections with the regents, or perhaps such favour may have been secured by more material inducements.

[13] F. Gaastra, *Bewind en beleid bij de VOC 1672–1702* (Zutphen, 1989), 41.

3. The Regents

The term 'regent' has been used so far without anything like a precise definition; the purpose of this chapter is to give as clear an idea as possible of who the regents were. The word is usually presented untranslated in English works and this is not a particularly happy usage, but there is no obviously more appropriate alternative, and so it seems best to keep the term and to try to give it something of its contemporary content. In seventeenth-century Dutch, the word meant more or less those who ruled, the governors: it referred in its narrow definition to the holders of local political power, more broadly to the holders of political power in general, and, most widely of all, to the governors of any public institution.[1] What we are concerned with here is to elucidate the nature of the regent group in its most precise sense: the members of the oligarchies or patriciates[2] of the towns, and particularly the voting towns, of Holland.

The best starting point is the *vroedschap*: clearly all members of this council were regents, they held their office for life, and they provide the undisputable core of the patriciate. The *magistraat*, on the other hand, gives rise to some difficulties: the burgemeesters were clearly regents, and were normally chosen from the *vroedschap* in any case; the *schout*, although he could be more the representative of the government of the province than a member of the local élite, was more usually from a local regent family, or by virtue of his power and influence was able to break into the local regent group; but the *schepenen* are another matter. As members of the *magistraat* or *gerecht*, they played an important part in run-

---

[1] Hence those well-known paintings with such titles as Regents of the Cloth Hall, of the Old Men's Home, etc.: these people were not regents proper, but only the governors of these institutions.

[2] I am using the term 'patriciate' here as a synonym for the regent group as a whole. Roorda, *Partij en factie*, 39–40, and G. Groenhuis, *De predikanten: De sociale positie van de gereformeerde predikanten in de Republiek der Verenigde Nederlanden voor ± 1700* (Groningen, 1977), 63–4, both use the term to include leading merchants and manufacturers as well as regents, but I find this unhelpful and prefer to call this broader social group—rather more vaguely, I concede, but it was not well-defined—the upper bourgeoisie.

ning their town, but only during the period—one or two years—in which they held office. Unless they were also members of the *vroedschap* or of an established regent family, they had subsequently no assured place in the regent élite. In towns where the office of *schepen* automatically conferred membership of an *oudraad*, it was usually restricted to men who were already members of the *vroedschap*. It seems, thus, that the post by itself rarely, if ever, brought with it membership of the regent group proper, though service in this capacity did undoubtedly confer considerable prestige. So, although the position of *schepen* is a marginal one which needs to be assessed according to the particular circumstances of each individual town, it can be taken as a general rule that within the political system of Holland this office is not by itself evidence of membership of the regent group. Where the *schepenen* were indeed regents it was because only members of this privileged group were appointed to the post; in such cases men did not become regents because they had been a *schepen*, but had become a *schepen* because they were already regents.

The case is much more straightforward with regard to the other offices attached to the town governments. This is perhaps best illustrated by the example of the *pensionaris*, formally at least the most important of such posts. Some pensionaries were clearly regents, but only because they were already such before their appointment; the office itself could not bring membership of the political élite. The pensionary was a salaried official, not a member of the oligarchy, and non-regent pensionaries remained outside the regent group despite the importance of their office.

However, membership of the *vroedschap* cannot be regarded as the sole criterion of regent status, as it is clear that some men who were not members of the local council were nevertheless regents. This was possible, for example, in towns with an *oudraad*: in Amsterdam men who were excluded from the *raad* because a close relative was already a member could become *schepen* and thus attain the *oudraad*, which in its turn opened up the possibility of appointment as burgemeester. This was the way in which the brothers Andries, Cornelis, and Jan Bicker were able to exercise power in Amsterdam in the late 1640s: the rules prevented close relatives from being members of the *raad* at the same time but this ban on consanguinity did not extend to all offices in the town government. Andries Bicker had been in the *raad* since 1622, which kept his brothers out of this body, but Cornelis served as *schepen* in 1628 and Jan in 1647, making them all by this latter date eligible for the position of burgemeester. In the ten years from 1645 the power of the 'Bicker league' was marked by the appointment of Andries as burgemeester in 1645 and 1649,[3] Cornelis in 1646, 1650, and 1654, while Jan made his single appearance in 1653.[4] Clearly, any definition of regent which excluded Cornelis Bicker would not be very helpful. In addition to such clear-cut cases as these, another major problem is that the outer limits of the regent group are difficult to define, particularly as it would be unrealistically pedantic to exclude from the political élite the close family of undisputed regents. For example, the son of a regent who was clearly destined to follow his father into the *vroedschap*, but could not do so during the latter's lifetime, was clearly a part of the wider regent group. So were female members of regent families, in so far as they were used to make or consolidate alliances between regent families through marriage. Also, marriage to a woman of a regent family could open up a way into the political élite for an outsider: the son-in-law also rises applied as well in the towns of Holland in the seventeenth century as in the Hollywood of the 1930s. So the immediate family, both male and female, of regents should also be considered to be members of the oligarchy. The next question is the extent to which the broader family connections of the regents can be seen as part of the oligarchy as well, and here it must be admitted that the point where regent ended and non-regent began is not something that can be defined precisely. The regent group proper was surrounded by a penumbra of relatives by birth or marriage who were something like candidate regents and whose future depended on circumstances, and especially on the demographic success or failure of the senior branches of their families.

The regent group was thus an oligarchy with as a core the members of the *vroedschap*, who held office for life and filled vacancies within their ranks by co-optation.[5] (As has been noted, this free-

---

[3] He had already been burgemeester eight times between 1627 and 1641, but none of his brothers had held the office before.

[4] J. E. Elias, *De vroedschap van Amsterdam* (Haarlem, 1903–5), nos. 57, 110.

[5] A useful survey of the modern literature on the regents can be found in D. J. Roorda, 'Het onderzoek naar het stedelijk patriciaat in Nederland', in W. W. Mijnhardt (ed.), *Kantelend geschiedbeeld* (Utrecht and Antwerp, 1983). Among more recent publications relating to the subject, J. J. de Jong, *Een deftig bestaan:*

dom of co-optation was limited, in some cases, at some periods, by the stadhouder making the new appointments from three-name short-lists.) In all the towns of Holland this was a very small group of men: the councils varied in size from less than twenty to something over forty members. Despite this relatively small size, there were frequent complaints in the course of the century from the smaller towns of the difficulty of finding suitable candidates for regent positions. This may have some whiff of plausibility for those small towns which were experiencing economic difficulties from quite an early stage, but the suspicion must be that the problem lay not in the lack of qualified men but in the shortage of lucrative posts. It is probable that the reductions in the size of some councils which took place around the mid-century (see above, Chapter 2) were intended to make it possible for all members of the *vroedschappen* to be provided with attractive employment—the aim being to limit the number of regents to the posts available. Whatever may have been the case in the smaller towns, there could be no question of any shortage of suitably qualified would-be regents in the larger towns, especially in the years of growth both in size and prosperity, which lasted until at least the middle of the seventeenth century, and probably rather later for the biggest of them. In these towns, the councils which might well have included most of the notable families of their towns in the sixteenth century necessarily excluded large numbers of wealthy and prominent families in the much larger and richer communities of the following century. This is most obviously the case in the giant Amsterdam, but was not much less of a potential problem in major towns such as Leiden, Rotterdam, and Haarlem. There was no attempt, however, to expand the size of the regent group to match the increase in the number of suitable candidates (something of this nature was suggested by Pieter de la Court, but he was a consciously rational reformer and in any case an outsider as far as the regents were concerned). The interests of the propertied classes were held to be sufficiently represented in practice by the existing regents—and, indeed, in general terms this was true. The regents did protect and promote the economic interests of a broad range of the trading and manufacturing bourgeoisie.

Het dagelijks leven van regenten in de 17de en 18de eeuw (Utrecht and Antwerp, 1987) and C. Schmidt, *Om de eer van de familie: Het geslacht Teding van Berkhout 1500–1950* (Amsterdam, 1986) are particularly interesting.

With regard to political power and the profits of office, however, the regents were much more selfish. They were a closed group with what might well be considered a natural tendency to exclude outsiders and to tighten coherence within the group by deliberate policies, including the use of endogamy. However, throughout most of the seventeenth century there were a number of circumstances—some endemic, some epidemic—which combined to bring about a greater degree of movement into and out of the élite than would have been the case if the oligarchies had been left undisturbed. These included demographic and economic factors, as well as the effect of recurrent political crises; and it can also be argued that the very structure of regent rule itself encouraged a definite if limited degree of mobility.

First of all, there is the question of demography, and specifically whether the regent group was able to maintain its numbers over time or whether, as seems to have been the case with many of the élite social formations in early modern Europe, demographic failure necessitated more or less constant recruitment from outside. Two contrasting dangers pulled regent families in different directions. On the one hand, too many children would dilute the wealth and thus possibly the social status of the senior branch of the family, and would certainly mean uncertain or unpromising futures for the younger children. Thus, in order to preserve wealth and power, restraint in child-bearing was called for. Also it may be that already in the seventeenth century a certain reluctance on the part of husbands from the upper bourgeoisie to endanger the health and even life of their wives through repeated pregnancies was beginning to emerge. The evidence is, however, ambiguous and there is no evidence at all of the deliberate use of effective contraceptive techniques—except abstention from intercourse and possibly coitus interruptus. Pulling in the other direction, however, were high infant and child mortality rates and the danger of childbirth to the mother. Repeated pregnancies were as likely to kill the wife of a regent as any other woman, or very nearly so, but, to put it somewhat coldly, from the point of view of a family's reproductive strategy a dead wife could be relatively easily replaced, and so the vulnerability of women was not perhaps a major demographic problem.

It was not so easy, however, to ensure that sufficient children survived into adulthood to prevent the family from dying out. It is clear that, in the eighteenth century, a considerable number of regent families failed in this most basic of tasks.[6] One—but only one—of the reasons advanced to explain this situation was that there seems to have been a decline in fertility within regent families in the eighteenth century as compared to the preceding one. To put it simply: they had too few children. The position is far less clear with regard to the seventeenth century, partly because of a lack of research, but also because the regent groups in the various towns were less stable as far as their family composition was concerned than they became in the following century. What research has been published is ambiguous,[7] but at the very least it can be said that some regent families were always liable to die out in the direct line, though we do not as yet know how important this factor was for the regent group as a whole. Also, families failing in the main line could be replaced by cadet branches, as appears to have been the case with major landholding families in England.[8] The question whether regent families would have been able to maintain them-selves if left undisturbed is, however, somewhat speculative as far as the seventeenth century is concerned as, on the whole, the oli-garchies were not left to work out their own demographic fortunes without disruption. Factors other than the purely demographic intro-duced a certain degree of social mobility into the political élite.

Certain aspects of the structure of local government, and of the rules and regulations controlling it, gave rise to a definite, if definitely limited, degree of movement into and out of the political élite. Specifically, the rules against consanguinity usually ensured that fathers and sons, brothers, and other very close relatives could not be members of the *vroedschap* at the same time. In most, if not all, towns, however, there was no such ban on relatives by marriage: the presence of a father- or brother-in-law was no bar to a man entering the *vroedschap*. This gave an excellent chance for outsiders to break into the regent group through the influence of a powerful regent family. For the ambitious regent, marrying a daughter or sister to a suitable man from a non-regent family

---

[6] See De Jong, *Met goed fatsoen*, 167–8; Kooijmans, *Onder regenten*, 120; and Prak, *Gezeten burgers*, 191.

[7] H. van Dijk and D. J. Roorda, 'Sociale mobiliteit onder regenten van de Republiek', *Tijdschrift voor Geschiedenis*, 84 (1971)—the authors themselves draw a number of fairly firm conclusions, but it can be doubted whether these are really justified by their evidence.

[8] L. Stone and J. C. Fawtier Stone, *An Open Elite? England 1540–1880* (Oxford, 1984), 108–9.

offered the opportunity of bringing a close but not banned relative on to the council. A similar marriage to a member of another regent family, whilst it might strengthen the family's position in one way, was unlikely to offer quite the same opportunities, especially as the man in question would probably be barred from entry into the council by the presence of a member of his own family. Thus, the nature of the political game, with the strategies employed by competing regent families and groups, were in themselves likely to bring about a modest degree of mobility in the regent élite. Naturally, such openings were only available to families which already possessed a certain standing and good relations with the existing regent group, otherwise a marriage alliance was hardly likely to have been considered in the first place. So, while the maintenance of the established regent families demanded a degree of endogamy, there were also good political reasons for a significant degree of exogamy.

The political problems associated with rapid economic growth do not seem to have created serious difficulties for the majority of the towns of Holland, perhaps because even in the seventeenth century the boom period for most of them was quite brief. On the other hand, for a very important minority, chiefly the bigger towns, the rapid growth which continued throughout much of the century had very significant consequences for local political life. To the extent that wealth was the most important, perhaps ultimately the only necessary, qualification for regent status (except for being a native of the province and religiously acceptable), the size and nature of economic development in these towns caused major problems. For the size of the richer merchant and manufacturing group increased at least as fast as the total population, and consequently the pool of families conventionally qualified for entry into the regent group grew considerably. This situation seems to have had a destabilizing influence on town politics. While the smaller towns complained of economic stagnation and sought to cut down the size of their regent groups, in the more economically dynamic towns out-groups of men of wealth and ambition formed, ready to take advantage of any weakness in the defences of the existing political élite in order to force an entry for themselves. Part at least of the notorious turbulence and regent factionalism of a number of towns may have been caused by the existence of such discontented outsiders.

In the last third of the seventeenth century and throughout the eighteenth, the situation reversed itself. Now economic stagnation and even serious decline in some towns lessened outside pressure on the regent élite. On the contrary, in these less promising economic circumstances office-holding became much more important as a way of maintaining the financial position of regent families. In this changed situation, membership of the regent group helped to safeguard individuals and families from the dangers of an uncertain economic environment: thus regent status brought or maintained wealth, rather than wealth demanding entry into the regent group as in the dynamic years of the earlier period.

The stability of the existing regent groups was most directly and obviously disturbed by the recurrent political crises of the seventeenth century, specifically through the *wetsverzettingen* of 1618 and 1672. *Wetsverzettingen* were unusual emergency changes in the membership, not only of the *magistraat*, but also of the *vroedschappen*, carried out on these two occasions on the authority of the stadhouder. (His right to carry out such changes was highly dubious in law, but his actual power to do so was established in practice in these years.) What particularly concerns us here is the effect of these *wetsverzettingen* on the composition of the regent élite, together with—although this is a much less obvious matter—the effects within the towns of Holland of the attempted *coup* by Willem II in 1650 and his unexpected death in the same year.

The basic argument advanced here is a simple one: that these crises brought drastic and rapid changes in the composition of the political élite in the Holland towns, after which they were allowed a period of consolidation, only to be shaken up and disrupted again by the next crisis. This process meant that from the late sixteenth to the late seventeenth century, the established regent oligarchies were periodically disturbed by the enforced purging of existing families and the infusion of new blood.

This pattern really begins, of course, with the take-over by the rebels of most of the towns of Holland in 1572 (Amsterdam only in 1578),[9] when a large proportion of the existing regent group fled, either because it was pro-Spanish or because it feared to be caught in such an exposed position if, as seemed highly likely, the

[9] Haarlem went over to the Revolt in 1572 but was taken by Spanish troops in the following year, and only returned to the rebel ranks in 1577.

revolt were to be suppressed.[10] The old regents were thus replaced by new men, committed to the Revolt, to the Reformed Church, or, perhaps, to both. In the succeeding forty-odd years, this new oligarchy was able to establish itself, developing into tightly knit groups, having shed its weaker members, and marked particularly by a considerable degree of intermarriage. Then came the remonstrant–contraremonstrant disputes, amounting almost to civil war, and growing in intensity during the Twelve Years Truce (1609–21). These events reached a crisis in 1618–19 with the execution of Oldenbarnevelt and a series of *wetsverzettingen* in the voting towns of Holland, which broke up this post-Revolt ruling élite.

The scale of the changes brought about in 1618 varied from town to town, and was obviously less in the contraremonstrant towns, though even here the dominant party often took this opportunity to rid itself of opponents within the oligarchy. So, although Amsterdam had staunchly supported both the contraremonstrants and the prince, the group in control nevertheless took the opportunity to strengthen its position by the dismissal and replacement of seven of the thirty-six *raden*. There were no changes in Enkhuizen or Purmerend, however, and even Dordrecht evaded any purge, though the reasons for this are a matter of dispute. (It was claimed that all the regents were so closely interrelated that it was impossible to victimize some without alienating all,[11] but this sounds like special pleading as much the same could have been said with as much or as little truth of any of the oligarchies of the Holland towns.) In other towns, in contrast, the disruption to the existing regent élite was considerable, particularly in those towns which had been the strongest supporters of Oldenbarnevelt, and where the remonstrant element was powerful in the *vroedschap*. Thus, in Rotterdam fifteen out of twenty-two councillors lost their seats;[12] in Haarlem nineteen out of thirty-two; and in Leiden and Hoorn over half the *vroedschap* was ejected.

---

[10] The extent to which the regent group was renewed in the course of the Revolt is as yet unclear. Some writers stress the degree of continuity (e.g. Koopmans, *Staten van Holland*, 41–5) but, though the break with the past was far from complete and circumstances differed widely from town to town, there can be little doubt that a significant change in the composition of the regent oligarchy took place in 1572 and the immediately succeeding years.

[11] J. Wagenaar, *Vaderlandsche historie* (Amsterdam, 1790–6), x. 281.

[12] There were twenty-four members in the Rotterdam *vroedschap*, but two places were vacant at the time of the *wetsverzetting*.

These purges allowed new families, riding on the surge of orangism and Reformed Orthodoxy (real or feigned), to gain entry to the regent group. As a knock-on effect, these new men would do their best to bring family members and other allies from outside regent circles into the town governments, thus facilitating some further renewal of the regent élite in the following decades. In the same period, a group of families—varying in size from place to place and including some of the wealthiest—would find themselves excluded from political power: the ejected regents and their families, their political allies, and all those tainted by remonstrant connections. Just as the increasingly closed nature of the oligarchies had excluded significant numbers of would-be regents before 1618, those excluded after this year would in their turn begin to constitute an out-group of considerable size, wealth, and standing, embittered by their experiences of 1618 and the subsequent harassment of remonstrants and their supporters by the victorious party.

The following thirty years gave the new oligarchy the opportunity to settle into power and form itself into another closed élite; some newcomers proved unable to establish themselves, or rather their families, in the regent group, but the rest were able to consolidate their hold on power in much the same ways as their predecessors. Then came the crisis of 1650, when the shock of Willem II's abortive *coup* was swiftly followed by his death from smallpox. These events probably had serious consequences for the regent groups of many towns, though the subject is as yet largely unexplored. At least, it seems likely that this combination of circumstances introduced another period which was favourable for changes within the oligarchies of the voting towns of Holland. Not only was the prestige of the house of Orange badly shaken by the reckless actions of the young prince, but his death left the orangists temporarily without a clear leader or unambiguous guidance. The decision of the States of Holland to dispense with the office of stadhouder deprived the orangist groups in the voting towns of a powerful source of outside support. The degree of influence which Frederik Hendrik and then his son had been able to exercise in the towns through their powers over the appointment of magistrates each year, and by the manipulation of their powerful patronage network, has never been fully or properly investigated, but it can hardly have been a negligible force in local politics. (Amsterdam, where the stadhouder had formal powers of appointment over *schepenen* alone, and not over burgemeesters or *raden*, was to some extent an exception.) Now this support was gone, and the balance of power in a number of towns seems to have shifted significantly, particularly as at least part of the patronage formerly exercised by the stadhouders fell to the States of Holland and could be used by the *raadpensionaris*, and certainly was by Johan de Witt, to strengthen the position of his supporters in the town governments.

Certainly, in the decade after Willem's death, changes slowly but surely took place in many towns, not through *wetsverzettingen* but through the natural erosion of the existing regent groups by death, and the replacement of deceased *raden* by men more in tune with the dominant regime in The Hague. This process is fairly clear in Rotterdam, for example, though the way in which it was achieved is not. Studies of other towns in the years immediately after 1650 would be extremely useful in this respect. However, the overall result seems tolerably unambiguous: by the middle of the 1660s most of the voting towns had evolved from their often orangist past into more or less fervent defenders of the True Freedom. Some towns, it is true, were largely untouched by this phenomenon—for example, Leiden and Enkhuizen—and Amsterdam as usual went its own way, being ready to swing against De Witt by the late 1660s, but in general the political situation must have been favourable in the 1650s and 1660s for the out-groups which had formed in the decades after 1618, allowing a significant number of their members to gain (or regain) entry to the *vroedschappen*. Certainly, in Rotterdam the new regents of these years included many from families which had been expelled from the town government in 1618, or had been strongly associated with the remonstrant movement, as well as representatives of the newly wealthy which this economically dynamic town was still producing. The new élite formed in this way by the amalgamation of the survivors of the post-1618 oligarchies with the returnees and newcomers of the period after 1650, however, had only a relatively brief period of undisturbed consolidation and enjoyment of the fruits of office, before it in its turn was broken up in 1672 as brutally and decisively as had been the case in 1618.

The French invasion was the immediate cause of the *wetsverzettingen* of 1672, which were characterized by large-scale popular violence, markedly orangist in nature. The membership of the political élite was again changed to an extent that varied considerably from town to town, and again the reasons for local peculiarities are not always immediately apparent. In Amsterdam, the faction (or party) led by Gillis Valkenier took advantage of the situation to exact revenge on its opponents for the defeat it had suffered over the choice of burgemeesters in the previous year, and sixteen members of the government of the town were replaced. In Enkhuizen, the town government emerged once again almost unscathed, but Rotterdam, true to its tradition, was possibly the most politically polarized town in the province, and no less than fourteen of the twenty-four *vroedschappen* were thrown out.[13] Hoorn also had over half its *vroedschap* replaced, while Dordrecht, despite its connections with De Witt and his brother, had only fourteen of its forty *raden* ejected, curiously enough a similar proportion to the notoriously orangist Leiden. Roorda[14] sees these local differences as a function of the nature and intensity of factional infighting, but, whatever the reasons for such variations, for the regent oligarchy of Holland as a whole the *wetsverzettingen* brought about large-scale changes in its membership. Also, the influence of the stadhouder on the choice of magistrates was reintroduced, and in this and other ways Willem III was able to support and promote his parties in the towns over the next three decades. Willem's death was succeeded by another stadhouderless period, which allowed some but probably not many ousted families to return to the oligarchy, and thus there was no further major disruption of the regent élite in Holland until the late 1740s. These years were also a period of economic decline for nearly all the towns, and thus pressure from the newly enriched—as there were less of them—fell off, helping to ensure that the early eighteenth century would be the most stable of all periods for the oligarchies of the voting towns of Holland.

The degree to which the regent élite was disturbed by these recurrent political crises can be disputed if we follow the line taken by Van Dijk and Roorda[15] that only individuals not families were affected by the *wetsverzettingen*. There may be some truth in this

---

[13] One of these, Adriaen Paets, a fervent supporter both of De Witt and of liberal religious ideas—and thus doubly suspect—was acting as extraordinary ambassador to Spain at the time of the *wetsverzetting*, luckily for him. On his return he was able to take his place in the Rotterdam *vroedschap* because of the prince's support, although he had apparently been replaced in 1672.

[14] Roorda, *Partij en factie*, 171, 238–9.   [15] 'Sociale mobiliteit', 310.

for the smaller and economically stagnant towns, but it does not seem to apply to two of the most economically dynamic towns: Amsterdam and Rotterdam. In Amsterdam, while three of the seven regents ejected in 1618 were quite quickly returned to the oligarchy, the other three were never restored either in their own persons or in their family (one case is ambiguous). Of the ten *raden* expelled in 1672, four of the families regained power later (though for one family this was only in the late eighteenth century), but five never returned (again, one case is ambiguous).

In Rotterdam, of fifteen families ejected in 1618, nine returned to power, either through the male or female lines, but only two of these before 1650 (and one only after 1672). Six families never regained their position in the oligarchy and one did so only after sixty-odd years. Even more strikingly, of the thirteen families expelled in 1672 (the Visch family had two members—cousins—in the *vroedschap* at the time), only two had managed to regain representation by the end of the eighteenth century. Admittedly, both towns were still growing in both wealth and size until at least the 1670s, and thus had pools of potential regents which were also still increasing, while in Rotterdam at least party divisions ran deep and reinforced factional differences, and so they cannot necessarily be seen as typical. Nevertheless, it is clear that for these towns, and probably for at least some of the other large towns too, the *wetsverzettingen* affected families as a whole and not just individuals.

In general, the history of both these towns in the seventeenth century suggests strongly that, in towns which were growing economically and as long as this growth continued, families conventionally well qualified for entry into the oligarchy would also continue to emerge. This process combined with political and demographic factors in towns which were expanding economically to facilitate both steady and convulsive changes in the composition of the regent élite. In contrast, the first half of the eighteenth century produced economic and political conditions which helped to stabilize these élites, leaving in the main only demographic factors to enforce some degree of social mobility.

Having discussed who the regents were, and the degree of mobility into and out of the oligarchy, the question whether they constituted a separate social and economic as well as political élite needs to be considered. Perhaps the least controversial aspect of the regent group as a whole is that it was wealthy; no historian has seriously suggested that the regents were not among the richest people in their society. Traditionally, the phrase used to describe the qualities of these councillors, the 'vroetscap en rijckheyt', reminds us that wealth as well as wisdom were supposed to characterize the regents and to justify their privileged position in society. By the seventeenth century, the regents were not necessarily the richest men in their towns, but a certain minimum prosperity was a prerequisite for entry into the regent group, and loss of it—certainly through bankruptcy—could and did mean the end of a regent's career. Poverty was not simply an economic failing, but a political and moral one as well.

Precisely how the regents compared with their fellow-citizens as regards wealth is less certain, and the evidence available is difficult to evaluate and quite possibly deliberately misleading. On the face of it, the best sources for the study of comparative wealth in the towns of Holland are the tax records, chiefly the accounts of the collection of the 100th and 200th Penny and the registers for the abortive *Familie-Geld*. The former were taxes on wealth, the other an income-tax which was never in fact imposed, but for which information was officially gathered in 1674. Unfortunately for our purposes, these tax assessments and collections were, in practice, in the hands of the town governments, and it is reasonable to suspect that there may have been more or less systematic under-assessment of the regents. On the other hand, the assessments which were made are not improbably low, and they do change for individuals—usually rising—over the years. Also, regents ejected from government do not seem to have had their assessments drastically increased in the aftermath either of 1618 or of 1672, which suggests that either these assessments were fair by the standards of the time, or that the victors in these years were behaving in a remarkably gentlemanly manner to their defeated opponents—which hardly seems to fit the circumstances on either occasion. In any case, the tax records must be used with caution, but used they must be as no other source provides comparable information for such a large part of the urban population.

Such evidence as we have suggests that the regents were drawn, as might be expected, from the richest section of Dutch urban society, but that they were only a part of that wealthy group. Many non-regents were at least as rich as the regent group, and some, certainly in the larger towns, were considerably richer.[16] Wealth was a necessary condition for entry into the regent group but not a sufficient one. This fact is of some importance, as it suggests that, for the seventeenth century at least, the regents were separated from the rest of the broader class of the richer merchants and manufacturers only by their political power, not by wealth. In theory, and to a great extent in practice also, this indicates their representative function. The regents did not just represent their own interests, economic and social, but those of the propertied classes in general as well. In so far as contemporaries justified the powers of the regent group in rational rather than historical terms, their individual wealth was taken to guarantee that they would pursue policies which favoured trade and manufactures—which in general was indeed the case. It is this embeddedness of the Dutch regent group in the broader economic life of their communities which explains the almost single-minded pursuit of the good of the economy which marks the policies not only of the towns of Holland but of the States of the province as well, and to a large extent of the Dutch Republic as a whole.

While the regent élite was recruited from families which had attained prosperity through trade and manufactures, it does seem that its members tended to drift away from direct involvement in such activities as they became established in the oligarchy. The degree to which this occurred during the seventeenth century is unclear, but a movement towards a certain professionalization is evident among the most powerful families at least. One indication of this tendency is the increasing frequency with which sons of established regent families were sent to university, usually Leiden, to study law. The proportion of regents with a law degree increased unmistakably in the course of the century. After graduation, scions of the most powerful families would register as advocates before the court of Holland and then seek some office in the government of their town—most obviously as one of the secretaries or even as *pensionaris*—until a place in the *vroedschap* became available, or until the death of a father or of an elder brother made promotion to the council possible. Such a concentration on a

---

[16] There is no systematic study of the comparative wealth of the regents in seventeenth-century Holland; my remarks are based on sporadic evidence in the existing literature and on study of the records of the 200th Penny tax and the assessment for the *Familie-Geld* in Rotterdam in the 1660s and 1670s.

political career left no room for direct involvement in business, and meant a *rentier* existence was necessary. So, just as the regent oligarchy tended—if not disrupted by political crises, demographic failure, and the like—to become more closed and exclusive, so it also tended to move away from active involvement in those trades and manufactures which were the mainstay of by far the greater part of the upper bourgeoisie. Thus there was the possibility of a cleavage opening up between the economic interests of the regents and those of the wealthy as a whole, and this is indeed what a number of historians have suggested did happen in the eighteenth century. However, while recent research has demonstrated the *rentier* nature of the regent oligarchy in this latter period, it has cast doubt on the idea that this created any real rift between them and the rest of the upper bourgeoisie, as these were also increasingly dependent on investments rather than active involvement in commerce or production. Be that as it may, during the seventeenth century, the forces and pressures which ensured a constant or occasional influx of new families into the regent élite also ensured that the oligarchy remained in close contact with the world of trade and manufacture, as these new families were usually still involved in business at the time of their entry into the regent group. Only when and if this supply of new families into the oligarchy dried up would the development of a significant difference of economic interest and experience between the regents and the rest of the upper bourgeoisie become a real possibility.

This drift away from trade observable among regent families leads naturally to a consideration of the financial benefits to be gained from involvement in local government and administration. In general, the profits of office in the towns of Holland seem to have been very modest indeed—at least officially. Some posts were, of course, extremely profitable. The *schout*, with his fixed percentage of fines levied and all the possibilities of the composition system at his disposal, could do pretty well—and very well if he was prepared to be ruthless. The *baljuw* of Rotterdam[17] was assessed in the *Familie-Geld* of 1674 at an income of f.6,570, and he was not a man with a reputation for uncommon ruthlessness or corruption; and the *baljuw* and *dijkgraaf* of Schieland, also a Rotterdam

[17] The official known in most towns as the *schout* was called *baljuw* in Rotterdam.

regent, was assessed even higher, at f. 7,300.[18] Similarly, the
receivers of certain taxes, for example the 200th Penny, a position
reserved for local regents, could make a considerable amount of
money quite legitimately, as they were paid a percentage of the
total receipts. In general, however, the profits of office available for
most regents were at best modest, and probably did not compare
with the opportunities for gain offered by the booming world of
Dutch trade and manufacture. The risks involved, however, were
minimal, and regent status may have brought privileged access to
certain forms of safe investment. Under Johan de Witt, for example, loans to the States of Holland were a much sought-after form
of investment, as they were utterly reliable in terms both of the
payment of interest and the repayment of capital (though the interest offered was notably low) in a world singularly lacking in secure
investments. Regents were much more likely than those without
political clout to be able to get their hands on part of such loans,
though it also helped to be a friend or political ally of De Witt
himself.[19]

Income from office may well have become much more important
for many, if not most, regents in the eighteenth century, as recent
studies suggest,[20] but this change is probably best understood as a
reaction to the worsening opportunities offered by trade and manufacture in the declining economies of most towns in this period. In
the much more buoyant seventeenth century, and particularly in
the larger towns which continued to grow until well into the second half of the century, continued involvement in business was still
attractive and offered the prospect of greater financial gains than
the profits of office. The Rotterdam regent Johan Timmers was
assessed in the mid-1660s for the 200th Penny at a respectable fortune of f. 50,000, but his younger brother Paulus, who remained in
the family's wine-trading business (until Johan's death opened a
place for him in the *vroedschap* in his turn), was assessed at twice

[18] The assessed incomes of some other individuals, drawn from the same register
(the *kohier* of the *Familie-Geld* for Rotterdam), can give some meaning to these
figures: an apothecary assessed at f. 2,190, a master sailmaker at f. 1,825, a silver-
smith at f. 1,642, a fruit seller at f. 1,460, and a baker and a ships' carpenter both at
f. 912.
[19] H. H. Rowen, *John de Witt, Grand Pensionary of Holland, 1625–1672*
(Princeton, NJ, 1978), 112.
[20] De Jong, *Met goed fatsoen*, 124–5, and Prak, *Gezeten burgers*, 145; but see
Kooijmans, *Onder regenten*, 113.

this amount. It seems unlikely that the two brothers, both well placed within the Rotterdam oligarchy, would have been dealt with by the tax assessors in significantly different ways, and the conclusion seems warranted that—for this family, at this time, at least—a regent career could be less financially rewarding than a business career. One example, of course, does not constitute any kind of proof, but the impression remains that during most of the seventeenth century more money was to be made in business than through a normal regent career. There were considerable profits to be made, but only for the exceptionally successful or powerful; the prospects for most regents were much more modest.

The security of official salaries and emoluments may have been important, however, in a society where safe investments were difficult to find, and for men wishing to concentrate on a regent career such sources of income may often have been of great importance in maintaining a family's financial position. On the other hand, a regent career was not a route to wealth, though it might help to preserve it. Those primarily concerned with profit had more alluring prospects elsewhere, until the Dutch economic boom began to fade in the last third of the seventeenth century. The number of posts which could bring massive financial advantages was very limited, and few of them were available to town regents.[21]

If the official and legitimate profits of office were relatively modest, was corruption a major source of profit for the regents of Holland, and were the possibilities of illegitimate gains an important part of the attraction of a regent career? One of the reasons why contemporaries regarded wealth as a necessary qualification for entry into the regent élite was that this was taken as some sort of a safeguard against misuse of public office for gain. Regents who were already rich were felt to be less likely to be tempted to go beyond the limits of the acceptable in their exploitation of the possibilities offered by their position. Unfortunately, the reality does not always justify this expectation, wealth being no prophylactic against greed. In general, however, corruption in the town governments of Holland, as far as one can tell, seems to have been

[21] An example of a very rewarding public career is that of the receiver-general, De Jonge van Ellemeet: see B. E. de Muinck, *Een regentenhuishouding omstreeks 1700: Gegevens uit de privé-boekhouding van mr. Cornelis de Jonge van Ellemeet, Ontvanger-Generaal der Verenigde Nederlanden (1646–1721)* (The Hague, 1965).

on a modest scale, and perhaps can be charitably renamed as compensation for poorly- or unpaid duties.[22] There were a number of notorious cases which came to light at the time, but the culprits usually seem to have been men of broken or threatened fortune, and not regents with a secure financial position. Johan Kievit, a Rotterdam regent with strong orangist connections, was forced into exile in 1666 because of his implication in the Buat affair.[23] The change of regime in 1672 gave him his opportunity to repair his fortune, and he took it as *advocaat-fiscaal* of the Maas admiralty with rather too much enthusiasm, and was convicted of large-scale peculation in 1689 and exiled for life.[24]

On the other hand, corruption, albeit on a rather petty scale, was rife, though the line between proper and improper practices was not always easy to draw. In particular, the various admiralties offered numerous opportunities for the unscrupulous regent, as Kievit's case reminds us: they not only had large amounts of money to spend and lucrative contracts to award, but were also responsible for the collection of the convoys and licences (import and export taxes). Malversation of funds and the acceptance of bribes by officials appear to have been more the norm than the scandalous exception—and what we know could well be only the tip of an iceberg. A central problem was that the whole system of administration was open to corruption because there were so very few checks and controls over what the regents did, certainly within their own towns. Perhaps the admiralties have become so notorious because here the machinery existed for the discovery of malpractices: formally the admiralties were Generality not provincial or urban institutions, and so they were subject to inspection by higher authorities not only at the provincial but also at the

---

[22] Cf. the discussion of the whole issue of official corruption in the early modern period in J. Hurstfield, *Freedom, Corruption and Government in Elizabethan England* (London, 1973).

[23] Buat had been carrying on a secret correspondence, as well as more open contacts, with the English on behalf of a group of orangists, among whom Kievit was one of the most prominent, who apparently hoped to achieve peace by overthrowing the existing regime in the Republic with English help. Buat's motive was his devotion to the interests of the young prince of Orange, but when this correspondence was discovered—through a piece of almost comical ineptitude on the part of Buat—by De Witt, it was regarded, not surprisingly, as treasonable. Buat was tried and executed; Kievit had to flee the country and was condemned to death *in absentia*.

[24] Melles, *Ministers aan de Maas*, 131–4.

Generality level. It was much more difficult to investigate or control what the regents did in their own towns, where their authority
was practically absolute. The way in which Barthold Cromhout
and Frans Oetgens used their position as powerful Amsterdam
regents to profit personally from the extension of the town in the
second decade of the century is a notorious example of what could
happen. They bought up secretly and cheaply land which they
knew the town would have to buy to carry out the expansion plan
they themselves were helping to push through.[25] The radical decentralization of political authority in this instance played into the
hands of corruption of this sort; particularism disguised and protected self-serving practices at the local level. The only power
within the state which could conceivably have done something to
counteract this tendency was the stadhouder, but the holders of
this office had little interest in the problem and nothing to gain
politically from interfering in the matter. Indeed, under Willem III,
the influence of the stadhouder may well have been used in such a
way as to aggravate the problem, as he was more concerned with
gaining support for his policies than with examining the political
and public morality of the politicians who were able to deliver the
goods for him (see Part 2, Chapter 2). Perhaps patronage and corruption are too similar in their nature to be kept securely apart,
and a political system which worked to such a great extent
through the one would have to live with the other.

The regent élite was recruited from the upper bourgeoisie and
did not constitute a separate and distinct group as far as wealth
alone was concerned; it was only a subsection of the richest part of
Dutch urban society. The composition of the wealth and the
sources of income may have been rather different for regent families, given their privileged access to certain forms of investment and
to the profits of office, but they were not a separate aristocracy of
wealth. However, the regents were clearly a separate group as far
as political power was concerned. Did this special political position
make them a distinct social group? In other words, were they a
distinct aristocracy within urban society, or were they developing
in this direction? Until quite recently, it was generally believed that
a process of aristocratization took place within the regent group,
beginning perhaps around the middle years of the seventeenth

[25] Elias, *Vroedschap*, pp. lxii–lxiii.

century, and this opinion was backed by a considerable amount of pictorial and anecdotal literary evidence. Recent studies of the eighteenth century have put this idea in question,[26] so where does this leave the regents of the previous century?

There can be no doubt that the position and power of the regents bred a certain arrogance in many if not all of them, and that this sense of social superiority expressed itself in marriage strategies and style of life in general. Yet it would be hard to demonstrate that they lived a very different life from that of their wealthy fellow townspeople. Culturally, in the broadest sense, the regents remained part of the upper bourgeoisie, and their language, amusements, type of housing, and education were more or less the same as those of the wealthier section of the population in general. It may be that this changed in the course of the eighteenth century—though the evidence now suggests that if it did the process was a more subtle and intangible one than has hitherto been thought—but for the greater part of the seventeenth century the regent group was a political élite only, not an economic or social one.

Examination of the marriage strategies pursued by regent families produces a fairly predictable picture, but one which is open to a variety of interpretations. For most of the seventeenth century at least, there was a considerable degree of marriage between regent and non-regent families, but equally the evidence suggests that the more firmly established a regent family was the more likely it was to seek marriages either within the regent group of its own town or—and this is a matter far too little investigated—with regent families in other towns. There were good reasons for both approaches: endogamy strengthened alliances within the regent group, and was an almost indispensable step in the formation of factions and even parties; on the other hand, links with outsiders could provide support in the form of sons- and brothers-in-law who were not blocked from entry into the *vroedschap* by too close blood ties with sitting regents. It has been argued that the tendency towards endogamous marriages among the regent élite was intensified during the two stadhouderless periods (1650–72, 1702–47), but the evidence is unconvincing.[27]

---

[26] De Jong, *Met goed fatsoen*, 243; Kooijmans, *Onder regenten*, 205–6; Prak, *Gezeten burgers*, 261.

[27] Van Dijk and Roorda, 'Sociale mobilitiet': the authors fail to take into consid-

In any case, even if established regent élites did tend towards endogamous marriages, rather than using this means to bring outsiders into the oligarchy, then the repeated political crises of the seventeenth century periodically interrupted this process of closure of the oligarchy. The new men brought into the regent group in 1618 and 1672 were generally of mature years, and already married; thus when they entered the oligarchy they not only brought their own families, but also pulled a range of families to whom they were connected, by marriage and otherwise, significantly closer to the political élite. Also, such periodic upheavals, together with the more gradual processes of change and renewal within the regent group, created a sort of penumbra of semi-regent families round the regent group proper. This is a social group which is particularly difficult to define or circumscribe, but consisted of families which had produced regents in the relatively recent past and those allied to such families. Indeed, it is often difficult to decide whether a given family should be considered a member of the regent group at a particular time or not; excluding all families not actually represented in the *vroedschap* at any given time offers a clear, but unsatisfactory, solution. A family which had produced regents in the recent past, and was to do so again in the near future, should surely be considered part of the regent group, even if none of its members were actually on the council at the time; and a whole range of cases with a greater or lesser claim to be included in the élite can be easily imagined. So, besides the fact that the regent group was only a politically privileged section of the upper bourgeoisie, it was also part of an ill-defined larger group with at least some claim to the status enjoyed by the regents and their immediate families. The situation may have been less fluid in the smaller towns, where the pool of eligible families must have been distinctly restricted, and by the eighteenth century the élite may well have become more stable and thus more easily demarcated from the rest of society, but for the bigger Holland towns for most of the

eration that the periods chosen as contrasts to the stadhouderless periods—i.e. 1618–50, 1672–1703, and 1747 onwards—each began with the introduction of a considerable number of new regents, most of them already married, through *wetsverzettingen*. This circumstance gives an artificial boost to the figures for exogamy in the succeeding periods. To put it another way: it was the *wetsverzettingen* which temporarily opened up the regent groups, otherwise regent behaviour in this respect was more or less the same with or without a stadhouder, which might have been expected.

seventeenth century the regents remained in an important sense a part of a larger social formation and not a self-contained urban aristocracy.

In seeking to discover whether, or to what extent, a process of aristocratization of the regent group took place, either in the late seventeenth or in the eighteenth century, it may be that we are hunting the Snark. As far as the seventeenth century is concerned, at any rate, the evidence is not only unsystematic and anecdotal, but its significance is often far from clear. For example, one development which has been adduced to indicate a tendency of the regents to adopt a separate, more aristocratic life-style and consciousness is the purchase of lordships (*heerlijkheden*). These gave their owners limited seigneurial rights over particular areas of the Holland countryside, and enabled them to adopt territorial titles. It has been argued that in this way the regents were beginning to ape the nobility, and adopt a style of life distinct from that of the rest of the bourgeoisie, but is such a view really in accord with the available evidence? Some very prominent seventeenth-century regents did adopt the name of their *heerlijkheden* to give themselves an aristocratic allure—such as the powerful Amsterdam regent Cornelis de Graeff *van Zuidpolsbroek*—but this practice seems to have been uncommon among the regents of Holland as a whole, and may well have been largely restricted to the highly competitive atmosphere of Amsterdam. Most regent owners of *heerlijkheden*, whether they bought them for economic or for social reasons, did not use the titles in ordinary social intercourse. Moreover, the number of regents who in fact bought lordships was probably not very great in any case, though local studies of the question would be useful. Some of the lordships held by regents were not really theirs at all: in Rotterdam, where the town government was more or less systematically buying up the *heerlijkheden* in the surrounding countryside, these were placed in the names of senior members of the *vroedschap*, but ownership remained with the town.

Similarly, the purchase of country houses and estates by town regents has been put forward as illustrating their adoption of a noble rather than a bourgeois life-style. However, there is a great difference between an English merchant's attempt to merge into the gentry through the purchase of a country estate and a Dutch regent's acquisition of a *buiten*. The name itself should give us

pause: it refers to something outside the town, with the latter as
the normal sphere of life. The terminology is that of the inveterate
town-dweller: the country house was a place for a summer retreat,
not a permanent residence. Also, many were distinctly modest
affairs; the grand mansions built by Amsterdam regents and merchants along the Vecht are not at all typical of the common run of
buiten in the seventeenth century. Moreover, in this wish for a
refuge from the dust and smells of town in the summer, the regents
were exhibiting a taste they shared with the upper bourgeoisie as a
whole. Neither the desire for, nor the possession of, a *buiten* was
restricted to the oligarchy, and the regent group remained firmly
rooted in the life and business of the towns.

Another misconception which has grown up on the basis of very
little evidence is that the regents were beginning to express their
cultural separateness by adopting the use of the French language.
There was indeed a growing admiration for French culture from
about the middle of the seventeenth century, however this was not
specific to the regents but affected the educated in general. The
idea that the regents came to despise the Dutch language seems, in
part at least, to rest on a misreading of the evidence; when Pieter
de Groot wrote that 'Le Flament n'est que pour les ignorants', it
was from his embittered exile in Antwerp, where the statement
may well have been true.[28] Other evidence suggests that, far from
deserting their own language for French, a very large number of
prominent regents were not at home with that language. It was
reported that, when an intercepted letter from the French ambassador, D'Avaux, to Louis XIV was read out to the States of
Holland in 1684, many of the members could not understand
French well enough to follow it.[29] Again, there is no hard evidence
here of a cultural separation of the regent group; there may well
have been an increasing cultural rift between the better educated as
a whole and the mass of the Dutch population, but that—though
very interesting in its own right—is a rather different matter.

The regent group, along with the rest of the upper ranks of
Dutch urban society, does indeed seem to have adopted a progressively more luxurious style of living. This can be seen in the richer
clothes of the subjects of portraits, in the steady improvements in

[28] F. J. L. Krämer, *Lettres de Pierre de Groot à Abraham de Wicquefort* (The
Hague, 1894), 401.
[29] Wagenaar, *Vaderlandsche historie*, xv. 181.

the size and amenities of the houses of the regents, in their purchase of country places and carriages, and in the increasing number of their servants. In such matters, however, they remained
representative of the upper bourgeoisie as a whole, at their most
extreme showing the same characteristics in exaggerated form. The
evidence available suggests that the regents had the same social and
cultural values as the rest of the upper ranks of Dutch society.

In one respect there was a growing differentiation between the
political élite and the rest of the upper bourgeoisie: the regents
were becoming more of a specialized profession, not an aristocracy. Whereas at the beginning of the century the great majority of
the regents in the Dutch towns were fully employed in trade or
manufacture, and some were indeed mere shopkeepers or crafts-
men, by the second half of the century there was a clear tendency
among families firmly established within the political élite to move
away from direct involvement in business and to become full-time
politicians and administrators. This process was partly obscured,
and partly slowed down, by the changes in the composition of the
regent group which occurred from time to time, but the underlying
trend seems inescapable. The sons of established regent families
would be sent to Leiden to study law, perhaps go on a more or
less Grand Tour, spend some time as an advocate before the Court
of Holland, and then move into a position in the administration of
their home town while waiting for a place in the *vroedschap* to
become available. This career pattern was wholly distinctive of the
truly established regent family, and was not shared even by those
with a less assured grasp on regent status.

4. Party and Faction

For nearly three decades now, discussion concerning the nature of politics within the voting towns of Holland during the Republic has been shaped to a perhaps unhealthy extent by the question whether what happened is best understood in terms of party or of faction. It seems clear that, as far as recent historical writing is concerned, the protagonists of the predominance of faction are in the ascendant.[1] However, before accepting the current orthodoxy which stresses the priority of faction over party in Dutch seventeenth-century politics, particularly at the local level, two points seem worthy of consideration: first, whether there is more to be said for the role of party, and of ideologies in general, than recent scholarship is willing to allow; and, perhaps more importantly, whether interpreting the political life of the period as if faction and party were mutually exclusive terms is not a misleading way of approaching the subject. The discussion here centres on the towns of Holland in the seventeenth century, but the implications for the politics of the province and even the Republic are not far to seek.

With regard to the first point, it is certainly not my purpose to explain everything in urban politics in party terms, but rather to suggest that the way towards a better understanding of political life in the voting towns of Holland is not to jettison the concept of party altogether, but to reinterpret the meaning and importance of party commitments and ideologies in relation to what can now be seen as the realities of factional politics, as well as to the varied and varying conditions of the individual towns.

What might be called the factionalist interpretation of Dutch politics in the Republican period was a reaction to the

---

[1] Cf. J. Aalbers, 'Factieuse tegenstellingen binnen het college van de ridderschap van Holland na de Vrede van Utrecht', *Bijdragen en Mededelingen betreffende de Geschiedenis der Nederlanden*, 93 (1978); and esp. S. Groenveld, 'Holland, das Haus Oranien und die ander nordniederländischen Provinzen in 17. Jahrhundert: Neue Wege zur Faktionsforschung', *Rheinische Vierteljahrsblätter*, 53 (1989), and *Evidente factiën in den staet: Sociaal-politieke verhoudingen in de 17e-eeuwse Republiek der Verenigde Nederlanden* (Hilversum, 1990).

conventional picture of these centuries, which was seen as basically
anachronistic not just because it described political developments
in terms of party conflict, but also because it conceived the
orangists and republicans as parties of a type which did not really
come into existence until the nineteenth and twentieth centuries.[2] It
can be doubted whether this is an adequate account of the historiography of this subject over the last hundred and fifty years, and it
certainly does less than justice to the subtlety of the writings of
Pieter Geyl, for example,[3] but this reaction against what seems to
have been experienced as a stifling orthodoxy has led to fruitful
new developments both in the topics studied and the methods used
to conduct research into them. Beginning with Roorda's seminal
study of the local conflicts in the towns of Holland and Zeeland
during the 'disaster year' (*rampjaar*) of 1672,[4] the focus of historians' interest has shifted significantly towards the local rather than
the national, and to the faction as an expression of individual and
group self-interest rather than to the party. In the process both
orangists and republicans have been dismissed as the anachronistic
creations of nineteenth-century historians with no basis in the lived
reality of seventeenth-century politics. At the present time, it seems
that the shift in attention towards provincial and urban politics has
been the most fruitful, while the concern with faction and the denigration of party is possibly leading us up a blind alley.

One positive result of this recent stress on faction is that it has
given us a better understanding of what was happening in the
towns, making it clear that to a great extent the stuff of politics at
this level was the competition for power between individuals, families, and family-groupings. What were largely at issue for most of
the time were positions and offices of profit and power, with politi-

[2] See Groenveld, *Evidente factiën*, 7–9 for a brief and forceful summary of this
position. The extent to which this has become the new orthodoxy is suggested by
the remarkably similar historiographical introductions to De Jong, *Met goed
fatsoen*; Kooijmans, *Onder regenten*; and Prak, *Gezeten burgers*.

[3] P. Geyl, 'Historische appreciaties van het zeventiende eeuwse Hollands regentenregiem', in *Studies en strijdschriften* (Groningen, 1958), is still one of the most
useful studies of the subject available, and in general a simplistic party-interpreta-
tion of the politics of the seventeenth or eighteenth century is not easily found in
the work of this historian.

[4] Roorda, *Partij en factie*. The subtitle of this work—'a testing of strength
(*krachtmeting*) between parties and factions'—does not really fit the contents. What
the study shows is a series of local conflicts of considerable complexity, involving
elements which can be described as factional or party-political, but not direct
conflicts between parties and factions.

cal considerations, in the sense of competing policies, remaining very much of secondary importance. This competition for office could express itself in fierce factional infighting, could be strictly regulated by contracts of correspondence or by less formal agreements, or rewards could be more or less fairly distributed among all regents, according to local circumstances. This type of politics lends itself splendidly to investigation and analysis by means of prosopography and genealogy, but such approaches can all too easily obscure other aspects of urban politics which are more difficult to evaluate. The degree to which political conviction or religious orientation may also have played their parts can be disguised by the very methods used by historians to investigate urban politics, despite the fact that these have proved so revealing in other respects—or perhaps because of this.

For example, genealogical studies have shown how closely interrelated the local oligarchies were, and have made it clear that the family, even more than the faction, was the basic element in the political life of the towns of Holland. This circumstance has been taken to mean that regents, in the main, took political decisions because of family interest and connections and not out of conviction, but it is not clear that this necessarily follows. For practical purposes the family can be defined in fairly narrow terms: the nuclear unit together with in-laws, uncles, and cousins; the wider family clan or connections might well have significance when it came to the awarding of jobs, favours, and other help, but not as far as direct participation in the political game was concerned. On the one hand, it is true that it was the family rather than individuals which maintained a grip on a place in the oligarchy; without the family the individual, however gifted, would never even have been able to make a start on a regent career (except in circumstances such as *wetsverzettingen*), while with a powerful family even the most mediocre of men could confidently look forward to a respectable regent career. Thus families rather than individuals were the basic components of factions, unless historians have been misled by the very genealogical techniques which they have used to analyse them. Yet this is not the whole story, for families were basic to the political system in another way as well: they were the guardians and repositories of political traditions and of ideologies in the broader sense. When we note that Johan de Witt was not averse to a discreet use of nepotism, despite his clear abhorrence of other forms of political corruption, this is a reminder that family members could be regarded as reliable political supporters with, most probably, a similar political orientation. In the circumstances of the seventeenth century, for a powerful politician to give positions of profit and influence to relatives was perhaps no more surprising than to find a modern political leader giving office to fellow members of his own party.

On a less exalted level than De Witt, families maintained stable political orientations for remarkably long periods in this century. Families which took the remonstrant side in the first decades of the seventeenth century can be reliably expected to be supporting De Witt and losing out again in 1672, just as they had done in 1618; and contraremonstrant families can also be expected to maintain a generally orangist position throughout the greater part of the century. Of course, individuals and even whole families changed sides for the usual reasons—conviction, opportunism, or a mixture of both—but continuity of family political orientation was the norm by which such not infrequent changes should be measured. Contemporaries assumed that membership of certain families implied a general set of political beliefs and attitudes, particularly in the case of families which had been associated with success or failure during one of the century's periods of marked political polarization. Regent families which had sided with Oldenbarnevelt against Maurits and the 'orthodox' calvinists were marked by this association for generations, and the families of the Loevestein captives of 1650[5] were likewise clearly labelled. Johan de Witt's first steps in provincial politics, before he had established his own distinctive identity, were under the banner of the Loevestein 'faction', and, indeed, it would not be too misleading to take his father's imprisonment during the crisis of 1650 as the key to his later attitude towards crucial issues of domestic politics. Thus, the fact that political groupings were composed of alliances of families does not necessarily mean that they were simply factions, in the sense of having no shared political aims or values other than the struggle for office and power. Such family associations within the oligarchies could also have distinct ideological flavourings.

There are a number of reasons, quite apart from those arising

[5] These were the six delegates to the States of Holland arrested by Willem II in 1650 and imprisoned in the castle of Loevestein. Subsequently, the republicans were often referred to by their opponents as the Loevestein faction.

from the use of a particular methodology in the study of town politics, why the significance of political issues, of 'party', has been underestimated, one of the most important being that the issues which divided the parties in the main only became real at provincial or Generality level.[6] There was no orangist or republican policy applicable to local politics; here both sides pursued more or less the same ends: self- and family-interests together with a general concern for the economic welfare and political autonomy of their own towns. The questions regarding the position of the stadhouder within the province, or of the princes of Orange within the Republic, had little direct influence on the practice of government at the local level, which is one reason why the urban oligarchies could adapt so easily, with sometimes only minimal changes of personnel, to major reorientations in the politics of the province. In day-to-day matters it was of no great significance to the regents whether the prince of Orange or the States of Holland was the more powerful political force within the province. There was perhaps some increase in the effective pressure on town governments by the stadhouder during Willem III's period in office, but this affected both parties and partly explains the very general agreement within Holland not to appoint a successor after the stadhouder-king's death. The inauguration of a second stadhouderless period does not appear to have been a serious party-political issue. The orangist regents were apparently not so orangist as to be prepared to surrender any real part of their local power to a stadhouder. Like their republican compeers, they were first and foremost the masters of local society and wished to stay that way. This was the regents' first principle of political belief, and the orangists shared it with the republicans. On the issue of the autonomy of the voting towns, the two sides were united.

It is perhaps for this reason that the remonstrant–contraremonstrant conflict hit the towns so hard, creating deeper and longer-lasting divisions within the broader regent group as well as the rest of the population of the towns than any other dispute throughout the seventeenth century. For the religious disputes

---

[6] In consequence, the apolitical nature of urban politics in Holland in the eighteenth century portrayed by De Jong, *Met goed fatsoen*, Kooijmans, *Onder regenten*, and Prak, *Gezeten burgers*, is not entirely convincing, as all three authors deliberately chose to ignore their particular town's role in provincial politics, which is precisely where party differences were most likely to show themselves.

of these troubled years did affect how the regents acted at the local level; they directly concerned the policies they were to adopt towards the Reformed Church within their towns, and led to sharp differences of opinion over the role which the official church was to play in local society. So a series of problems could and did occur over the appointment of ministers, the policing of sermons, and the suppression or not of popular agitation. On all these issues ideological considerations determined what decisions were taken on practical matters of local government. Never again, until 1672, and then only briefly, would the Dutch towns be so directly affected and divided by political issues. Normally, the differences between the parties did not have such resonance at the local level. For example, disputes over foreign policy—over peace or war with Spain in the years before 1648, or concerning the proper policy to adopt towards Louis XIV's France—were important, of course, but did not polarize local communities in the way the religious disputes of the early years of the century had done. Even when rival foreign policies involved contrasting economic interests, conflicts at the local level do not seem to have cut so deep or involved such a large proportion of the urban population.

So, it would be a mistake to allow the more spectacular episodes of conflict on party lines to obscure the fact that for most of the time urban politics moved in far less turbulent waters—although personal and factional rivalry could be vicious, its reverberations were generally much more restricted in their effects on the local oligarchies. Also, if it is true that most party issues only came alive at provincial level or higher, then it is distinctly relevant to stress that the majority of the regents of the voting towns of Holland seem to have shown remarkably little interest in affairs beyond their own town, and very few appear to have nursed ambitions at other than the local level. This general attitude revealed itself in a number of ways, but one of the most telling is the circumstance that in most of the oligarchies a relatively small number of men monopolized appointments to important posts outside the towns. Apart from the case of the delegates to the States of Holland— where urban interests were likely to be directly involved in many if not most of the issues to be decided—appointments to the *gecommitteerde raden*, the States General, Council of State, the *Rekenkamer*, etc. tended, in most towns, to circulate among a rather limited number of members of the *vroedschap*. These active members were presumably interested in such matters, and also not too worried that prolonged absences from their home towns would weaken their positions there. The attitude of the majority of the regents, in contrast, reveals not so much a provincial cast of mind but an even further developed particularism centring on their own towns. In such an atmosphere, party politics, even of the limited seventeenth-century sort, was often going to take a back seat, or at least appear to do so.

Yet party allegiances were present and were important, forming a vital component of the traditions and identity of regent families. They were all the more important as they implied or reflected a whole *Weltanschauung*, including attitudes towards religion. It is important, however, not to be too idealistic in our definitions of what political parties should look like: the claim to have discovered divisions within the oligarchy of Middelburg in Zeeland with marked religious and political characteristics[7] has been criticized as showing no more than practical or emotional preferences for or against domination by a prince of Orange rather than a true ideology,[8] but this seems to be setting far too stringent a standard for the use of the term 'party'. Just such practical and emotional motives were probably at the root of party allegiance in the Holland towns in the seventeenth century—but does that make the political loyalties of this period so different from those of later times? The nature of the surviving evidence, however, does make it difficult to assess the significance of political beliefs for individuals and families in this period. There is very little direct evidence of the beliefs and motivations of regents during the seventeenth century; in particular, there are very few collections of private papers or correspondence deriving from ordinary regents. What has survived usually relates to major figures—who were thus far from typical—involved in national politics, and is of an official or semi-official nature—one thinks of the papers of Oldenbarnevelt or the correspondence of De Witt. Perhaps personal and political relations were so face-to-face in Holland that it was unnecessary for most regents to conduct business by letter; clearly in the towns themselves immediate personal contact with friends and colleagues was

---

[7] M. van der Bijl, *Idee en Interest: Voorgeschiedenis, verloop en achtergronden van de politieke twisten in Zeeland en vooral in Middelburg tussen 1702 en 1715* (Groningen, 1981).

[8] Groenveld, 'Holland', 95.

easy, and even on the provincial level both distances and travelling times between the towns or between them and the political centre, The Hague, were relatively short, given the good communications system which existed in the province, including the passenger-barge services on the canals which provided regular and reliable all-weather transport.[9] Just as future historians of our own time will curse the telephone, except in so far as records of phone-tapping survive, so perhaps we should blame the short distances and efficient transport arrangements which obtained in Holland for the paucity of certain types of evidence. Also, Dutch regent families seem to have lacked either the longevity or that family piety so characteristic of the aristocracy in other European countries which has led to the preservation of private archives into the present century.

In consequence, much of the evidence which can be used to investigate political allegiances is at best tangential and more usually simply ambiguous. Official records are generally unhelpful, as voting divisions within councils are very rarely given, because of the prevailing collegial ethos which placed the emphasis on maintaining at least the appearance of unanimity. Usually such divisions within the oligarchy are only traceable when something has gone wrong—during *wetsverzettingen*, for example, when sides became all too apparent, or when the disputes became so serious that one side or the other was prepared to break the otherwise sacrosanct confidentiality of regent business. Religious records, on the other hand, can be important evidence for political matters. This is obviously the case in the first decades of the century, when choosing sides in the religious dispute was in itself a political act, but even later, when all regents were supposed to be members of the Reformed Church, remonstrant links can sometimes be demonstrated in formally orthodox regents. Similarly, readiness to act as elder or deacon, on the one hand, or as political *commissaris* on the local church council, on the other, might well be significant indicators, not only of a regent's position with regard to the role of the Reformed Church, but also on a broader range of political issues (compare the discussion in the following chapter of the relationship between religious and political orientations). However, in general such evidence is suggestive rather than decisive, and even

[9] J. de Vries, *Barges and Capitalism: Passenger Transportation in the Dutch Economy (1632–1839)* (Wageningen, 1978).

such uncertain material is not always available for most of the regents in many of the towns for much of the century.

In considering the whole question of party and faction in Dutch politics in the Republican period, historians should perhaps take a warning from a rather earlier episode in English historiography. Namier's work on eighteenth-century English politics tried to demonstrate the artificial and unrealistic nature of interpretations based on party ideology, and stressed in contrast the importance of political alliances based on patronage and family connections.[10] On the whole this approach has worn well—though, predictably enough, ideology is making something of a comeback even for Namier's chosen period,[11]—but when the method was applied to the early eighteenth century, and *a fortiori* when it was used to explain political conflicts in the Civil War period, the results were unconvincing.[12] The road to the obvious is not always straightforward, and it has taken English historians much labour to reach the conclusion that there are periods when strong ideological divisions exist, and that when they do such beliefs are likely to affect political action. The existence of such divisions in England in the seventeenth and early eighteenth century marked these years off from the relatively cool (in ideological terms) middle years of the eighteenth century.

It may well be that something similar is true of the Dutch Republic, where purely factional explanations of politics seem to work reasonably well for the greater part of the eighteenth century, but where the need to take political and religious convictions into serious account in relation to the early eighteenth century,[13] and at least at key points in the previous century, seems evident.

However, in any case, the point to stress is perhaps not that party is more important than has recently been allowed, but that setting up faction against party is not a very helpful way of

[10] L. B. Namier, *The Structure of Politics at the Accession of George III* (London, 1929) and *England in the Age of the American Revolution* (London, 1930).
[11] L. Colley, *In Defiance of Oligarchy: The Tory Party 1714–60* (Cambridge, 1982), 7 and ch. 4 in general.
[12] The Namierite approach to the early eighteenth century was thoroughly undermined by G. Holmes, *British Politics in the Age of Anne* (London, 1967), and subsequent scholarship has completed the demolition. The historiography of the English Civil War over the last thirty or forty years defies summary, but it is increasingly clear that succeeding waves of 'revisionism' have failed to make the war go away, or to obscure the fact that serious political and ideological issues were involved.
[13] Van der Bijl, *Idee en Interest*.

improving our understanding of the nature of practical politics in seventeenth-century Holland. The dichotomy between party and faction is, it can be argued, to a considerable extent a false one, as the two were far from being mutually exclusive. Rather, the faction can be seen as the basic form of organization for political action at town level in the seventeenth century, and the activities of factions could include party motivations or not, according to time, place, and circumstances. Or, in other words, the faction was not an alternative to the party, but on the contrary was the only form of political organization which was effectively available for the achievement of party objectives. It was an imperfect instrument for the pursuit of ideological goals, but the same could probably be said of any political organization at any time, for the need to gain or maintain power, and all that goes with it in terms of rewards for the faithful, is all too often at odds with the ostensible ideological purpose.

For the most part, political conflicts in the voting towns of Holland were fought out within the regent group itself and its penumbra of closely related families. Only in exceptional periods, such as the crisis during the Truce (1609–21) and in 1672, were broader sections of the population brought into the local political struggles. So in normal times there was no place for a party organization on later lines, with leadership, platform, propaganda, and popular appeals; politics was confined to the politically privileged élite itself. It is true that the regents were influenced in what they actually did and did not do by public opinion, and that this climate of opinion was shaped or expressed by a pamphlet literature of considerable volume and wide appeal, but the degree to which competing regent groups were prepared to appeal for support outside the oligarchy was distinctly limited except in times of extreme desperation or ambition.

Rather than seeing party and faction as direct competitors, it would seem better to recognize that they acted on two different levels of the political system, or that they were different in nature as well as aim. Faction was a permanent part of the structure of the political life of the oligarchy in the voting towns of Holland; faction was the way the system worked. It could act as a component of the party system or cut across it according to circumstances. There is a good example of this in a letter from the Rotterdam regent, Adriaen Paets, to Johan de Witt explaining how factional considerations had led to some arrangements that were less than ideal from the point of view of the partisans of the True Freedom. However, there was a brighter side. 'It is true that, for the working out of that plan the assistance was sought of two people, one of whom is not of our sentiment and the other is incapable of forming any sentiment about affairs, but that it is equally true that the concessions made for their help were without damaging consequences for the future, and allow us the power to provide the States of Holland with a firm and honourable counsellor and the coming meeting with generous delegates . . .'.[14] He ends with pious comment: 'I hope that all will turn out for the best, and that this town, once the debts of the new regents have been paid, will outstrip all the other members in the matter of liberty.'[15] The faction could be the local organizational base of a party, or it could be purely concerned with the control of power and profits, or more likely it would be both in a great variety of different proportions.

The temperature of provincial, and Generality, political debate, and the urgency of matters in dispute, were important variables with regard to the degree to which local factions took on a party-political flavour. Clearly, at times of crisis, most obviously during the Truce and in 1672, party feeling became more acute and the regent group at local as well as provincial level became more polarized, as indeed urban society outside the regent group was both becoming more involved in the political system than was possible at more normal times, and was being similarly divided along ideological lines. At times of heightened political conflict the party nature of the opposed local factions became obvious, whereas in quieter times it might be obscured or, indeed, absent. However, at the same time, these periods of crisis also created openings for men motivated purely or largely by opportunism, as such periods of acute political divisions gave outsiders the rare chance of breaking

---

[14] ' 't is waer, dat tot uytwerckinge van dat dessein versocht is de assistentie van twe luyden, waervan den éénen niet en is van ons sentiment in veele saken en d'ander incapabel, om eenig sentiment over saken te formeren, maer dat is van gelycken waer, dat de toesegginge van hare hulpe was sonder schadelycke engagementen in het toekomende en dat sy ons liet het vermogen, om Hare Edel Groot Mog. van een eerlijk en cordaet conseiller en de naeste vergaderinge van genereuse gedeputeerden te versien . . .'

[15] '. . . ich hope, dat alles ten besten sal uytvallen en dat dese stadt, nadat de schulden van de nieuwe regenten sullen wesen geacquiteert, alle d'andere leden in het point van de liberteyt sal vooruyttreden . . .', in N. Japikse (ed.), *Brieven aan Johan de Witt* (Amsterdam, 1919–22), ii. 295–6.

into the otherwise impregnable regent élite by taking on the colours of one party or the other. In 1672 and in the run-up to 1618 such ambitious men played a significant part in the organization of orangist opposition in towns dominated by supporters of Oldenbarnevelt and De Witt, and the successful ones were indeed able to break into the regent élite on a tide of orangism. It is perhaps as significant that such party colours were adopted by these ambitious outsiders, as that the sincerity of their commitment to orangism can be legitimately doubted. In fact, commitment to the ostensible purposes of the oppositional movement seems to have been more genuine in 1618, probably due to the important religious component of the disputes at that time, than in 1672, as many of the new regents who came to power in the latter year quite quickly proved to have no very deep allegiance to the broader aims of orangist policy. So, in these periods of crisis, both genuine and powerful party feelings were revealed, but at the same time the naked self-interest of factional infighting was also displayed at its most uninhibited. It is thus no surprise that these crises are difficult to interpret, and send powerful but contradictory messages about the nature of political life in the voting towns of Holland.

As far as can be judged from the existing literature, the strength of party allegiances, and the importance of party divisions, varied greatly not only from time to time but also from town to town. At the one extreme there were towns such as Rotterdam, where remonstrant influence was strong in the early decades of the century, not only within the regent group but also within the potential recruiting ground of regents, the upper bourgeoisie, in general. In such towns there was a remarkable continuity of party loyalties, embodied in families and their traditions, linking the supporters of Oldenbarnevelt to those of De Witt, by way of the States-party opponents of Frederik Hendrik's war policy in the 1630s and 1640s. Here not only families remained politically consistent, but structures of alliances between families were also far from ephemeral. At the other extreme were towns where factional conflict seems to have been undisturbed by political ideas and ideals.

Sometimes, however, this lack of party motivation in factional conflict can be misleading as far as what it seems to tell us about the nature of town politics is concerned. For example, the conflicts within the oligarchy in Hoorn in the late 1660s and early 1670s came to a head ostensibly over the question of the preservation of an old privilege which gave the citizens at least the appearance of influence over the selection of burgemeesters, but it has been convincingly shown that this issue of principle was something of a red herring. On the contrary, what seems to have been the problem was widespread corruption in the town government, with the crassest example being the involvement of a number of leading regents in large-scale malversations in the Hoorn chamber of the East India Company.[16] The whole affair is particularly unsavoury, but should not be seen as demonstrating the essentially non-party nature of politics at the local level. Both majority and minority factions in the Hoorn *vroedschap* were supporters of De Witt, and there is little trace of orangism in any of the regents in this town, so any disputes which occurred could not take on a party coloration. It is perhaps as interesting that neither of the factions even pretended to be orangist, which might have been a useful ploy if political convictions had mattered nothing to the participants.

Some towns were dominated by one party—Leiden and Haarlem, for example, were notoriously orangist for most of the rest of the century after the defeat of the remonstrants in 1618—while in others the regent group was divided along party lines, but in all competition for office and for the perquisites of office was a permanent factor, with nothing necessarily connecting it with the issues that divided the parties at the provincial or state level. The ideological component of the greater part of local political concerns was minimal if not non-existent, except in the case of religion, which is why the Holland towns were almost drawn into civil war on the remonstrant issue. In that instance a party issue was of immediate relevance for policy at the local level, but such integration of local and national conflicts was, thankfully, rare, otherwise the picture of town politics in Holland would have been much more violent, and antagonisms much more irreconcilable, than they in fact were. In general, local power struggles generated powerful antagonisms on the individual and family level, but these were only rarely exacerbated by the extra boost of genuine ideological divisions. These came at the provincial and national level.

---

[16] D. J. Roorda, 'Een zwakke stee in de Hollandse regentenaristocratie: De Hoornse vroedschap in opspraak, 1670–5', *Bijdragen voor de Geschiedenis der Nederlanden*, 16 (1961).

5. Religion, the Reformed Church, and Urban Politics

Religion in general, and the Reformed Church in particular, played an important role in the politics of the towns of Holland, not only in the first decades of the seventeenth century, when the clash between remonstrants and contraremonstrants was a dominant issue, but throughout the century. The Reformed Church had a peculiar position in the political life of the Dutch state because it functioned as one of the few unifying symbols which the decentralized and heterogeneous Republic possessed. As the official church it had a political significance which the other churches and sects lacked: while membership of the church or attendance at its services was not imposed on the inhabitants of the country at large, it was nevertheless in an important sense the state church and all holders of public office at every level were supposed to be members. Its physical occupation of the churches unwillingly vacated by the catholics, often the most prominent buildings in the towns as well as the countryside, was a very visible expression of its unique position in the Dutch Republic.

The influence of the Reformed Church on the political process during the seventeenth century is of particular importance because, for much of the period, there was a close relationship between Reformed orthodoxy and orangism which gave both persuasions extra political force. Reformed support for the house of Orange was established during the Truce crisis and remained a determining structure of Dutch political life until the end of the Republic, and perhaps later, but was of especial force during the seventeenth century. Conversely, Reformed orthodoxy was a central component of orangism, and lent it a passion and a popular appeal which a purely secular political stance might well have lacked. However, when looking at the role of religion in town politics it is necessary to avoid over-simplification. First, all regents were members of the Reformed Church, formally at least, and this became increasingly the case in practice as well as in theory as the century progressed.

Secondly, not all ministers of the Reformed Church were orangists,[1] though this often seemed to be the case at the time.

With regard to ensuring that all regents should become members of the church, this was not at all easy to achieve, especially in the early decades of the century, and many towns retained formulas which did not require magistrates or regents in general to be full members of the church. In these cases, regents had to be at least— according to one variant of the formula—'de Gereformeerde religie toegedaan' (committed to or favouring the Reformed religion). This phrase, or a similar form of words which amounted to the same thing, seems to indicate regular attendance at the services of the church, but not that actual membership which would have exposed the regents not only to the surveillance of the church council in moral matters but also to pressure to undertake the onerous and not always congenial tasks of elder and deacon. Nevertheless, after the expulsion of the remonstrants from the town governments in 1618 (and these were in any case members of the church before their expulsion after the synod of Dordt in the following year),[2] all regents had to be at least nominally attached to the Reformed Church, which included the Walloon Church[3] but not, of course, the new remonstrant churches which were set up in the aftermath of the defeat at Dordt, or any of the dissenting protestant sects. The regents had their special pew (the *herenbank*) in the main church of their town, symbolizing the close relationship between state and church which it was felt should, and to a large extent did, exist. So, all regents were part of the Reformed Church, but some were more firmly attached to its doctrines than others, and on the whole orangists were more ready to work sympathetically with the church than their opponents. In studying the careers of individual regents, it is perhaps as important to note their relationship to the church as any other aspect of their lives. As especially prominent men in their towns, the regents could be

[1] Cf. M. Th. Uit den Bogaard, *De Gereformeerde en Oranje tijdens het eerste stadhouderloze tijdperk* (Groningen, 1954).

[2] The remonstrants or arminians (after the Leiden professor of theology, who can be considered as the founder of the group, Jacob Arminius) favoured a broader interpretation of what constituted Reformed orthodoxy than was acceptable to their opponents—in particular, their proposed modifications to the doctrine of predestination caused outrage. They were defeated at the synod of Dordt, expelled from the Reformed Church, and eventually set up their own separate church.

[3] The Walloon (*Waalse*) church was a French-speaking calvinist church with a separate organization from the Reformed Church, but in full communion with it.

expected to accept the responsibilities this position brought with it, and in relation to the church this meant service first as deacon then as elder. This was certainly the proper relationship between town government and official church as the latter saw it. Those regents who were willing to serve on the church council in these offices are likely to have taken a rather more positive view of the church's role in public life, and perhaps also to have been more sympathetic to its general reverence for the princes of Orange than those who avoided such service. In contrast, those regents who were prepared to act as watchdogs for the magistracy on the church council (as *commissarissen politiek*) were possibly showing that for them control rather than co-operation was the watchword in the relationship between the civil authorities and the Reformed Church, and taking on such an office may well be an indication of republican sympathies.

The association between the States party and liberal protestantism, particularly of the moderate remonstrant variety, is tolerably clear but, after the defeat of 1618–19, could only be expressed in indirect ways. The link was at its closest in the decade or so before 1618, when the supporters of Oldenbarnevelt were marked by both a stress on the provincial autonomy of Holland expressed through the States, and by support for the remonstrants in their struggle with the forces of self-styled orthodoxy. This period marked the formation of the distinctively republican element in Holland politics, and the stamp of its formative years stayed with it for the rest of the century at least. However, after this period, open membership of the remonstrant church was denied to the urban oligarchs, and so the question of the religious attitude of republican regents becomes largely a matter of inference from indirect evidence. It would be going too far to suggest that in general republican regents were hypocrites who only remained in the Reformed Church because it was essential to their careers. These men were no more hypocrites than most in public life at the time, who found it possible to believe sincerely and whole-heartedly in the teachings of the dominant church of their country. Republican suspicions of the influence of the Reformed Church, apart from a revulsion inspired by the events of the years leading up to 1618–19, stemmed from its general support for the position and power of the princes of Orange, and its tendency, both in foreign and domestic concerns, to put religious rather than political or economic considerations first. It was possible to believe sincerely in the teachings of the Reformed Church without also believing that it should be allowed, as a human institution, to interfere in matters that properly belonged to the magistrate. Republican regents tended to be more sympathetic to the remonstrants, and in general less ready to respond to pressure from the Reformed Church to take effective action against protestant dissenters and even catholics. For example, one clear consequence of the defeat in the government of Amsterdam of the party which had triumphed in 1618 was a much more lenient attitude to the beleaguered remonstrants, and indeed to nonconformists in general from the mid-1620s onwards.[4] The difference between orangists and republicans in such matters, however, was to a great extent a matter of nuance and style rather than fundamentally different policies. The great majority of regents of whatever political colour was reluctant for purely expedient reasons to take any steps towards the persecution of dissenters in any systematic way, though for the republicans expediency was likely to be reinforced by principle. Similarly, both parties showed themselves ready to pass laws against the practice of the roman catholic faith, but neither side was prepared to enforce such laws with any rigour. Again, the reasons may have included principle, particularly where republican regents were concerned, but the practical difficulties facing any effective action are likely to have been the decisive factor.

In some towns the differences between republicans and orangists with regard to religious attitudes and preferences were more marked. In Rotterdam, for example, where the remonstrants had been very strong before 1618, the regents of the States party, although necessarily members of the orthodox church, seem nevertheless to have retained strong links with dissenting groups. While Van der Goes's comment in 1671 that the Rotterdam *vroedschap* was full of arminians[5] may have been an exaggeration—or an over-simplification—it is true that many of the republican regents in this town can be found to have had links with the remonstrants and, in a much more radical direction, with the collegiant movement, particularly during the first stadhouderless period.[6]

---

[4] H. A. Enno van Gelder, *Getemperde vrijheid* (Groningen, 1972), 82–3.
[5] C. J. Gonnet (ed.), *Briefwisseling tusschen de gebroeders van der Goes 1659–1673* (Amsterdam, 1899), ii. 321.
[6] For the considerable activity which the collegiants developed in Rotterdam,

Rotterdam may well have been an extreme case in this respect, but if so its regents were only displaying in exaggerated forms characteristics which they shared with a large proportion of republican regents.

On the other hand, the orangist regents had in common with the republicans a concern to keep the Reformed Church under strict political control. In normal times they were no less concerned than their fellow regents to restrict the church and its ministers to their proper concerns, as they saw them, and to prevent them from interfering in political matters. At times of political crisis, the orangists could and did benefit from the intervention of rabidly orangist ministers into the political life of their towns, but in general they shared to the full the common regent view that political matters were their affair and that the church should keep out of them. This attitude by the regents could lead to conflict in two areas especially: the appointment of ministers and the content of sermons.

The role of town governments in the selection of ministers for the Reformed Church in their towns was never properly regulated at the provincial level. Attempts had been made in the 1580s and 1590s to reach an agreement which would be valid for Holland as a whole, but no formula could be found which was acceptable to both the church and the regents. To simplify a rather complex matter, the civil authorities wanted the power to veto what they felt to be unsuitable appointments, while the church was only willing to allow town governments a consultative voice. In consequence, appointments of ministers were always potential causes of discord, particularly as church and magistrate tended to look for rather different qualities in their pastors. The regents were above all concerned that ministers called to their town should be 'peaceable' men, while the church was likely to prefer those with rather more evangelical bite. In the case of sermons, it was all too likely that ministers would slant their exhortations in directions unwelcome to the regents, though outside the periods of crisis the weapons available to the magistracy were sufficient in most cases to keep preachers circumspect. Cases such as that of the fervently orangist Rotterdam minister, Ridderus, who preached what were

together with some indications of their links with the local regents, see J. C. van Slee, *De Rijnsburger collegianten* (Haarlem, 1895), 95–135 and J. Melles, *Joachim Oudaan* (Utrecht, 1958).

felt, not only by the Rotterdam *vroedschap* but also by the *gecom-mitteerde raden* (to whom a mysterious report of the matter was sent), to be seditious sermons during the second Anglo-Dutch war, remind us of the financial control the regents had over ministers of the church. As the accusation was that Ridderus had preached that Oldenbarnevelt had been a traitor, that God would punish the Republic if it continued to be ungrateful to the house of Orange, and that he and all pious men were dissatisfied with the 'maxims' of the existing government in Holland, it is perhaps not surprising that he had his salary suspended.[7] The civil authorities paid the salaries of the ministers of the Reformed Church, as well as own-ing the church buildings, which illustrates the officially supported status of the church, but also gave the magistracy considerable power.

A striking example of the suspicions which the regents as a whole entertained with regard to the Reformed Church is the insti-tution of the office of *commissarissen politiek*, representatives of the town government on the local church councils. Such political observers, representing the States of Holland, were well established for provincial synods, but in the course of the century they began to be introduced at the town level as well. There is evidence that they were deeply resented by the church councils,[8] all the more so because of the feeling that, if the regents had been prepared to take the responsible role in church affairs proper to their position in society, then they would have been adequately represented among the elders and this distasteful form of supervision would have been unnecessary. It may well be that this particular, rather draconian and often offensive, manner of keeping the church in line was more especially the work of dominant republican groups, and that those regents accepting the job of *commissaris politiek* were among the most fervently anti-orangist—though they were unlikely to be too openly tainted with heterodox religious connections or sympa-thies.

One of the chief reasons for keeping a close eye on the ministers of the Reformed Church was the belief that they had great influence on the populace as a whole, and thus were capable of

---

[7] Price, 'Rotterdam Patriciate', 111–12.

[8] Whether this was generally true has been questioned by Groenhuis, *De predikanten*, 28, but he admits that they were often introduced as a result of serious conflict between town governments and church councils.

76   *Town Politics in the Province of Holland*

stirring up popular feeling against the authorities. The demagogic role, and success in that role, of ministers seems borne out in particular by the events during the Truce crisis and again in the troublesome summer months of 1672. In particular, the difficulties which contraremonstrant ministers were able to cause for remonstrant town governments was a dreadful warning to the regents of the dangers of pushing the Reformed Church too far, and one which remained with them for the rest of the century. The Amsterdam minister Adriaan Smout demonstrated another aspect of the real influence of the Reformed clergy in the 1620s when he successfully attacked the Amsterdam directors of the VOC[9] for their neglect of the widows and orphans of some of their seamen who had been lost at sea, forcing them to make excuses and change their policy.[10] Such influence seems to have been real, though perhaps less great than nervous regents often supposed.[11] It does appear that, when there was general and serious dissatisfaction with a town government, the ministers of the Reformed Church were nearly the only alternative possessors of moral authority, able to act in some sense as representatives of the *burgerij.*

However, such influence is less easily explicable than the popular power of the clergy in most other countries of seventeenth-century Europe. The population of the voting towns of Holland was far from homogeneously Reformed. Not only regents were attracted to the remonstrants either in the early years of the movement or later, and throughout the seventeenth century a not insignificant proportion of the population were protestant dissenters, particularly mennonites. The real problem, however, is presented by the catholics. The proportion of the population of the Republic which was catholic in one sense or another, in these years before the existence of official religious censuses, has long been a matter for dispute between experts—not to say partisans—but the precise figures are perhaps less important here than the general picture, which is not really in dispute. For the greater part of the seventeenth century, somewhere in the region of 40–50 per cent of the total population of the Republic was catholic, so why did this large proportion of

---

[9] The Dutch East India Company (*Vereenigde Oost-indische Compagnie*).
[10] R. B. Evenhuis, *Ook dat was Amsterdam*, ii (Amsterdam, 1967), 158–9.
[11] On this question in general, see Groenhuis, *De predikanten*, 31–8.

non-members not undermine the popular influence of the ministers of the Reformed Church?

First, the population of the towns of Holland had a significantly different religious profile than the population of the Republic as a whole. The overall figure for catholics in the total population was inflated by the existence of certain regions, in North Brabant in particular but not only there, which were almost entirely catholic. In the voting towns of Holland the proportion of the population which remained loyal to the catholic church was notably less than in the population as a whole, though still considerable at perhaps 15–20 per cent for most towns (see Chapter 6). (Moreover, as the towns recruited much of their population from the surrounding country areas, and as these were more catholic than the towns, at least in south Holland, then the proportion of catholics at least held steady against confessional erosion in the course of the century, and may even have grown.) Secondly, it may be that the very presence of such large, but not overwhelming, numbers of dissenters and catholics stimulated Reformed militancy and sense of confessional cohesion. The heterodox were present in large enough numbers to cause alarm, but not enough to intimidate. On the other hand, religious riots against catholics were remarkably rare, though tensions occasionally rose high in years of external threat.[12]

Perhaps the answer is that it was the large-scale orangism of the mass of the population which explains the apparent influence of the Reformed ministers: they were, in this sense, preaching to the converted. The Reformed Church provided a platform for, and a prominent articulation of, popular orangism rather than creating it. Moreover, it may well be that the church acted as a focus for resentment of regent rule, and suspicions of its trustworthiness. It appears to be the prevailing orthodoxy that there were few or no class or social antagonisms in Dutch society in the seventeenth century, but it is hard to escape the conviction that in an important sense orangist mobs were expressing deep-seated social resentment, if not loathing, of the regent regime. At times of crisis, this resentment tipped over into positively paranoid fear and suspicion. The regents were believed to have sold the country out to Spain in 1618 and to France in 1672 (both, of course, catholic powers), and in

---

[12] Dekker, *Holland in beroering*, 39. There were serious anti-catholic riots in 1747, but nothing approaching this scale of violence occurred in the seventeenth century.

these circumstances the representatives of the Reformed Church could at least be trusted to be unswervingly loyal to the Dutch state—as the whole survival of the Reformed Church depended on keeping all catholic powers at bay. This was not an entirely irrational reaction: the regents not only strove to keep all power in their own hands, they also regarded information about foreign and domestic politics as none of the public's business. In such circumstances excessive secrecy could reap its own rewards in the readiness of an ill-informed public to believe even the wildest of rumours. However, whereas in the popular view the regents could be up to anything, the ministers of the Reformed Church could be trusted—the tendency towards a confusion or conflation of religious orthodoxy with patriotism was present even in such a religiously pluralist society as the Dutch Republic.

Whatever the reasons for, or the reality of, the popular influence of the Reformed Church, the regents certainly believed in its importance. This is demonstrated not only by their concern to monitor and, if possible, control the activities of the church and its ministers, but also through the extent to which they were prepared to make concessions to its demands. The general question of the treatment of catholics and dissenters is better dealt with at provincial or Generality level (see Part 2, Chapter 6; and Part 3, Chapter 5), but with regard to the local level of politics it is clear that the magistracy felt that they could not simply ignore the strictures of the ministers of the church. First of all, they were themselves members of the church, and were bound to heed the guidance of their ministers in spiritual matters. Moreover, with regard to the catholics the difference in their attitude from that of these ministers lay largely in the area of what was thought to be practical politics. The regents in general shared the church's abhorrence of catholicism, but believed that any attempt at effective action would be disastrous, so they paid lip-service to Reformed demands for restrictions of the *stoutigheden der papisten* (the naughtinesses or insolence of the papists) but did as little about it as they could get away with. With regard to protestant dissenters and radicals, the situation was rather different, as enough regents throughout Holland displayed sympathy with liberal protestant ideas to ensure that such religious movements were protected from Reformed intolerance. However, even here there were limits to the freedom of action available to the town magistrates. Extreme radicals could be, and were, persecuted by the local authorities; in particular, socinianism continued to be anathema to the orthodox, and magistrates frequently had to take some action against publications accused of this heresy and their printers, though often with apparently deliberate inefficiency.[13] The early quakers too were often subject to official harassment, but the quietistic collegiants were generally left alone after the persecution of the remonstrants (with whom they were easily confused in the early years) died down. Some matters continued to be sensitive issues well into the period of the pre-Enlightenment in the last years of the century. It is interesting to note, for example, that the magistrates of Rotterdam put pressure on Pieter Rabus, in response to strong protests from the local Reformed Church, to tone down the treatment of radical religious and philosophical ideas in his periodical, *De Boekzaal van de Geleerde Wereld*. Serial publications in Latin or French could apparently be more or less ignored, but a publication in Dutch was an entirely different matter, and Rabus had to censor his approach to ideas likely to offend against Reformed orthodoxy.[14]

A question that would repay investigation is the extent to which the Reformed Church offered a field of public action for men excluded from the regent élite. The offices of elder and deacon offered to men of wealth and ambition a public role of importance and prestige, and an affirmation of their standing in local society. Other than these church offices there were few if any such positions in the society of the towns of Holland outside the government itself—the boards of charitable institutions perhaps, or the position of *vredemaker*,[15] in some towns the position of *schepen*. There is some evidence to suggest not only that service on the church council was the recourse of those with thwarted political ambitions, but also that the body of former and actual elders and deacons could form a sort of embryonic opposition group to the regents.

It is hardly surprising that former elders and deacons of the Reformed Church figured prominently among the new magistrates appointed by Maurits in 1618, but in Rotterdam at least the same was also true of the new regents of 1672. This may possibly have

[13] Enno van Gelder, *Getemperde vrijheid*, 174–9.
[14] J. J. V. M. de Vet, *Pieter Rabus (1660–1702)* (Amsterdam, 1980), 272–5.
[15] The *vredemakers* constituted a body for the settlement of minor civil disputes; the actual name of the institution differed from town to town.

been a result of the peculiarly heterodox reputation of the
Rotterdam *vroedschap*, but it may equally well be that the opposition groups in the most strongly republican of towns tended to
centre round the leaders of the local Reformed Church. In relatively normal times, the church-centred activities of prominent men
could be a politically harmless outlet for the desire for public
recognition, but in more disturbed periods the combination of personal identification with religious orthodoxy and thwarted ambition could produce a politically explosive force.

In general, while it would be a mistake to suggest a complete
identification of orangists with Reformed orthodoxy, and of republicans with liberal calvinism or even protestant dissent, nevertheless
a general tendency of this nature does seem to have existed in the
oligarchies of the towns of Holland. The connection seems to have
been rather stronger the other way around: firm supporters of
Reformed orthodoxy were very likely to be orangist, and equally
those with liberal religious sympathies were likely to be republican
in their political coloration.

6. Catholics, Dissenters, and Politics

Another circumstance which affected the atmosphere in which politics took place in the towns of Holland in the seventeenth century was the existence of significant groups of people who were outside the ranks of the official church. In principle, of course, protestants who were not members of the Reformed Church had no role in the political life of their town, and the catholics would have been banned even more definitively if this had been possible. In practice matters were not always as clear cut as this suggests: catholics or quasi-catholics may have remained in the governments of some towns in Holland into the second or third decades of the century, and the more respectable dissenting protestant groups had sympathizers, if not open adherents, among the regent élite for much of the century. More important than such tenuous or disguised influences, however, was the sheer size of these groups in the population as a whole, and in the towns in particular, which meant that they could not simply be ignored by the authorities. The existence of large numbers of people outside, and possibly hostile to, the Reformed Church, was an important element in deciding what was and was not politically and practically possible in the towns of Holland during the seventeenth century.

Such religious outsiders maintained a presence in the regent group in the late sixteenth and the early decades of the seventeenth century, and even in later years the orthodoxy of some town councils was not beyond question. Whereas catholics or catholic sympathizers were probably the most important nonconformists in the oligarchies of the Holland towns at the beginning of this period, they very largely, if not entirely, disappeared from them after the second decade of the seventeenth century. On the other hand, protestant dissent in a variety of shadings continued to have some representation among the regents. The remonstrant influence, after a temporary near-eclipse after 1618, reasserted itself quite quickly, and regents with remonstrant leanings or connections made their way back into some at least of the *vroedschappen* by the middle years of the century. Usually those regents with heterodox sympathies conformed to the official church on the surface but maintained regular contacts with catholics or dissenters, particularly among their own relatives. While catholic influence appears to have become negligible, certainly after the troubles during the Truce, the degree of regent involvement with the remonstrant church and with other heterodox groups such as the collegiants, especially in the years of high religious excitement in the middle decades of the seventeenth century, would repay investigation. In the third quarter of the century, the government of Rotterdam was notoriously sympathetic to the remonstrants, and a number of members also had significant collegiant contacts in this period. Similar links between regents and respectable, and sometimes even radical, dissent existed in other towns as well, though the case in Amsterdam of Coenraad van Beuningen's involvement with heterodox movements and then descent into religious mania is a trifle extreme.[1]

Such connections may have brought the regents as a whole the covert support of those sections of society which were less than unquestioningly loyal to the Reformed Church, but religious heterodoxy, either actual or suspected, could also draw down upon the regents, and certainly upon individuals among them, considerable popular hostility. This was particularly likely to be the case at times of high political tension. The way in which the suspect religious attitudes of the regents could alienate significant sections of the urban population was shown clearly enough in the run-up to the crisis of 1618, when a large proportion of the regents of the towns of Holland were more or less fervently, and for more or less idealistic reasons, attached to the remonstrant cause, and regularly found themselves the object of violent demonstrations by 'orthodox' mobs. Once stated, the theme was to re-emerge often enough in the course of the century to become an underlying structure informing Dutch political perceptions. It is noticeable that the attacks on Wittian regents in 1672 echoed those on the supporters of Oldenbarnevelt half a century earlier in their combination of orangism and accusations of disloyalty to the Reformed Church. Clearly, in the popular mind orangism, orthodoxy, and patriotism were closely allied, and regents lacking in one part of this triad were likely to be suspected of deficiencies in the others as well. In

[1] C. W. Roldanus, *Coenraad van Beuningen: Staatsman en libertijn* (The Hague, 1931), 54–8.

1672, whereas there is little substance to the accusations of lack of patriotism—lack of courage is perhaps a rather different matter—in many cases there may have been at least some truth to justify the suspicions of religious heterodoxy.

A characteristic of both the catholics and the protestant sects was that they were not drawn from distinct and separate sections of the Dutch population. They were represented on all levels of society, with the formal exception of the political élite, and were thoroughly integrated into all aspects of the economic and cultural life of the towns. Consequently, they could not be easily marginalized and treated as an alien element within the majority community, and this in itself provided considerable protection against effective persecution.

Whereas the general image of the protestant dissenter at the beginning of the century was of the humble mennonite drawn from the artisan and small-shopkeeper sections of the lower middle classes, with the defeat of the arminians and the setting up of a separate remonstrant church came an important change in the profile of dissent. It was now also strongly represented, qualitatively if not quantitatively, among the wealthier and better-educated sections of Dutch society. Moreover, the various baptist groups had moved a long way from their subversive reputation of the early sixteenth century, and by the beginning of the following century had become a byword for piety, industry, and trustworthiness—the archetype of the economically valuable Dutch citizen.

Many prominent families in the towns as well as in the countryside remained loyal to the old church, or returned to this loyalty in the course of the seventeenth entury, and the catholics remained well represented in the wealthier and better-educated sections of Dutch society, even attracting some notable converts, especially following the proscription of the remonstrants after 1619.[2] They were progressively excluded from the political élite, but seem to have suffered relatively little in social and economic terms. However, the precise social profile of the catholic population of the voting towns of Holland is difficult to assess, and possibly changed significantly in the course of the century. It is not just that there is some difficulty in finding out how many catholics there in the towns at any given time, but that for a considerable period in the

---

[2] Some leading remonstrants converted to catholicism and others, like Grotius, were rumoured to have done so.

beginning of the century it is not clear who were and who were
not to be considered catholics. After the almost complete collapse
of the organization of the catholic church in the course of the
Revolt, it was only slowly that a new system of pastoral care was
established by the church on missionary lines. For the first decades
of the seventeenth century there are very few church records, most
non-Reformed (under official pressure) had their children baptized
in the public church, and many people may very well not have
known themselves whether they were catholic or not—or, indeed,
what the difference was. As the new ecclesiastical organization
took hold towards the mid-century, usable figures for catholic
communicants become available, and in the second half of the century more and more catholics had their children baptized in their
own churches, and so reliable estimates of catholic numbers
become possible. Thus any estimate of the size of the catholic proportion of the urban population for the early seventeenth century
is likely to be seriously misleading, not only because of the lack of
reliable statistics but also because of the fluidity and lack of
definition of the religious loyalties of many people in these years.
From about the mid-century on, however, it becomes possible to
make estimates which have some relation to the realities of the
time. These suggest that the proportion of catholics in the Holland
towns was less than that in the population as a whole, but still
substantial. In Amsterdam, for example, catholics formed something in the region of 20 per cent of the population in the late seventeenth century,[3] and in Rotterdam about 15 per cent;[4] while a
recent study of Haarlem in the early years of the century suggests a
figure of 12 per cent for the active catholic population,[5] though
this could be a serious underestimate of those who were more
catholic than anything else.

The number of catholics in the towns of Holland seems likely to
have increased in the course of the seventeenth century, not only as
a result of the progressively better self-identification of the catholic
section of the population, but also because of the high levels of
immigration from the countryside to the towns. The towns could

[3] H. Nusteling, *Welvaart en werkgelegenheid in Amsterdam 1540–1860* (Amsterdam
and Dieren, 1985), 19.
[4] G. J. Mentink and A. M. van der Woude, *De demografische ontwikkeling te
Rotterdam en Cool in de 17e en 18e eeuw* (Rotterdam, 1965), 48.
[5] J. Spaans, *Haarlem na de Reformatie: Stedelijke cultuur en kerkelijk leven,
1577–1620* (The Hague, 1989), 104.

only grow at the pace they did, or even perhaps maintain their existing populations, with the help of large-scale immigration from the surrounding countryside or, in the case of Amsterdam, from much further afield as well.[6] In the southern part of Holland large areas of the countryside were overwhelmingly catholic, and so for many of the towns of this area the process of immigration brought with it an increase in the size, both absolute and relative, of the catholic population. This process also led to a significant change in the social composition of the catholic group, specifically to a large increase both absolutely and proportionally in the numbers of the poor. This change must have been the primary reason why at least some town governments encouraged the setting up of separate catholic poor-relief organizations, which took a considerable strain off the *diaconie* and other official instances.[7] Whatever the precise size or social composition of the catholic element in the population of the towns of Holland, the *papisten* were certainly numerous enough to present the authorities with major problems if they were mishandled.

The existence of substantial numbers of catholics and protestant dissenters in the province as a whole, but in the towns in particular, made the relatively tolerant religious policies of the regents a practical necessity. It may well be that many, even most, regents had no desire to pursue a policy of religious repression—except for a flurry of vindictive actions against remonstrants immediately after 1619; but, in any case, the sheer size of the groups outside the Reformed Church made effective persecution simply impracticable. Toleration was the product of force of circumstances, rather than of principle.

There was an ideological element in Dutch religious toleration, in the form of a general dislike of persecuting people over details of belief and practice in matters which, some at least were prepared to argue, following the Erasmian tradition, were simply beyond human comprehension. It is true that even to the most liberal-minded of protestants roman catholicism remained an evil

[6] The interpretation of the excess of deaths over births in the towns of early modern Europe is a complex and controversial question—cf. A. Sharlin, 'Natural Decrease in Early Modern Cities: A Reconsideration', *Past and Present*, 79 (1978)—but the high level of immigration into the towns of Holland in this century can hardly be doubted.

[7] C. W. van Voorst van Beest, *De Katholieke armenzorg te Rotterdam in de 17e en 18e eeuw* (The Hague, n.d.).

system, but in the course of the century ordinary catholics were coming to be seen by the more tolerant of protestants as the victims of spiritual oppression by their own church rather than themselves deserving further punishment. Also, the more extreme forms of protestant dissent were generally condemned: 'socinian' seems to have been used as a code-word for forms of heterodoxy felt to be beyond the pale for decent Christians (probably because the socinians were regarded as denying the divinity of Christ). However, the numbers of such people were so low—or they were prepared to keep a low enough profile—that they did not constitute a major problem and could largely be ignored. The prosecution of Adriaen Koerbagh in Amsterdam, for example, seems to have been the result of his breaking the tacitly accepted rules of the game: he did not keep his head down, but published his ideas both repeatedly and under his own name, in the end leaving the authorities little choice but to respond to Reformed pressure and bring him to trial.[8] In general, as long as catholics and protestant dissenters did not threaten public order, the regents were unlikely to act against them, and it would be somewhat cynical to deny any element of principle in this attitude.

Yet it would be equally misleading to ignore the extent to which circumstances encouraged such toleration. Another consideration which helped to edge the policies of the regents of the towns of Holland towards a relatively tolerant stance was distrust of the potential political influence of the Reformed Church. Interference in political matters was anathema to the regents, and they were distinctly ambivalent about helping to strengthen the position of the public church as long as it maintained its relative independence from control by the civil authorities, and thus its potential for causing political problems. The desire for a more comprehensive official church, which would also be more subservient to the civil authorities, lay behind much of the regent support for the remonstrants in the early years of the century. It was hoped that a church with a more flexible theology and looser discipline would draw in a greater proportion of the population than a rigidly orthodox one was likely to achieve, and the remonstrants proved themselves prepared to give a much more unequivocal obedience to civil government than their opponents. The model the regents had

---

[8] Enno van Gelder, *Getemperde vrijheid*, 180–2; H. Vandenbossche, *Adriaen Koerbagh and Spinoza* (Leiden, 1978).

in mind was probably something along the lines of a Dutch version of the Anglican church. Such a church could be expected not only to provide a more effective unifying force for the new state, but also to be a more pliable instrument in the hands of the political élite.

There was also, of course, an established tradition of, if not positive toleration, then at least a reluctance to persecute which was rooted in the Spanish period. Before the Revolt, the towns of Holland, at least as much as anywhere else in the Netherlands, had resisted considerable pressure from the Spanish government in Brussels to enforce the edicts against heresy, and on the whole enforced these measures with deliberate inefficiency. There were local aberrations, most notably in Amsterdam as the result of internal political circumstances, but on the whole the regents were unwilling to persecute, particularly at the behest of outside authorities, fellow citizens who caused no trouble in other ways simply because they were protestants. After the Revolt, although the new town governments took over the churches for Reformed worship and banned the exercise of the catholic faith, this proved as far as they were prepared to go. They were not prepared to ban the services of the mennonites or other protestant dissenters, nor were they ready to proscribe catholic beliefs. They paid frequent lip-service to the complaints of the Reformed Church regarding the impudence of papist practices and the enormities of the radical sects, but in some ways the situation suited them as it deprived the official church of a religious monopoly in practice, and catholics and dissenters provided them with a built-in constituency of supporters. For these latter, regent rule was the best they could hope for; any other system would be likely to produce a government more ready to listen to the demands of the Reformed Church and thus increase the pressure on religious outsiders in general.

However, after all this has been said, probably the fundamental reason for the policy of religious toleration was severely practical—effective repression was simply not possible, at least not without unacceptable economic and social costs. Especially in the case of the catholics, who may have constituted less than a third of the population of the Holland towns but almost half that of the Republic as a whole, any serious attempt at coercion would have had disastrous effects and even then would almost certainly have failed. Local authorities would have resisted any such policy as stubbornly as they had done before the Revolt, and with the likelihood of much greater success, in defence of their autonomy as much as anything else. Apart from the army, there was no repressive apparatus available to local authorities which was capable of carrying out such a task, and the use of the army for such a purpose would have been wholly unacceptable to the regents, except in the direst of emergencies, as they were far too afraid of setting precedents that might help the stadhouder to increase his power at their expense.

The case of the disturbances at Zijdewind, a small village near Alkmaar, illustrates and illuminates a number of these issues. The attempt by the local *baljuw* to disperse catholic worshippers here in 1649 was met with violent resistance and caused acute embarrassment on all sides. The States of Holland did not want the catholic issue stirred up at a time when secret negotiations with a visiting papal envoy were taking place, nor did catholic leaders for similar reasons, and the affair was hushed up as far as possible. An interesting aspect of the matter is that the local catholics seem to have believed that the Treaty of Münster must have secured them freedom of worship, otherwise the king of Spain would never have signed it.[9] Apart from anything else, this is a reminder that the Dutch Republic did not live in a vacuum, and that throughout most of the seventeenth century it was dependent to a significant extent on alliances with catholic powers—France up to 1648, and the Austrian Habsburgs in the last quarter of the century. Under these circumstances it would hardly have been politic to embark on a necessarily high-profile campaign against Dutch catholics.[10]

The priorities of the regents, besides the maintenance of their own power, were public peace and economic prosperity. Both of these would have been severely damaged by a serious attempt at religious repression. It is an interesting reflection of the values of the period that one of the most frequently used arguments, for the toleration of protestant dissenters at least, was their economic usefulness. It became a cliché of contemporary social comment that

[9] J. J. Poelhekke, *Geen blijder maer in tachtig jaer: Verspreide studiën over de crisis-periode 1648–1651* (Zutphen, 1973), 106 ff.

[10] Admittedly, neither France nor Austria showed reciprocal sensitivity, but this was a reflection in part simply of the unconscious bigotry which typified most catholic governments in this period, and in part of the greater vulnerability of the Republic. The Dutch needed these alliances more than their catholic allies did—or at least were prepared to pay more for them.

the mennonites in particular were hard-working, honest, and in general a positive economic asset. Negatively, it was argued that repression would disturb trade in general and in particular dry up the flow of economically useful immigrants. Although as far as I am aware the argument was not used, the importance of cheap labour from catholic areas of the Dutch countryside and even the neighbouring catholic territories in the Holy Roman Empire (especially seasonal workers) may have been an important additional consideration in forming an economic justification for religious toleration.

There was also an important element of self-interest—or, a harsher judgement would add, corruption—in the attitude of the civil authorities towards the catholics. In the course of the century, as it slowly became accepted that the catholics would perform their religious services in formal secrecy—although in the crowded towns of Holland everyone must have known what was going on, as long as the catholics made a pretence at secrecy all was well— the local police officials, the *schouten* or *baljuwen*, levied a sort of unofficial tax on them in return for not disturbing their meetings or, in some cases, for protecting these gatherings.[11] The profits to be gained in this way were probably substantial, and so the officials directly responsible for enforcing the laws against catholic worship had a strong financial motivation for ensuring that both this worship and the laws against it continued.

[11] Price, 'Rotterdam Patriciate', 110.

7. The *Schutterij*, Popular Influence, and Public Order

The extent to which people outside the regent élite had an influence on the politics of the voting towns of Holland in the seventeenth century is a question which has largely gone by default. Yet, although historians may have played down the extent to which the town governments were vulnerable in the face of popular violence, this was something the regents themselves could not afford to forget. Although in form, and to a very large extent in practice, the regents were the absolute rulers of their towns, this unquestioned legal supremacy of the magistracy could not disguise the fact that there was a serious flaw in their power: they lacked effective repressive forces immediately to hand to suppress popular disorder. Awareness of this weakness made the regents extremely sensitive to any public criticism which might stir up discontent among their subjects, but it also encouraged them to avoid policies which might cause widespread resentment. The importance of this factor cannot be measured only by counting actual riots; the ever-present threat of popular violence, as much as its reality, influenced the way in which the town governments acted. The nature and extent of this influence, however, is difficult to estimate either in general terms or in specific cases.

This vulnerability of the regents in the face of the reality or the threat of public violence is the theme of this chapter, but it must be conceded at the very beginning that, in his recent book on rioting and disorder in the Republic in the seventeenth and eighteenth centuries, Dekker has on the contrary emphasized the effectiveness of the forces, from civic militia to the army, available in Holland for the control of popular violence during this period.[1] This contradiction is, in part at least, more apparent than real: Dekker is concerned to argue that, in comparison with many contemporary states, and in particular with France, the ability of the authorities to maintain and restore order seems impressive. This may well be

---

[1] Dekker, *Holland in beroering*, 120.

true, but it does not follow that the regents were not extremely vulnerable to mob violence, particularly in the short term. Unlike the ruling groups in many other countries, the regents of Holland lived in the centre of their densely populated towns, in houses opening directly on to the street in most cases. They were a very visible group, and both their persons and their property could be attacked with relative ease. It was this vulnerability in the first hours or days of disorder, rather than any confidence on the part of the authorities in their ability to restore order in the medium term, which deeply affected the psychology of regent rule.

In the towns themselves the chief means of maintaining order was the *schutterij*, the civic militia. Some towns employed a paid body of soldiers—certainly Amsterdam did so—but most town governments were dependent on their *schutters* for the control of popular violence. The nature of the *schutterij* was determined by the classes of society from which it was recruited. In theory, the *schutters* had to provide their own equipment and thus were drawn from the relatively well-off middle and lower-middle classes in the towns, probably that range of society from artisans and small shopkeepers upwards. Thus they represented a solidly bourgeois element and could usually be relied on to act effectively against mob action or other disorders coming from the poorer sections of society. It is usually said that the *schutterijen* were officered by regents, but this is something of a misconception. There were in most towns not enough regents to provide captains, lieutenants, and *vaandrigs* for all the militia companies and, moreover, regents were unlikely to be keen to take on the tedious chores of everyday militia duty. Certainly in Rotterdam only the two colonels of the *schutterij* were always regents, and their duties appear to have been largely honorific, while the other officers were drawn partly from junior members of regent families but largely from the upper bourgeoisie in general.[2] It seems likely that this was the case in most if not all of the voting towns, but this would not necessarily mean a weakening of the reliability of the militia as men from such backgrounds could normally be relied on to support the existing authorities.

However, if disaffection, for whatever reason, was rife among the middling classes of a town, then the *schutterij* could prove an

[2] Price, 'Rotterdam Patriciate', 273.

unreliable instrument in the hands of the regents. Even if the officers could be trusted, the ordinary *schutters* were not necessarily prepared to obey their orders, act effectively, or, indeed, turn out to serve at all; and in extreme circumstances they too could turn against their rulers. An unambiguous demonstration of the powerlessness, at least in the short run, of the urban authorities when disaffection took hold of the local militia was given by events in Alkmaar in 1609. During a dispute which centred on the attempt of local gomarists to rid the town and region of five arminian ministers,[3] the rank and file of the *schutterij* took a hand: they organized a demonstration against the newly chosen town government, claiming it was in breach of ancient privileges, forced their officers to support their action, took over the town hall and the gates of the town, and kept control of the town for eight weeks.[4] This was an action of arminian *schutters* against a gomarist magistracy, and similar disturbances in many towns during the remonstrant–contraremonstrant clashes revealed the unreliabilty of the *schutterij* in such circumstances. In the highly charged atmosphere of the summer of 1672, disaffection within the civic militias was probably even more widespread. These were periods of serious political and religious divisions in the towns of Holland, spreading far outside regent ranks, and this was shown by the unwillingness of the propertied classes to come to the support of the authorities—even when they were not themselves among the demonstrators. Indeed, far from being the natural supporter of the town governments, from another perspective the militia could be seen as in some sense representative of the citizenry and thus in potential opposition to the regents.[5] In the course of the violent disorders of the summer of 1672 came calls for the *krijgsraden* (the council of the officers of the *schutterij*) to be made a sort of watchdog over the town governments on behalf of the population in general.[6] Nothing came of this, as the new regents who came to power

---

[3] Arminius and Gomarus were the Leiden professors of theology who became symbolic leaders of the opposed religious camps at the beginning of the century; the terms remonstrant and contraremonstrant cannot properly be used before the submission of the Remonstrance to the States of Holland in 1610.

[4] J. den Tex, *Oldenbarnevelt* (Haarlem and Groningen, 1960–72), iii. 162–3.

[5] In this context, it is significant that the civic militia was commonly known as the *burgerij*, which is also the Dutch term for the citizens of the towns.

[6] P. Geyl, *Democratische tendenties in 1672* (The Hague, 1950), 35–8; Roorda, *Partij en factie*, 76.

as a result of the disorders and, *a fortiori*, the prince had nothing
to gain by such a change, but the demand in itself is significant as
an indication that the militia could be seen as a body representing
the broader middling groups of society as against the regent élite
and its close allies. Indeed, in the early years of the Revolt, the
States of Holland had found it expedient to promulgate a formal
ban on any involvement or consultation of the *schutterijen* in political matters (1581). This action suggests that they were indeed
regarded as potentially serious political rivals of the regents, with
some credibility as representatives of the opinions of the citizenry
at large. The potential of the militias for effective intervention in
civic affairs was shown during the Truce crisis, when many town
governments found that they could not rely on the *schutters* to
suppress popular disturbances. In the 1620s also, the Amsterdam
schutterij was the centre of opposition to the town government's
more lenient attitude towards the remonstrants; the action was
largely confined to one company and failed to divert the magistrates from their path, but it looked serious for a time. In general
it can be said that the ban of 1581 did not entirely succeed in
excluding the militias from involvement in urban politics.[7]
Representation of the interests of the middle ranks of urban society
remained a latent role for the civic militia throughout the seventeenth century.

A complication with regard to the composition of the *schutterij*
is the question of the degree to which it was in practice, as well as
in theory, drawn from the propertied classes. In his study of the
troubles in Haarlem in the late 1740s, De Jongste has demonstrated
that one of the problems the government of this particular town
had to face at this time was the extreme unreliability of its *schutterij*.[8] Haarlem had suffered a severe economic decline in the late
seventeenth and early eighteenth century, and this appears to have
weakened in particular that section of the propertied classes which
was supposed to provide the militia. It seems to have been the
lower and middling ranks of the bourgeoisie—the artisans, shopkeepers, small-scale traders and entrepreneurs—who were hit most
heavily by the general depression of the town's economy. As a

[7] P. Knevel, 'Onrust onder de schutters: De politieke invloed van de Hollandse
schutterijen in de eerste helft van de zeventiende eeuw', *Holland*, 20 (1988).
[8] J. A. F. de Jongste, *Onrust aan het Spaarne: Haarlem in de jaren 1747–1751*
(Dieren, 1984), ch. 3.

consequence, in some quarters of the town there were too few men
with the required property qualifications for service in the militia
and many of the *schutters* actually recruited seem to have been too
poor to provide their own equipment. Thus, significant sections of
the *schutterij* were more sympathetic to the demands of the rioters
than they might otherwise have been. Haarlem in the 1740s, of
course, was a town which was already quite far down the road of
economic decline. By the second half of the seventeenth century,
similar social forces may have been operating in those towns in
Holland which had started to decline in wealth and population
during this period, but they are hardly likely to have been present
in the larger and still buoyant towns. It is possible, then, that, in
the economically weaker towns, the *schutterijen* may have become
less representative of the solid bourgeoisie in the course of the
seventeenth century, and thus even less reliable a tool in the hands
of the magistracy in the last decades of the century than they had
been in the first.

In general, it seems to have been the case that, if the *schutters*
were prepared to turn out and to obey orders, then popular violence could be kept in check without too much trouble. However,
such whole-hearted co-operation by the militia came most readily
when disaffection was limited to the poorer sections of society.
This seems to have been the case with regard to riots about food,
which normally had no middle-class participation or noticeable
sympathy.[9] It was not easy to control large and often violent
crowds in the physical setting of the densely populated and closely
built-up towns of Holland. Given solidarity between the regents
and the broader bourgeoisie, it was possible in most cases, though
it would have been more difficult where the local militia had had
to resort to recruitment from the poorer classes themselves. In
other sorts of disorder, however, disaffection was not confined to
the poorer levels of society but spread through the bourgeoisie as
well, and in these cases the problems facing the magistracy were
much more severe.

In the case of riots over taxation or, *a fortiori*, of disturbances
arising from deep religious or political divisions where the bourgeoisie was at least as much affected as the lower orders, the
schutterij could not be relied upon to act with any enthusiasm or

[9] Dekker, *Holland in beroering*, 27–8.

effectiveness, and in extreme cases they could become the focus of disaffection rather than its suppressor. As has been seen, there is some evidence that in the summer of 1672 the officers of the civic militia in a number of towns took on, or were forced to assume, something of a representative role for the disaffected *burgerij*.[10] Recruited from the middle groups of Dutch urban society, the *schutters* and their officers were highly sensitive to the opinions and attitudes of their fellow citizens, among whom they had to live and work. In particular, it was difficult for them to use force against men and women they had to deal with in their everyday lives. The officers especially were obvious targets of popular pressure, and may not have felt they had a great deal of choice in regard to how they acted. Certainly in Rotterdam the account of the troubles of the *rampjaar* given by a republican regent leaves no doubt that the militia, and in particular their officers, were a subversive influence, at least in the eyes of the losing party.[11] Thus, the civic militia was not a mindless tool in the hands of the magistracy; the social origins and loyalties of its members meant that they were as, if not more, likely to respond to pressure from their fellow bourgeois as to the orders of the regents.

This is a reminder that a certain vulnerability was a fundamental operating condition of regent rule. The regents were not isolated in country estates, but lived among those they ruled and were both highly visible and immediately accessible in times of raised emotions. One of the most interesting aspects of regent rule in general, but one that is also perhaps the most difficult to assess, is the extent to which the actions of the political élite were affected by this awareness of the danger of alienating too great a proportion of the citizenry at the same time. In theory and in law the power of the regents verged on the absolute; the revolt against Spanish absolutism and centralization had produced a political system within which absolutism itself had triumphed at the level of the town governments. However, as in all absolutist regimes, there was a

[10] Roorda, *Partij en factie*, 70–6, and *Het rampjaar* (Bussum, 1971), 65.
[11] [W. Vroesen], *Waaragtig verhaal van de muiterij binnen de stad Rotterdam . . .* (n.p., 1785). This invaluable though far from impartial account has been attributed to a number of Rotterdam regents, but internal evidence points clearly to one of the town secretaries, Willebord Vroesen, as the author. This attribution is supported by a marginal note by (presumably) Cornelis van Alkemade in a contemporary MS version of this work in the Leiden University library (Price, 'Rotterdam Patriciate', 444–5).

considerable distance between what was formally and legally possible and how far in practice it was politic to go. The regents had to take serious account of the susceptibilities of the people of their towns, and in particular of the broad range of the bourgeoisie. The government of Delft was especially tactless in 1616 when it increased the excise on corn at the same time as it reduced it on wine. This was seen as preferential treatment for the better-off and provoked large-scale rioting which the *schutterij* proved unable or unwilling to control; only when the *gecommitteerde raden* sent troops into the town could order be restored.[12] In general, the regents preferred to avoid this sort of trouble, even at the cost of some modifications of policy.

As has been noted, the regents and their families lived in the towns, though in the course of the century they increasingly tended to remove to country retreats in the summer and, until this scourge died out after the 1660s,[13] when plague threatened also. Their houses and other property were in their towns as well, so both their persons and their property were vulnerable in the face of mob violence. In fact, one of the characteristics of the Dutch urban mob throughout both the seventeenth and eighteenth centuries was that it tended to attack property rather than persons.[14] Plundering and even demolishing the houses of regents who had become the focus of popular resentment was much more common than direct physical attacks on their persons, though it may be that only the decision of some of the more notorious republican leaders to flee in 1672 saved their lives. It may well be that Pieter de Groot, as a symbol of republicanism in both his family and himself,[15] and as the protagonist of the vilified negotiations with the French, was lucky to have survived to write his sour comments on events from the relative security of Antwerp.

For the regents of Holland were open to attack: they mostly walked about town rather than using carriages (rather from convenience than modesty, as these were not a very efficient way of get-

[12] A. Th. van Deursen, *Het kopergeld van de gouden eeuw* (Assen, 1973–80), iii. 59–60.
[13] L. Noordegraaf and G. Valk, *De Gave Gods: De pest in Holland vanaf de late middeleeuwen* (Bergen, NH, 1988), esp. 47.
[14] Dekker, *Holland in beroering*, 85–92.
[15] He was the son of Hugo de Groot (Grotius), the great scholar but less impressive politician, who had been a close collaborator of Oldenbarnevelt, was arrested with him, and imprisoned, before escaping into lifelong exile.

ting round most of the towns of Holland), and the assassination attempt on Johan de Witt as he walked, accompanied by only two servants, through the streets of The Hague in the evening of 21 June in the dangerous summer of 1672 reminds us, as it certainly reminded his fellow republicans among the regents of Holland, of their vulnerability to physical violence. Personal intimidation was certainly the order of the day in the critical summer months of the *rampjaar*. In such circumstances, the fact that relatively few people were killed or seriously injured by mob violence in the course of the century (probably far more were killed by the forces of order) is remarkable, and seems to point to the highly symbolic nature of such violence and the degree of control with which it was carried out—with plundering, for example, being clearly distinguished from theft: property was destroyed not stolen.[16]

Rioting was, of course, an extreme response, and a sign that the regents had already failed in a fundamental aspect of their policy, which was the maintenance of peace and order in their towns. It was with the aim of averting such dangerous disorders that the regents tried to keep as close a control as possible over any influence which might stir up discontent. The influence which the ministers of the Reformed Church were believed to have on public opinion was the reason they were under such close surveillance by the town authorities. The activities of rabble-rousing religious leaders during the remonstrant–contraremonstrant troubles became a horrible warning to the regents of what could happen if the *predikanten* were allowed to get out of hand. Oldenbarnevelt, even during his trial, was capable of dredging up yet older cautionary tales, and blamed the loss of Flanders and Brabant on the activities of the calvinist extremists in the towns of these provinces in the years immediately after the Pacification of Ghent. Although most ministers of the Reformed Church were mindful of their religious duty of obedience to ordained civil authority—and of where their salaries came from—there were sufficient orangist firebrands throughout the century to remind the regents of the potential threat from this direction, and to reinforce their determination to have only 'peaceful' men admitted to the ministry in their towns. A sharp ear was kept on the contents of sermons, especially in contentious times, and this concern about the possibly subversive

---

[16] Dekker, *Holland in beroering*, 87.

influence of the church as an institution was the chief reason why many governments appointed political observers to the church councils of their towns, to prevent actions they regarded as improper interference in political affairs.

Similarly, the regents as a group were concerned to monitor and control the dissemination of information and argument about public affairs by means of the printed word and image. The intention was to ensure that political matters in general remained the exclusive preserve of the regents, with the mass of the population receiving only a limited amount of strictly controlled information. In this way the regents hoped to minimize the chance of popular discontent. However, the deserved nemesis of secrecy is paranoia, and an ill-informed public all too often proved less ready to trust its rulers than they must have hoped. The most obvious examples of serious public disorder arising, at least in part, out of ignorance coupled with distrust came during the Truce crisis and, more briefly, in 1672. Conspiracy theories were rife in these years, and although we can now be tolerably sure that Oldenbarnevelt had not sold the Republic out to the Spanish, and that De Witt and his supporters had not betrayed the Republic to Louis XIV's France, many people at the time appear to have believed these accusations. These are extreme cases, but they are perhaps symptomatic of a general distrust between regents and populace arising in part out of the defective information available to those outside the oligarchy.

However, the problem was not simply that the regents tried to keep the public ignorant of what was going on politically, it was also that their attempts at censorship failed.[17] They got what sometimes looks like the worst of both worlds: there was insufficient open discussion of public affairs, but a wealth of clandestine comment. The regent regime attempted to control the flood of pamphlets on public affairs, but failed. Individuals were prosecuted and punished, often severely, but the numbers of pamphlets produced and distributed continued to rise inexorably.[18] The policing resources available to town governments were in general inadequate for the task of tracking down the printers of what were felt

---

[17] See G. de Bruin, *Geheimhouding en verraad: De geheimhouding van staatszaken ten tijde van de Republiek (1600–1750)* (The Hague, 1991) for the practical problems with regard to political secrecy in the Republic.
[18] See, most recently, C. E. Harline, *Pamphlets, Printing and Political Culture in the Early Dutch Republic* (Dordrecht, 1987).

to be subversive pamphlets, never mind their anonymous authors.[19]
There were, of course, plenty of publications supporting the
authorities, but these were private initiatives and in the decentralized Republic there could be no organized government 'information' service; official publications were very largely limited to the
texts of treaties or ordinances, and such material could hardly out-
weigh the influence of critical pamphlets designed specifically and
skilfully in style and language, as well as in the prejudices to which
they appealed, to suit the tastes of a popular audience.

The regents also showed their concern—or perhaps 'apprehension' is the more appropriate term—about public opinion in the
circumspection they employed in dealing with the Reformed
Church, and the regard they regularly displayed for the susceptibilities of the orthodox. Of course, individual town governments did
at times treat the leaders of the church within their towns in a
heavy-handed way, and there was a certain amount of bullying of
recalcitrant ministers, but in general the town governments preferred to rub along with the church, maintaining where possible an
atmosphere of amicable co-operation. Even where the authorities
had no intention of acceding to the demands of the Reformed
Church in practice, whenever possible they avoided direct con-
frontations. The actual treatment of catholics may have become,
more or less steadily, more tolerant as the century wore on, but
the public attitude of the town governments and the content of the
laws corresponded much more to the Reformed view of society
than to what was happening in practice. In general, however, it
was the economic policies of the regents which reflected their concern to maintain the fragile peace of their towns. Perhaps rightly,
they seem to have believed that general prosperity was the best
guarantee of the public peace, and their attempts to improve the
economic fortunes of their own towns—though an element of con-
scious public service cannot be gainsaid—were also aimed at limiting the likelihood of widespread disaffection.

Despite the best efforts of the regents, however, public disorders
and rioting were an important component of political life in
Holland, and particularly in the towns, either in fact, or as a possibility or a threat which had always to be taken into account. Apart
from the immediately and obviously political riots during the

---

[19] Enno van Gelder, *Getemperde vrijheid*, 166–7.

Truce period and in 1672,[20] there were a considerable number of disturbances in the voting towns with, to say the least, political implications, especially food riots and protests against particular taxes. Such local upheavals were a frequent reminder to the regents throughout the century of the dangers consequent on pushing their subjects too far. Food riots were rare before the end of the century, Dekker recording only two (in Leiden and Gouda in 1630) before the 1690s when five took place. Disturbances over taxes, usually excises, were more common in the seventeenth century, with about seventeen being recorded. More or less politically inspired disturbances also occurred in 1652–3 in reaction to the Dutch setbacks in the war with England, taking on a distinctly orangist complexion in a number of towns.

Compared with the often massive civil violence in other European countries in the seventeenth century, this is perhaps an unimpressive catalogue and rather justifies the traditional view of the Republic as a relatively peaceful country over revisionist interpretations stressing discontent and disorder.[21] Yet it is possible to reconcile the two views to some extent: the Republic did enjoy a considerable degree of civil peace but, after the traumatic shock given to the regent regime in the years up to 1618, even infrequent riots were sufficient to keep the authorities acutely aware of their vulnerability. The relative paucity of rioting outside the two great crisis periods must in part be attributed to the general prosperity of the towns, but also to the circumspect policies of regents who were always aware of the dangers of upsetting too many people at the same time.

Nearly all these riots were to some extent political, as they aimed to change the policies of the town governments, but the different types of riot involved different mixes of participants. The food riots, hardly surprisingly, were the work of the poorer sections of the urban population, whereas the tax and political riots involved nearly all levels of the citizenry.[22] On the other hand,

[20] Dekker, *Holland in beroering*, does not include the civil disturbances during the Truce crisis in his general survey of rioting in the Republic, as he considers them as more nearly constituting a civil war than a series of riots. He has a point, but the omission is none the less unfortunate.

[21] Dekker, *Holland in beroering*, 142–5.

[22] I have not found Dekker's distinction between religious and political riots useful in this context: nearly all the religious riots in the seventeenth century were inevitably political as well, and political riots often had significant religious content.

although for the most important periods of rioting, during the Truce and in 1672, we have only anecdotal and invariably biased evidence as to who did the rioting, in most cases it seems tolerably clear that it was not the undifferentiated, monstrous spawn of contemporary fears, *het grauw* (the mob), which caused the most trouble. Certainly, among those convicted of involvement in the various tax riots, there were many from artisan and small-shopkeeper backgrounds, and it is plausible that such people were also dominant in the more overtly political disturbances as well.

However, in 1672 and almost certainly in the disturbances during the Truce, dissident regents and ambitious members of the upper bourgeoisie were involved not only in the exploitation but also in the organization of the riots. It is important here to distinguish between the basic motivation of the crowds and the attempts to channel their violence. The religious and political emotions and fears which led to the disturbances of these years were spontaneous; they could be stirred up but not created by agitators. However, the precise targets and timing of these popular movements could be influenced by politically ambitious intriguers. At least we can be reasonably sure that such men tried to give direction to the discontent, though the extent to which they succeeded in determining what actually happened is uncertain. What is clear is that, in these years of crisis, the riots were used with some success to put pressure on the dominant regent groups, and that the most astute or well placed of the intriguers rode to political office on the wave of these popular disturbances. It was possible for such men to use these expressions of widespread disaffection to gain power for themselves or their families because the rioters had no idea of changing the political system; they wanted changes in specific policies or, at most, in personnel, but had no coherent alternative to the existing regime to propose.

A major riot which took place in Rotterdam in 1690, directed primarily against the *baljuw* Van Zuylen van Nievelt, sums up some of the interest and many of the problems involved in the study of such violent episodes. Dekker sees it basically as a tax riot, while older studies have suggested the guiding hand of dissident regents and thus have presented it as primarily an offshoot of conflict within the oligarchy of the town.[23] The violence was

---

[23] Dekker, *Holland in beroering*, 34; Mees Azn., *Rotterdamsche oproer.*

considerable, but highly focused, directed chiefly at the house and property of the *baljuw*, and the local militia could or would not control the mob. This seems to be a similar case to the riots, notably again in Rotterdam, of 1672: genuine popular feeling was probably directed and certainly exploited by dissident regents, for Van Zuylen van Nievelt, besides being particularly hard-handed and probably corrupt in the way in which he carried out his duties as *baljuw*, was also the dictatorial head of the prince's party in the Rotterdam *vroedschap*. The dissident regents were here able to take advantage of Willem III's heavy involvement in England and Ireland to bring down his political boss in Rotterdam, but their success was short-lived as the prince eventually found time to enforce his will on the town and, with the amoral pragmatism usual in his approach to Dutch domestic affairs, reinstate the probably corrupt but certainly politically reliable *baljuw*.

There were ideas present in seventeenth-century Holland which envisaged a change in the nature of the government, most noticeably in the work of the brothers Johan and Pieter de la Court. They argued for a considerable extension of the group participating in politics, to include most of the solid bourgeoisie.[24] The aim was not democracy, but a strengthening of the rule of the propertied classes against the mass of the people, who were seen as irrational, orangist, and religiously orthodox—three closely related concepts, one suspects, for the De la Courts. These and similar theories emanated from small intellectual coteries of upper bourgeois if not regent background, and were often programmatically republican. They do not seem to have appealed to any particular constituency outside their own rather narrow ranks, nor to have had even the remotest chance of being put into practice. Neither were there any readily available democratic programmes to which opposition pamphleteers and rioters could appeal. Their place was taken by a naïve orangism and by recourse to vague notions of burgher privileges, but, in the main, orangism was not seeking a fundamental change in the form of government either. In the seventeenth century orangism was not monarchist, and certainly this was not its attraction as far as the people of the towns of Holland

---

[24] Th. van Tijn, 'Pieter de la Court: Zijn leven en economische denkbeelden', *Tijdschrift voor Geschiedenis*, 59 (1956); M. van der Bijl, 'Pieter de la Court en de politieke werkelijkheid', in H. W. Blom and I. W. Wildenberg, *Pieter de la Court in zijn tijd (1618–1685)* (Amsterdam and Maarssen, 1986), 74–5.

were concerned. Increasing the power of the princes of Orange was apparently seen as a way of making the existing system work better, as a way to ensure that the regents ruled as they ought rather than overthrowing their power altogether.

The appeal to local privileges to ensure some participation in government by elements of the bourgeoisie was partly based on actual historical circumstances, as towns like Dordrecht and Hoorn still preserved some vestiges of citizen involvement in the choice of magistrates. Largely, however, it was based on a creative and normative view of history rather than what had actually been the case: the feeling was that there ought to be some involvement of the more respectable bourgeoisie in government and particularly in the choice of magistrates, and that therefore such participation must have existed in the past; if there was no existing evidence for such practices then this could only mean that the regents had tampered with the historical record. The perspectives for change arising from such attitudes, however, were relatively limited. Even in 1672 the changes proposed were very minor, such as giving the *krijgsraad* formed by the officers of the *schutterij* some form of monitoring role over the activities of the town government, and received very short shrift from the authorities once the *wetsverzettingen* had taken place.[25] In consequence, riots might help to change policy—strengthen the position of Maurits in 1618, ensure the elevation of Willem III in 1672, in each case accompanied by changes in the personnel of the town governments—but the system itself remained effectively and essentially unchallenged.

So, although popular volatility and the doubtful reliability in some circumstances of the *schutterij* were permanent problems for the regents in their attempts to maintain peace and order in their towns, the system of government was never seriously brought under threat. The principle of oligarchic rule was not really challenged, only from time to time what the regents did. Even so, their task was not always easy, and did not necessarily become any simpler in the course of the seventeenth century. On the one hand, the intensity of religious conflict undoubtedly declined, probably quite soon after the crisis of 1618–19, while never becoming negligible. However, the problems arising from economic change were present throughout the century, though varying in type. At first it was the

[25] Roorda, *Partij en factie*, 241–4.

problems associated with rapid growth—for example, housing problems and dislocation arising from temporary setbacks—which were predominant; later, and in some towns much earlier than others, it was economic stagnation and decline which, initially at least, fuelled urban volatility. Boom or bust, violence was never far below the surface in the towns of Holland in the seventeenth century.

Women had no formal role in the political life of the towns of Holland at all, but they, of course, constituted about half the population, and can be assumed to have had an influence individually and collectively on what happened in their towns. It has been argued that those outside the privileged élite could and did have an influence on the way that town governments were able to act; as far as women are concerned, the question in this context is whether they can be regarded as having any distinctive effects on the political process, perhaps through different points of view or separate agenda for action or reaction. However, it has to be confessed that it is difficult to say anything very much about these questions in our present state of knowledge, and it may well be that the nature of the surviving evidence will never allow us to explore them to any great depth. Nevertheless, in a discussion of the social context of politics in the towns of Holland in the seventeenth century, it is as necessary to be clear about where the gaps in our knowledge and understanding are as to indicate the findings of new research, and the whole question of women's role in Dutch society at this time is one where our ignorance is particularly galling.

It needs to be stressed that here, as in much of human history, women were not only formally excluded from politics altogether, but such an exclusion was not even thought worthy of comment at the time, either for or against, so self-evident was it that politics was not women's realm. This is a fundamental characteristic of Dutch political life: it was man's business. In many ways this is hardly surprising, as it was and had been the norm for European society for hundreds if not thousands of years, yet it is worth reminding ourselves of the fact that whatever social and economic changes were taking place in the towns of Holland, the position of women does not seem to have been on any practical or even theoretical agenda. By the end of the seventeenth century, Holland had moved a long way towards becoming recognizably modern in terms of economic organization and social structure. It could be argued that culturally the changes which had taken place were even more marked, but in the present state of our knowledge it appears that the position of, and attitudes towards, women had remained very largely unchanged.

Yet there were important aspects of the life of the Holland towns which might have been expected to lead to at least a degree of change in this respect. There is some evidence, for example, that the economic role of women was, or could be, important, though this question has so far not been given the attention that it perhaps deserves. An intriguing sign that contemporary society was prepared to recognize a significant economic role for women, and in a formal sense too, comes in the tax lists (for the 200th Penny and the *Familie-Geld*, for example): in these it is often the case that widows, and not their eldest sons, are listed as the responsible tax-payers, and thus, presumably, as at least the titular head of the family's business and financial interests.[26] Also, although the subject has not received systematic treatment, anecdotal evidence suggests that women played an important role at least in small-scale trading and shopkeeping—one remembers that Vondel's shop (selling silk-goods and stockings) flourished while his wife was alive, but failed quite quickly thereafter; although Vondel himself (distinctly ungraciously one feels) blamed his son, the lack of his wife's guiding hand seems the more likely cause of his business failure.[27] Certainly, women were very important at the level of stall-holding and street-trading in general, and among the poorer sections of the population women's earnings, though on average 40–50 per cent less than those of an unskilled male worker,[28] appear to have been vital to the family budget.[29]

Another area of notably prominent activity for women was provided by the particular needs of the catholic mission church in the Republic. In the difficult circumstances of a church that had lost its

[26] On the subject of widows, as they enjoyed greater legal freedom than either married women or those who had never married, it is perhaps a trifle surprising that the murder of husbands by their wives was not more common—or at least suspected to be—than appears to have been the case.

[27] J. Melles, *Joost van den Vondel* (Utrecht, 1957), 85.

[28] Nusteling, *Welvaart en werkgelegenheid*, 115.

[29] The eighteenth-century evidence given by D. Haks, *Huwelijk en gezin in Holland in de 17de en 18de eeuw* (Assen, 1982), 156–7 for the importance of women's work in the economy as a whole as well as for the economics of the household seems relevant for the previous century as well.

old economic and organizational infrastructure, wealthy unmarried women and widows came to provide indispensable support for the priests in their mission stations (*staties*). As *klopjes*—women living a quasi-religious manner of life, but without the discipline imposed by belonging to a conventional order of nuns—they were able to achieve a degree of influence in the day-to-day running of the church in Holland (and, of course, in the Republic as a whole) that proved in the end unacceptable to the catholic hierarchy. It is not really surprising that a church which was profoundly conservative both theologically and socially should have regarded the perfor-mance of such a prominent role by lay people, and most especially by lay women, with the deepest suspicion.[30] Women were soon to be reduced to proper subordination again, but for a period in the seventeenth century some women were able to play a part within the catholic sector of Dutch society at least as important as that of the deacons, if not the elders, in the Reformed Church—and thus what might be considered a semi-political role in the broadest sense of the term.

There is also a deal of anecdotal evidence regarding the dominant role of women within the Dutch household. Sir William Temple was told of a burgemeester who, on visiting a respectable house-hold, was unceremoniously picked up by a strapping maidservant and carried into the house on her back to prevent the dirt on his shoes from sullying the spotless interior of her mistress's home.[31] This seems to have been in the nature of a tale told to amaze Temple, who gives a somewhat ingenuous impression at this early stage of his stay in the Republic, but, in general, Dutch wives had the reputation of showing distinctly less deference towards their husbands than contemporary moralists would have liked.[32] Yet it may very well be that such stories of domestic tyranny should be understood in a distinctly different way, as symbolic of the increas-ing confinement of women to the domestic sphere, at least among the regents and the upper bourgeoisie in general, and such obsessive concern for cleanliness and order in the household as evidence of frustrated energies. It is possibly significant that there is no parallel

[30] E. Schulte van Kessel, *Geest en vlees in godsdienst en wetenschap* (The Hague, 1980), chs. II and III.
[31] P. Zumthor, *La Vie quotidienne en Hollande au temps de Rembrandt* (Paris, 1959), 158–9.
[32] Haks, *Huwelijk en gezin*, 155–6, but cf. E. Kloek, *Wie hij zij, man of wijf: Vrouwengeschiedenis en de vroegmoderne tijd* (Hilversum, 1990), 155–6.

cliché about burgemeesters' wives exercising excessive political
influence. If it is true that women, at least in these higher reaches of
Dutch society, were coming to be seen as suited properly only for a
domestic role, then it is not at all clear how this tendency is to be
interpreted: it can be seen as a trait of the emerging middle classes
which was to find its acme in the Victorian image of the domestic
angel, or as evidence of the emulation of aristocratic mores by the
Dutch bourgeoisie. Such interpretations might be seen as rather too
speculative, but one important practical consequence of the general
attitude to women which was prevalent in this society appears to
have been that they received less, or less useful, education at all levels of society than males. Even in the highest levels of the bourgeoisie, women's education was both different and distinctly
inferior to that of men. Constantijn Huygens, secretary to Frederik
Hendrik, and a poet and *homo universalis* of European renown,
ensured that his sons, including the future eminent scientist
Christiaen, enjoyed the most rigorous of humanist educations, but
his daughters as adults proved hardly able to write intelligibly even
in Dutch.[33] Moreover, no contemporary appears to have found such
a discrepancy at all strange, and the occasional well-educated
female intellectual, such as Anna Maria van Schuurman, was
treated as a freak of nature rather than as a model for emulation.

Women were not only excluded from the actual politics of the
time—they were also debarred from the imaginary politics of the
theorists. The brothers De la Court certainly excluded them from
their extended bourgeois oligarchy and, in most political writings,
this exclusion was taken for granted. Woman's possible inclusion
in political life had not even reached the stage where it was argued
against; the question had effectively not yet been put.

There was, however, one semi-political area of Dutch social life
where women did have a significant part to play, and this was in
demonstrations, riot, and disorder. As was the case throughout
Europe, as far as research has reached,[34] women were prominent in
all aspects and phases of public disturbances in the towns of
Holland in the seventeenth century, including the more violent
episodes.[35] Women had certain advantages in this area, which were

[33] H. A. Hofman, *Constantijn Huygens (1596–1687)* (Utrecht, 1983), 37–8.
[34] N. Z. Davis, *Society and Culture in Early Modern France* (London, 1975), 182–3.
[35] Dekker, *Holland in beroering*, 51–60; however, Kloek, *Wie hij zij, man of wijf*,
141, casts doubt on this picture of female behaviour.

the reverse side of the denigratory image held about them by society in general. As they were considered less rational and more susceptible to emotion than men—something like a species of grown-up children—they tended to be punished less severely than their male counterparts, for they were held to be less than fully responsible for their actions. This was a humiliating response to female action, perhaps, but a useful one none the less. Moreover, it appears that male *schutters* or soldiers were less ready to use extreme forms of violence against women, especially shooting, which again allowed women to take the lead in riotous activities with a degree of impunity. More positively, however, rioting can be seen as almost the only form of participation in politics available to the vast majority of the urban population outside the political élite, and this applies with especial force for women. Rioting was almost the only way women had of directly influencing how their society operated, and it is not fanciful to see their participation, and in particular the violence which they displayed, in public disorders as a, perhaps unconscious, expression of resentment of their exclusion from whole areas of public life, when their social and economic experiences must have taught them rather different lessons about the capabilities and responsibilities of women.

II

The Politics of the Province of Holland

The purpose of this part is to outline the distinctive characteristics of the political system of the province of Holland in the seventeenth century with, again, as in the preceding part, the emphasis on how it worked in practice rather than in constitutional theory. One of the aims of this section, as it will be of the third part also, is to try to demonstrate how a system which on paper looks almost perfectly designed for deadlock, inefficiency, and the promotion of internal strife, in fact was able to work notably well for much of this century. Even the near-breakdown of the system during the Truce crisis can be interpreted as an oblique tribute to the coherence of Holland's political society, as in the event civil war was avoided and the bloodshed which occurred was remarkably limited. Within this broad picture of relative stability, however, there was constant change, observable not only in the fluctuations between the periods when the States were dominant and those when the stadhouder was the effective head of government, but also particularly in the way in which the position of the stadhouder evolved in the course of the century. What happened in this province is of vital importance for our understanding of the politics of the Republic as a whole, and what follows can only be considered as a tentative approach to a surprisingly neglected subject.

Politics in Holland at the provincial level is a somewhat elusive matter. First, because the province and its affairs were so important a part of the political life of the Dutch Republic as a whole that its politics merge almost imperceptibly into those of the state; but also because the towns were so important within the province that its political life can to a considerable extent be seen as little more than a projection of that of the towns. Thus, shading into local politics on the one hand and affairs of the whole state on the other, the specifically provincial contents of the political experience of Holland remain hard to pin down. This is particularly true of the role of the successive princes of Orange as stadhouder of Holland; their motives and above all their power within the province are inseparable from their powers and positions in the other provinces and, even more importantly, in the central political and military institutions of the Republic. To a rather less marked extent—or at least less consistently—the *raadpensionaris* of Holland was also a figure in national politics and derived from this position a measure of power and influence which he could deploy on the provincial stage. Yet the role of Holland within the Dutch

Republic is so predominant that, whatever the difficulties, some attempt to isolate the provincial level from the national is necessary to an understanding of the political life of this state. Without some perception of the nature of Holland politics, of the structures and circumstances determining political decisions in this most powerful of the Dutch provinces, the politics of the state as a whole cannot be properly understood.

Holland was by far the most populous and wealthy province in the Republic. Its population had more than doubled in the hundred years before 1622, and continued to grow into the second half of the seventeenth century, by which time, however, first the countryside and then the smaller towns had started to be affected by demographic stagnation and even decline. In the last third of the century even the biggest towns had begun to falter demographically. During this period the population of the province rose from about 672,000 in 1621 to something in the region of 880,000 towards the end of the century, compared with estimated total population figures for the Republic as a whole of 1.5 rising to 1.9 million at about the same dates.[1] In wealth it seems likely that Holland's share was even greater. Throughout the century, Holland was officially responsible for meeting nearly 60 per cent of the Republic's expenditure on common affairs, chiefly military, and in practice the proportion may well have been higher, as Holland paid its quota more regularly and fully than any of the other provinces, and was even prepared at times to subsidize other provinces when the issue was urgent enough, and when the policy concerned was in accord with the interests and prejudices of its political leaders.

Holland was the dynamic centre of Dutch economic expansion in this period; some of the other provinces shared in the boom to a greater or lesser extent, notably Zeeland and Friesland, but were nevertheless only pale shadows of Holland. The population growth, the expansion of the towns, and the explosive development of trade and manufactures brought enormous changes to the economic and social life of the province, a transformation to an urbanized and commercial—perhaps one would be justified in calling it a bourgeois—society, yet the political system which governed this dynamic society remained in form at least deeply conservative.

[1] J. A. Faber *et al.*, 'Population Changes and Economic Development in the Netherlands', *Afdeling Agrarische Geschiedenis Bijdragen*, 12 (1965), 60.

Just as the old system of oligarchic rule remained undisturbed at the town level, so at provincial level the system remained structurally the same as it had been before the economic and social changes of the sixteenth and early seventeenth century, except for the disappearance of the previous sovereign—and even here his representative, the stadhouder, remained, with functions and prerogatives which derived to a significant extent from the situation before the Revolt. In a living refutation of the *ancien régime* metaphor of the body politic, the head—the count—of the political system had been removed in the course of the Revolt (formally only as late as 1581), and the rest of the body left to carry on as if all that had been lost was a useless and burdensome appendage. That matters were more complex and difficult than this in practice, with the stadhouder, for example, fulfilling some of the functions of the old sovereign while in theory supreme authority was deemed to lie with the States of the province, is one of the curiosities of the political system in the seventeenth century which make it such an intriguing subject to study.

Holland also retained the principle of absolute political equality between the towns represented in the States, but this theory ignored another practical problem which the economic changes of the sixteenth and early seventeenth century had brought into being: the disproportionate size, wealth, and power of Amsterdam. Quite apart from the permanent, if often latent, tension between the States as a whole and the stadhouder, among the towns there was the major structural problem of Amsterdam demanding the influence within the province which its financial power appeared to justify, but which the system as it stood could not allow—in formal terms, at least. The way in which this imbalance was accommodated—or not—is another theme which pits the formal system against the demands of practical politics.

In a century which has been characterized as peculiarly violent and rebellious by many historians, the domestic politics of Holland can be seen as remarkably peaceful in the main, yet this is not the whole truth for there were three points during the seventeenth century when the latent tensions and conflicts within Dutch society threatened to burst out of the controls and restraints of normal political behaviour and to plunge the country into anarchy or civil war. These were the conflict over the remonstrant movement, which erupted during the Truce and came to a head in 1618–19;

the struggle for power between Willem II and the States of Holland, which resulted in the attempted *coup* by the prince in 1650; and the political upheavals in Holland and Zeeland in the summer of 1672, consequent on the military disasters of the previous months. In each of these crises, the province of Holland was the arena in which these conflicts were chiefly fought out and the decisions here determined the future of the Republic as a whole.

These crises reveal the interaction of various themes: in particular, the rivalry between the princes of Orange as stadhouders of the province and the States of Holland, and the problematic relationship between the Reformed Church and the civil authorities at both town and provincial level. Close attention to these periods of near-breakdown reveals problems and uncertainties deep within the political system which were obscured in more normal times by the compromises and general pragmatism which were necessary to make such an apparently unpromising system work as well as it did in practice—most of the time.

The Truce crisis was the most serious of the three, as it was the nearest the Republic ever came to civil war, and even perhaps disintegration, in the seventeenth century.[2] In Holland it revealed sharp divisions between the members of the States which undermined the latter's ability to keep the situation under control; it made clear for perhaps the first time since the death of Willem of Orange the political potential of the office of stadhouder; and the religious dispute showed how important the symbolic role of the Reformed Church was, despite the relatively small size of its membership.

As the crisis deepened, a basic weakness of the States of Holland was revealed: its inability to act effectively when there were irreconcilable conflicts between its members. While Oldenbarnevelt was able to take the majority of towns with him in his policy of extending support and protection to the remonstrants, the determined opposition of a minority of towns led by the critically important Amsterdam effectively nullified his efforts. The practical autonomy of the voting towns not only made it impossible for the States to force the decisions of the majority on to the dissenting

---

[2] See the treatment of this crisis from contrasting perspectives in Den Tex, *Oldenbarnevelt*, iii; H. Gerlach, *Het proces tegen Oldenbarnevelt en de 'Maximen in den Staat'* (Haarlem, 1965); and A. Th. van Deursen, *Bavianen en slijkgeuzen: Kerk en kerkvolk ten tijde van Maurits en Oldenbarnevelt* (Assen, 1974), Pt. II.

towns, but it allowed the minority to dispute the legality of majority voting in such important matters. The increasing ineffectiveness of Oldenbarnevelt's leadership provided Maurits with an opportunity to increase his own power, especially as he could act in concert with Amsterdam and the other contraremonstrant towns, thus obscuring the extent to which this was a constitutional clash between stadhouder and States.

Maurits's role in the whole affair was ambivalent in the extreme. It is difficult to decide whether his most important function was in exacerbating the conflict or in resolving it. On the one hand, it is at least possible that the disputes between the remonstrants and their orthodox opponents could have been kept under control by the States, as other serious doctrinal problems were later in the century, had it not been for Maurits's public and decisive support for the contraremonstrants. On the other hand, his actions in 1618 did effectively resolve the crisis with a minimum of bloodshed and violence; they left a legacy of bitterness, it is true, but did not in the end undermine the sense of unity of province or Republic. In the stadhouder's favour, it can be said that the religious dispute was much more serious than those which came later in the century, not because the doctrines in question were more important than those in, say, the Cocceian controversy (see Chapter 6 of this Part), but because at this earlier period the whole position of the Reformed Church was much more fragile and uncertain than it became later when the church had an established and understood place within the Dutch polity. In these circumstances, Maurits's intervention on the side of the contraremonstrants brought a swift resolution to a problem which, left to Oldenbarnevelt's policies, might have festered for years. Yet the intriguing question remains whether an equally satisfactory conclusion might not have been brought about if the stadhouder had fully and honestly supported Oldenbarnevelt. It is also very much the question whether the fact that Maurits's intervention did not lead to civil war was the result of luck or good judgement.

In the event, 1618 marks the beginning of a new and much more important role for the stadhouder in the political life of Holland. After Willem of Orange's death the stadhouder had been overshadowed by the *Advocaat van den Lande*, but for the rest of the seventeenth century—except for the period 1650–72—it was the stadhouders who played the leading role in the politics of the

province. This transformation was a result of the way in which the
Truce crisis was resolved, though it might perhaps be more accu-
rate to say that this crisis revealed the power which was latent in
the office. However, the way in which these potentialities were
exploited in 1618–19 also had very important consequences. The
arrest and subsequent execution of Oldenbarnevelt, together with
the *wetsverzettingen* backed by the threat of armed force, intimi-
dated the regents at the time and later, but also provided the
nascent republican movement with a demonology. The Truce crisis
was to figure prominently in the political theory and mythology of
the rival parties in the Republic for the rest of the century, and the
ability of these events to arouse controversy has perhaps not totally
abated even now.[3]

Equally obvious was the crucial, yet weak and insecure, place of
the Reformed Church in the political life of the province revealed
by this first crisis of the century. The toppling of Oldenbarnevelt,
along with a section of the established oligarchies of the voting
towns, was a dramatic demonstration of the importance of the
church in Holland. The champions of orthodoxy saw the remonstrant movement as a threat to both the doctrinal purity and the
freedom from political tutelage of the public church. In turn, the
maintenance of the doctrine and independence of the church was
seen as vital to the integrity of the Republic by many who were
not strongly committed to the theological positions of the contraremonstrants. The weakness of the church's hold on the religious life of the province[4] only induced an extra degree of paranoia
among the orthodox. They felt they had no room for manœuvre or
compromise; it was feared that the least concession could lead to a
collapse before the forces of erastianism, unprincipled pragmatism,
and crypto-catholicism. Yet, despite its apparent and felt weakness,
the Reformed Church was able to rally sufficient backing to defeat
Oldenbarnevelt and his supporters. This was partly due to the
peculiar circumstances of the time, which brought the church powerful allies who opposed the policies of the Advocate for quite different reasons. However, the political importance of the church

[3] Gerlach, *Het proces tegen Oldenbarnevelt*, clearly took a somewhat partisan,
though largely justifiable, position, but this hardly explains the degree of heat displayed in hostile reviews of his work.
[4] A. C. Duke, 'The Ambivalent Face of Calvinism in the Netherlands 1561–1618',
in M. Prestwich (ed.), *International Calvinism 1541–1715* (Oxford, 1985).

was not merely the result of the particular conditions of these years. Although the position of the church did not remain unchanged, and although the remonstrants were followed in time by more successful liberalizing movements within its ranks, it nevertheless continued to play a unique role in the politics of both province and Republic. Even in Holland, with its remarkable degree of religious heterogeneity, Reformed orthodoxy retained its ability to act as the symbolic expression of patriotism.

A further important influence on the development of the internal crisis was popular violence, especially in the towns. There is more than a little uncertainty about the causes of the riots which took place in these years, and about the motivations of the rioters, but their importance is hardly open to doubt. These were the first clear demonstrations in this century of the power of popular action even in this most undemocratic of systems. From this point onwards it was clear that rioting could be a formidable force in the politics of the province, given favourable circumstances such as serious divisions within regent ranks. Even if it was often stirred up and manipulated by members of the élite for their own purposes, it was never an entirely reliable weapon in their hands, and it could move in unpredictable directions. For the historian, it is perhaps most fascinating through the glimpse which the slogans and war cries of the crowds give us of the ideas and perceptions current in areas of the population which are all too often a closed book to us.

The second crisis of the seventeenth century, which came to a head in 1650, was ostensibly about very different matters, namely the control of military expenditure and, by extension, of the foreign policy of the Republic. The determination of the States of Holland to reduce spending on the army implied a rejection of the adventurist foreign policy of Willem II. The treaty of Münster in 1648, which had finally brought to an end the long war with Spain, had been signed against the opposition of the young prince, and he hoped to resume the war in a renewed alliance with France. The States of Holland were determined on peace and retrenchment, and this fundamental difference in policy again brought them and the stadhouder into conflict, but on this occasion the former were considerably more united than they had been in 1618. Most importantly, the States were led in their opposition to the prince's policy by Amsterdam.

In 1650, Willem II could hope for no substantial support in

Holland, either from the regents or from the populace of the voting towns. The policy of peace and reduction of expenditure appealed to taxpayers and all those who could expect to do better in peacetime, and were possibly already benefiting from the improved conditions of trade.[5] Such interests far outweighed both numerically and in terms of political influence those who stood to profit from a renewal of the war. Also, the States of Holland could plausibly present themselves as the defenders of the rights and privileges of province and town against the stadhouder and a subservient States General. Whereas, during the Truce, Oldenbarnevelt and his supporters could be made to appear as innovators who were attempting to alter the nature of the Reformed Church and its relationship to the civil power, in 1650 the leaders of the States could present themselves as pious champions of the status quo, and it was Willem II who appeared to be willing to put at risk the tried and tested way of doing things in order to pursue his own personal ends.[6] It is, then, hardly surprising that he should have made little dent in the solidarity of regent resistance in the province, or that in the main the regents could rely on the loyalty of their citizens on such an issue.

The crisis which erupted in the summer of 1672 arose out of very different circumstances from either of the first two, but developed along lines which were in important ways very similar. The dramatic failures of the Dutch army and the advance of the French forces to the very borders of Holland brought about a panic which took the particular form of a paranoid suspicion, not of the competence, but of the patriotism of the States-party regents who had dominated the province under De Witt. Persistent popular unrest in the voting towns of Holland (and of Zeeland) led first to the appointment of Willem III as stadhouder, and subsequently to the assassination of De Witt and large-scale *wetsverzettingen* in the towns. The particular nature of this crisis meant that it had its own distinct characteristics, but, nevertheless, the way in which

---

[5] J. I. Israel, *Dutch Primacy in World Trade 1585–1740* (Oxford, 1989), 197–207.

[6] Not all contemporaries saw matters this way: see e.g. the views of the chronicler, Lieuwe van Aitzema, as related in G. N. van der Plaat, 'Lieuwe van Aitzema's kijk op het stadhouderschap in de Republiek', *Bijdragen en Mededelingen betreffende de Geschiedenis der Nederlanden*, 103 (1988). Aitzema was noted for his realism, not to say cynicism, but he was—according to this interpretation—inclined to see the States of Holland rather than the prince as the disrupters of the established political order in this case.

Holland responded to the situation showed such similarities to the earlier crises as to suggest the existence of long-standing structural elements in the political system which largely determined the way in which the province would respond to such challenges.

Most obvious of these structural factors was the dichotomy between stadhouder and States, which meant that if one failed recourse was had to the other. In the circumstances of 1672, the failure of the Wittian regime to ward off or contain the French attack led to the demand for alternative leadership, and it would seem that the only conceivable replacement for the republican system of De Witt was a return to the dominance of a stadhouder. This had nothing to do with the personal qualities or abilities of Willem III, as these were as yet unproven and, in any case, the vast majority of those agitating in his favour knew nothing about him except that he was the latest in the line of the princes of Orange. Two points deserve emphasis: it was the regents as much as the populace who saw the prince as their saviour; and there seems to have been no conception of any other way of dealing with the problem—no serious consideration was given to any reform of the political system. If a government by the *raadpensionaris* and the States was found wanting, then the only practical alternative, it would seem, was the stadhouder.

A particularly intriguing line of continuity was the confusion of patriotism with Reformed orthodoxy. This had been a powerful motif during the Truce crisis, but much less prominent in 1650, although it was present in the demands for a religiously motivated foreign policy. In the panic of the summer months of 1672, it came to the surface again: part of the popular suspicion of the regents was a distrust of their religious orientation. The popular response to the French military successes was a readiness to believe that the regents had sold their country down the river, but it was equally clear that those least likely to have done this were those of unimpeachable Reformed purity. In consequence, in the attacks on the sitting regents and the criteria by which their replacements were judged, considerations of religious orthodoxy played a prominent part.[7] In these tense months popular distrust was turned on regents with the taint of remonstrant connections as well as on the supporters of De Witt. To be a wholly reliable patriot, at least in

---

[7] This was certainly the case in Rotterdam (Vroesen, *Waaragtig verhaal*; Price, 'Rotterdam Patriciate', ch. 6).

times of widespread panic, it was necessary to be orthodox in religion; the loyalty to the state of all others could be much more readily impugned.

An interesting variation on 1618 was that in 1672 the *wetsverzettingen* were not carried out by the prince in person, but were the immediate result of popular pressure. The sitting regents were forced to resign their places under the threat of physical violence, and short-lists for their replacements were then sent to the prince. So Willem's role was less dramatic than Maurits's in 1618: he did not tour the towns forcing the governments to submit, but received the resignations which the rioters forced out of their regents. In practice, the stadhouder's influence on events appears to have been rather greater than this description would suggest. In particular he seems to have had a considerable influence in one way or another over the composition of the short-lists which were sent to him, and so in effect he probably had as much control over the appointment of the new regents as Maurits had had in 1618.

Again, the degree and extent of popular violence in 1672 connects the events of this year with the Truce crisis rather than 1650. Indeed, in 1672 the rioting in the voting towns of Holland played an even more direct role in the upheavals than in the earlier period. It was sustained popular pressure by means of more or less violent demonstrations which brought about, first, the elevation of the prince to the stadhoudership, and then, after a second wave of rioting, the *wetsverzettingen* of late August and September. Pressure from their own citizens forced the regents first to propose the restoration of the stadhoudership, with the fanatically republican Rotterdam in the van, and then to offer their own resignations to the prince. This whole episode was a stark reminder of a fundamental weakness of the oligarchy: its lack of coercive power. The town governments of Holland relied on the co-operation of their citizen militias, or on troops brought in from outside. When, as in 1672, the *schutterijen* were not only unwilling to act against the rioters, but in many cases were the hot-beds of opposition to the regents, and when the head of the army was unwilling to release troops to restore order in the towns (partly for severely practical reasons, but clearly political considerations were also involved), then the regents were helpless in the face of popular violence.[8]

    [8] *Contra* Dekker, *Holland in beroering*, 95–8, 108–9, 120.

It is worth stressing that, despite the degree of violence and popular distrust of the regent oligarchy that was evident in 1672, there was no real question of changing the basic nature of government within the province. As in 1618, the changes came in personnel and not in the system. Even at their most extreme, the petitions and pamphlets expressing public feeling looked only as far as some sort of machinery for checking the conduct of the regents, but nothing very practical was suggested, and there is no evidence that anyone in authority took such suggestions seriously. As soon as the new regents were firmly in power, they were able to reimpose order on the towns—with the support of the prince, whose interest in the popular movements ended after the restoration of the stadhouder-ship and the *wetsverzettingen*—greatly helped by the easing of the atmosphere of panic in the population at large which came with the stabilization and then improvement of the military situation in the autumn and winter. While some conception of reform was already emerging in the late seventeenth century, it remained the property of self-consciously radical intellectuals. It seems that any move towards practical reform of the political system would have to wait: only in the eighteenth century would it prove possible to found political movements on such ideas.

The relationship between the States of Holland, the stadhouder, and the other institutions of provincial government were rather clumsily improvised in the first years after the Revolt in 1572, but within a system which had formally stabilized—not to say stag-nated—by the end of the 1590s, the real balance of power between the various elements continued to fluctuate in practice until the violent end of the Republic in 1795. In particular, the two poles of political power and influence within the province were the States of Holland and the stadhouder, and the political life of the province was determined by the permanent—if often only latent—tension between these two opposed powers.

1. The States of Holland

Supreme political authority within the province of Holland and West Friesland (to give it its full name) lay with its States, but this statement of the conventional constitutional position disguises some real difficulties. From the first months of the Revolt, the political life of Holland had centred on the States, but equally almost from the beginning the relationship of the States to the stadhouder on the one hand and to the Generality, i.e. the central institutions of the Republic, on the other, had presented problems of competing authorities and competence, and it is hardly an exaggeration to say that these proved in the long term to be insoluble at the formal level. In terms of practical politics, however, the ill-defined and ambiguous relationships between States and stadhouder, and Holland and the Generality, did not cause too many problems for most of the time. It was only on rare occasions, such as in the three major crises of the seventeenth century, that they threatened to disrupt or perhaps even destroy the relatively smooth workings of the Dutch political system.

The States of Holland seized effective power in the course of the Revolt, and from 1578—when Amsterdam was brought over to the side of the rebels, thus finally uniting the province—for all practical purposes, whatever ambiguities there may have remained in constitutional terms, possessed sovereign power over the province. Of course, Philip II's sovereignty was formally recognized until the Act of Abjuration in 1581, and until this date all the official Acts of the States were issued in the name of the king against whom they were in revolt, but from this point on the formal and the actual situations merged and the authority of the States within Holland became clear. The only restrictions on this control regarded the degree to which membership of the Union with the other provinces making up the Republic limited provincial autonomy, and the extent to which the powers of the stadhouder were capable of limiting or even rivalling those of the States, in practice if not in theory. The position of the stadhouder will be discussed in the next chapter, but what needs to be stressed at the very outset is that even the most powerful of stadhouders had to work with and through the States. The States of Holland could be persuaded; they could be coerced; the constituent towns could be induced to send compliant delegations to The Hague; but the States could not be ignored or bypassed—the only way to rule Holland was through its representative body.

The States of Holland was composed of nineteen members: the nobles or *ridderschap*, and the representatives of the eighteen voting towns. There was more than a touch of arbitrariness about this membership as far as the towns were concerned. In the course of the Revolt the representation of the towns had increased from six to eighteen, and what was rather odd was not that there were very great disparities in size and wealth between the towns which maintained or achieved membership of the States, but that while some very small towns—such as Purmerend and Monnickendam—were able to gain representation, others were not. The reasons for the inclusion of some and the exclusion of others are not at all clear, and accident seems to have played some part. While all the larger towns (with the important exception of The Hague) gained admission, together with all the towns of any size at all in the Northern Quarter of the province, some of the smaller towns in the Southern Quarter failed to achieve lasting representation. A number of them appeared in the States from time to time in the first years after the Revolt—among others, Woerden, Oudewater, Geertruidenberg, Heusden, and Muiden—but a combination of the difficulty they had in sustaining the cost of regular delegations to the States with the reluctance of the established members to share power with these small fry determined their eventual exclusion.[1]

The six towns which had been represented in the States before the Revolt—Dordrecht, Haarlem, Delft, Leiden, Amsterdam, and Gouda—were recognized as the 'great' towns, but their privileges as such were of very limited importance, and were shared by Rotterdam as the leading newcomer. Apart from this relatively minor distinction, all the *stemhebbende steden* (i.e. towns represented in the States) were equal in formal power, despite their considerable differences in size and wealth. With the exception of the first few years after the Revolt, when military threats often constrained them to sit in a less vulnerable town, the States met in

[1] Koopmans, *De Staten van Holland*, 30–2.

The Hague, a neutral place within easy reach of all the major towns and not inaccessible even to the more remote of the smaller towns of the Northern Quarter, given the relatively rapid and frequent transportation available within the province both summer and winter.[2]

The increase in the number of towns represented in the States meant a decline in the relative political weight of the *ridderschap*, though not to total insignificance. There were recurrent disputes over who were entitled to be 'beschreven' as members of the *ridderschap*, but in practice the princes of Orange (who were normally recognized as the first noble of the *ridderschap*[3]) were able to determine its membership for much of this period, and were even able to engineer the appointment of nobles from outside Holland as long as they were in the possession of a suitable lordship (*heerlijkheid*) within the province. However, it seems that Oldenbarnevelt, during his period of political domination, was able to exercise a predominant influence over admission to this body; and, during the first stadhouderless period, deceased members were replaced by their eldest sons, or failing that were replaced by co-optation by the remaining members. A problem peculiar to republics was that there was no authority within the Dutch state which could create new nobles, thus families which died out could not be replaced. In Holland this was already becoming a problem by the later seventeenth century, and was not solved by the recruitment of a few members of the rather more prolific nobilities of the land provinces by Willem III.

The influence of the nobility in Holland has perhaps been seriously underestimated by later historians. Certainly, the nobles in Holland retained much of their superior social standing and prestige, but it remains to be demonstrated that they were able to play any significant independent political role. Despite their formal responsibility for the whole of the countryside of the province, they in fact lacked a power base and had none of the control over taxation, for example, which gave the *stemhebbende* towns such leverage. It would seem rather that the nobles enjoyed considerable prestige and, in more practical terms, profitable offices and emolu-

---

[2] De Vries, *Barges and Capitalism*, 34–42, 63–93.

[3] Not always: for a few years in the 1630s J. W. van Brederode was recognized as first noble rather than Frederik Hendrik, and during the first stadhouderless period Brederode again took precedence.

ments, but were politically almost completely dependent on the stadhouder. The only times when this was not true was when they were dependent instead on the chief minister of the States of Holland. Before 1618, Oldenbarnevelt's peculiarly strong position within both state and province enabled him to build up a clientele within the *ridderschap*, which had to be broken up as part of Maurits's *coup*; and again under De Witt the absence of a stadhouder brought the nobles into dependence on the *raadpensionaris*. In our present state of knowledge, there does not seem to be any convincing case for attributing to the nobles an independent influence in the political arena.[4]

Within the States of Holland, each of the nineteen members—the nobility and the eighteen towns—had one vote (voice or *stem*), with no weight being given in formal terms to differences in wealth or size. Decision-making was complicated by a number of factors. First, there was considerable resistance to taking decisions by majority vote. As in the councils of the towns, it was felt that decisions were best made collegially, with the States acting as a single body, or that at least the decencies should be preserved by maintaining the fiction of such unanimity. This conception of the proper way of reaching decisions could only be reinforced by the understandable reluctance of the larger towns, particularly Amsterdam, to be outvoted by an alliance of the smaller towns. In their turn these smaller towns were concerned that they might be railroaded by their more powerful neighbours into having to accept unwelcome policies, and they therefore clung to the idea of unanimity to protect their interests. Such considerations, together with the deeply entrenched particularism so characteristic of the towns, led to an insistence that important matters required the agreement of all the towns. There was always the possibility of some dispute as to what questions were important enough to exclude decisions by majority voting, but war and peace and, emphatically, money matters were clearly included. This principle meant that reaching decisions, particularly on important issues, could be difficult, but it prevented a dictatorship of the majority and put a premium on negotiation, compromise, and realism. In general, the system worked remarkably well—though not without frequent and acrimonious complaints from the weaker parties in any particular dispute—and occasions

---

[4] However, see Aalbers, 'Faktieuse tegenstellingen'.

when no agreement could be reached because of irreconcilable differences between the towns were surprisingly few.

Normally the towns were represented in the States by multi-member delegations, the size and composition varying in accordance with the custom and practice of the individual towns. These delegations did not have plenipotentiary powers, but were strictly bound by instructions from their principals in their home towns. Before each meeting of the States, the *stemhebbende* towns were sent the agenda (the *poincten van beschrijvinge*) for the coming session, so the relevant body in each town could instruct its delegation regarding what to say on the matters to be discussed. In principle, and usually in practice as well, the delegations could not and did not deviate from these instructions, and if they did they could be called to order by their principals. The only way in which a delegation could properly change its vote, in response perhaps to the discussion which had taken place in the States, was by referring back to its town government for new instructions. This system of referring back (*ruggespraak*) was not as clumsy and time-wasting as it might appear at first sight. The distances the delegations, or their spokesmen, had to travel were quite short in most cases, and could usually be covered in a few hours; meetings of the local *vroedschappen* were frequent and special meetings were not difficult to convene; in consequence, fairly rapid responses from the towns to changing circumstances were possible. The spirit of collegial decision-making and compromise often influenced the nature of the instructions given in any case: it was typical, for example, for a delegation which reported back that the weight of opinion in the States was against them, to be told to persist in their original opinion for a further round of voting, but that if they still remained in a hopeless minority they should then conform to the majority opinion.

This strict control of the delegations to the States by their principals in the towns underlines the fact that it was the towns themselves—or rather, of course, their governments—which were held to be voting, with the delegations being merely their instruments. In an important sense, thus, it can be said that the States were not really supreme, but that final authority rested collectively with the town governments, and that the States were the institutional expression of that political power.[5] The States were not superior to

[5] J. V. Rijpperda Wierdsma, *Politie en justitie: een studie over Hollandsche staatsbouw tijdens de Republiek* (Zwolle, 1937), 15.

the town governments but were an expression of their authority. This is one reason why the States found it so difficult to discipline or coerce dissident town governments: quite apart from the dangerous—to all towns—precedent which might be set, it was not entirely clear how one part of the sovereign could legitimately enforce its will on another part. An action by the States was a collective action of the towns (and of the nobles, of course, which complicates matters but does not affect the principle involved) and was not in formal terms superior to the act of any one town. A further consideration is that there was no machinery for the effective coercion of dissident towns; exhortations could be made and delegations sent to put pressure on recalcitrant members, but it was not clear what could be done if they continued to be unreasonable. Whatever the practical necessity for individual towns to bow to the will of the majority, they were under no legal—or indeed moral—obligation to do so.

This constitutional situation was reflected in the voting system which operated in the meetings of the States. This was not, indeed, a voting system at all in the modern sense: the question would be put to the assembly, and then the delegations (each speaking through a single spokesman) would give their opinions, often at length, in a strict order of precedence. The *ridderschap* spoke first, which was not insignificant as their spokesman was usually the *raadpensionaris*, followed by Dordrecht and the other great towns, then Rotterdam, speaking first among the lesser towns. After all had had an opportunity to give their opinion, the *raadpensionaris* would then sum up the feeling of the meeting, and this summary would then be submitted to the members for their approval—again in strict order of precedence. This procedure to some extent reflected political reality as well as theory. Despite the formal equality of all the members, the larger towns expected and usually received greater consideration than the smaller. The speaking order allowed the major towns to set the terms of the debate, and it would seem—though our knowledge of the actual workings of the States is disturbingly limited—that the lesser towns usually followed the lead given by the earlier speakers. Indeed, it seems to have been the convention that the lesser towns would not oppose anything on which the larger towns had reached an agreement. Only when the leading towns were in dispute—which was often enough in all conscience—

would the smaller towns try to sway the debate by adding their weight to one side or the other.

The differences in size between the towns did cause problems, however, and this was particularly the case with Amsterdam. Like any other town, it only had one vote in the States, yet it was about three times as big as the next largest town and dwarfed most of the others. Indeed, by the 1670s it contained within its boundaries almost a quarter of the total population of the province and quite probably an even greater proportion of its wealth. In these circumstances it was difficult to confine Amsterdam within the voting conventions of the States of Holland. Given its very large contribution to the finances of the province, it expected its opinion to be given particular weight in the deliberations of the States. In practice, Amsterdam was indeed accorded much greater consideration than the smaller towns, but the system was incapable of dealing with Amsterdam's pretensions to the satisfaction of all parties. When the leading town did not receive what it felt was its proper consideration, serious trouble could result. During the Truce crisis, Oldenbarnevelt's position was fatally (literally) undermined, not so much by the opposition of the stadhouder as by that of the government of Amsterdam, which felt that the Advocate, supported by a majority in the States, was paying too little attention to its opinions and interests. Less dramatically, De Witt found his position in the late 1660s significantly weakened when Amsterdam moved against him for similar reasons (see Chapter 5 of this Part). It was unusual, however, for disputes to reach such a pitch: in normal circumstances the interests of the greater towns, and of Amsterdam in particular, could be accommodated while remaining within the forms of strict constitutional equality represented by the voting system in the States.

Besides the threat of major political problems arising from the difficulty of accommodating the giant Amsterdam within the formal system of the States, there was the frequent—indeed almost permanent—minor irritation of how to deal with other dissident towns. The political system within Holland relied heavily on reasonableness and accommodation, and there was no effective machinery for dealing with towns which decided to be awkward and not go along with the majority. The problem was not just the theoretical one that the legal grounds for coercing a minority were unclear, but more importantly the severely practical consideration that if a precedent were once set of the majority in the States successfully forcing its opinion on an individual town, then no town could feel sure that it might not be treated in this way at some point in the future. In the Dutch politico-legal system precedent tended to be taken as establishing right, and it was in no town's interest that such a power should be established. Consequently, no town was going to speak in favour of the coercion of one of its fellow members of the States for fear of setting a precedent that might be used against itself. In these circumstances, a pragmatic approach to dissent was the only practical response. In effect, this meant that dissent by a large town, or group of towns, had to be dealt with by accommodation, but that lesser towns could be safely ignored until their opposition faded away through its own futility. This was not a perfect method, but in the main it worked—though when it did not the results could be very serious.

The most important minister of the States of Holland was the *raadpensionaris* (usually called the grand pensionary in English works). This office had a curious history, showing how particular circumstances and personalities could affect the development of political institutions in a lasting way. The post originated as the paid (thus, pensionary) legal adviser of the *ridderschap* in the States, but in the course of the Revolt it increased in political importance, and from 1585 Oldenbarnevelt made it, under the title of *Advocaat van den Lande*, the most powerful political office in the province, and indeed in the Republic. After his fall and execution, there was a reaction against this dominance and the post was renamed *raadpensionaris*, emphasizing its advisory and subordinate function *vis-à-vis* the States, and attempts were made to limit its political potential, partly by carefully composed instructions to define and control the activities of its holder. The office retained its potential to become politically central, however, and demonstrated this whenever it came into the hands of an able man at a favourable time.

Whatever his power and influence in practice, the *raadpensionaris* remained a paid official and thus in formal terms inferior to both the nobles and to the regents representing the towns in the States, and even to the members of the governments of the voting towns: they were the politicians and he was their servant.[6]

---

[6] See Rowen, *John de Witt, Grand Pensionary*, 141 for a discussion of this point in relation to Johan de Witt.

Oldenbarnevelt's salary was only f. 1,200, but he was able to amass a considerable fortune through gifts from various sources. Subsequently, the salary was raised, in part at least to limit the incumbent's dependence on such sources of income: Adriaen Duyck (1621–31) received f. 3,000, De Witt f. 6,000 in the last years of his career, and Fagel f. 12,000. Indeed, De Witt's instruction introduced a specific ban on accepting gifts.[7] The formal duties of the *raadpensionaris* were to advise the States on legal matters, including issues that would nowadays be considered political or constitutional, to put the questions for discussion to the assembly of the States (acting at the same time as spokesman for the *ridderschap*), and to sum up their deliberations. He was also bound to carry out the instructions of the States over a wide range of matters. The administrative support given to the *raadpensionaris* was rudimentary in the extreme, consisting chiefly of a handful of secretaries who were more an extension of their chief's household than officials of a civil service. Despite these formal and practical limitations, however, the office had to become politically important as it was the only one which could provide political leadership for the States—except for the stadhouder of the province, and he could not be expected to serve the States' needs in quite the way they might have wished.

In effect, the Advocate or *raadpensionaris* from Oldenbarnevelt onwards became something like a prime minister for Holland and, by what seems in retrospect an inevitable extension, of the Republic as well. Even under a powerful stadhouder such as Frederik Hendrik or Willem III, the *raadpensionaris* was an indispensable political instrument, and could be an important ally of the prince of Orange, as was Fagel for Willem. In the absence of a stadhouder, the *raadpensionaris* naturally took over the leadership of the Republic—Oldenbarnevelt had done this even with a stadhouder—as the career of De Witt shows, and as became evident again during the second stadhouderless period in the early eighteenth century. The *raadpensionaris* had his power base, of course, in the States of Holland. He was instrumental in drawing up its agenda for discussion, he advised and summarized the debates, and formulated its conclusions. In addition, he had permanent session in the *gecommitteerde raden* (see below) and was appointed to all

---

[7] Fruin, *Staatsinstellingen*, 233.

the important committees set up by the States. He was in effective
control of the finances of the province, and conducted its relations
with the other provinces, particularly through the States General.
In addition, certainly under Oldenbarnevelt and De Witt, he conducted the foreign affairs of the Republic, not as a formal part of
the duties of his office but by means of a series of *ad hoc* commissions and informal procedures. For example, the formal correspondence of the ambassadors of the Republic was carried on with the
States General through its *griffier*, but during the periods of dominance by Oldenbarnevelt and De Witt the real, business correspondence was directed to the *raadpensionaris* of Holland.

The ill-defined nature of the duties and powers of the *raadpensionaris* meant that the actual influence of the office varied considerably according to the character and abilities of the incumbent,
and to the circumstances obtaining, especially the presence or
absence of a stadhouder, and the character of the stadhouder when
present. At the beginning of the century, Oldenbarnevelt as
Advocaat van den Lande had practically unchallenged control over
the political leadership of Holland and the Republic. Maurits,
although stadhouder of Holland and other provinces, was content
at first to confine himself very largely to military affairs, and only
later did he begin to challenge the Advocate's supremacy.
Subsequently, the stadhouders of Holland were never again content
to play second fiddle to the *raadpensionaris*, and formed a structural counterweight to the latter's power—except during the stadhouderless periods. After 1618, when there was a stadhouder in
office the *raadpensionarissen* did not act as leaders of the opposition—except perhaps, and briefly, Adriaen Pauw[8]—but as more or
less loyal collaborators, and varied from powerful politicians in
their own right such as Fagel to the politically characterless Cats.[9]
In general the stadhouders were influential enough to make sure
that strong politicians with inconvenient policies were not chosen
for the office.

After the States themselves, the most important political body

---

[8] Adriaan Pauw, from a powerful Amsterdam regent family, was *raadpensionaris*
from 1631 to 1636, but was too independent-minded a politician to suit Frederik
Hendrik and was manœuvred out of office. He had a second period in the post at
the beginning of the first stadhouderless period (1651–3).
[9] A. Th. van Deursen, 'De raadspensionaris Jacob Cats', *Tijdschrift voor
Geschiedenis*, 92 (1979) is an attempt to rehabilitate Cats as a politician of substance in his own right, but is not entirely convincing.

was the *gecommitteerde raden* (commissioned councillors), a standing committee of the States in permanent session dealing with legal, military, and financial matters. Despite this very broad competence, its importance seems to have been more administrative than political—policies were made elsewhere. Its role in the day-to-day running of the affairs of the province was obviously of particular importance when the States were not in session. Although it is usual to speak simply of the *gecommitteerde raden*, there were in fact two such bodies, one for the main or southern part of Holland and the other for the Northern Quarter of the province. Apart from being a wholly typical example of the deep-seated particularism of the Dutch political system, this division can be traced to the military circumstances following the fall of Haarlem to the Spanish in 1573, which effectively split Holland into two separate zones. However, an administrative measure designed to meet a particular emergency was continued after 1576, when this militarily imposed division of the provision ended. This separate council for the Northern Quarter fitted in too well with the northern towns' particularism and fear of being dominated by the larger and more numerous towns of the South for it to be abolished once it had come into existence. (Unless otherwise indicated, the term *gecommitteerde raden* will be used to refer to the main body, that for Holland south of the IJ.)

The *gecommitteerde raden* had a membership of ten: the senior member of the *ridderschap*, nominees from the six great towns (Dordrecht, Haarlem, Delft, Leiden, Amsterdam, and Gouda) plus Rotterdam and Gorinchem, with the tenth nominated in turn by Schiedam, Schoonhoven, and Den Briel. The town representatives held this office for three years, except for the nominees from the three smaller towns, who had two-year stints. The members were formally appointed by, and were responsible to, the States, but as in practice the nominations from the towns were always confirmed by the States, they were in effect the representatives of their home towns. They were drawn from the local regent group, and were usually men of considerable standing and, if possible, ability, as membership involved important administrative duties as well as power and prestige. The *raadpensionaris*, although not a member, attended their meetings and had considerable influence on their deliberations, not only because of his office, but because he usually had far greater experience of government at the centre than the members themselves with their relatively brief periods of service.

Thus, the composition and mode of appointment of the *gecommitteerde raden* again emphasizes the power of the voting towns within the political system of the province. They were not content with having control over the decisions of this important committee through their influence in the States, but in effect bypassed the States to appoint its members themselves. In these circumstances it is hardly surprising that the *gecommitteerde raden* had major problems in dealing with recalcitrant towns. No more than the States themselves were they a suitable body to do more than cajole and threaten, and in practice their ability to enforce compliance with their directions was very limited. Where the government of a town was prepared to be stubborn in a political or judicial matter, there was little the *gecommitteerde raden* could do but keep up the pressure and try to save face.[10]

The *gecommitteerde raden* are a good example of an institution which arose to deal with the particular problems of the early years of the Revolt, continued as an indispensable administrative body, but never achieved the political importance that might have been expected. The reasons for this are not hard to find. Institutionally, the fact that its members were chosen, in effect, directly by the towns and for short periods of office only, prevented this body from developing into a council which could give coherent political direction. It was not a committee where the leading politicians could come together to formulate and direct policy (in contrast, for example, to the committee system of Long Parliament). Moreover, while the *raadpensionaris* might have been prepared to consider the *gecommitteerde raden* a suitable instrument of government, this was hardly true of the stadhouders. The committee was too much under the direct control of the towns in membership and policy to be a very effective instrument in the hands of the stadhouder, and this was a further reason why its political role was restricted.

[10] An example of this difficulty is given by the case of Leonard van Naerssen in Rotterdam. He was accused in 1653—thus in the politically difficult days of the first Anglo-Dutch War—of using seditious language about the government of Holland, but the best efforts of the *gecommitteerde raden* and the *Hof van Holland* could not persuade the government of the town to release him for trial by a provincial court. The *vroedschap* of Rotterdam advised him to petition the States for pardon on the grounds that he had spoken carelessly (Price, 'Rotterdam Patriciate', 76–7), and he was allowed to escape punishment.

2. The Stadhouder

The stadhouder was the other pole of political power and leadership in Holland apart from the provincial States, and was the main moving force in the political life of the province for a good part of the century. Yet the office was formally a subordinate one: the stadhouder was appointed, empowered, and instructed by the States. In this sense, and in perhaps only this sense, there is a parallel with the position of the *raadpensionaris*, who was also a subordinate official of the States capable of attaining supreme political leadership. No more than in this latter case is the formal constitutional position an adequate account of the strength of the stadhoudership in the practical politics of the seventeenth century.

Both the office and powers of the stadhouder in Holland were egregious anomalies even for a political system not remarkable for its constitutional consistency. Formally, the position of stadhouder, as the representative of the sovereign in Holland, should have disappeared with the repudiation of Philip II in 1581, or perhaps after the death of Anjou in 1584, but it did not, and the post became an important component of the congeries of powers and offices which enabled the princes of Orange to attain a quasi-monarchical position within the Dutch Republic after 1618. It must be stressed that the stadhoudership was a provincial, not a national, office, and the powers of the princes of Orange as stadhouder were probably less in Holland than in any other province. However, the effective power of the princes in the Republic did not derive simply from holding the office of stadhouder in most of the provinces; in their case it is certainly true that the whole was greater than the sum of the parts. In this chapter, however, we are concerned not with the role of the princes of Orange in the Republic as a whole, but as stadhouder in Holland, though the way in which the power of the princes outside Holland affected their ability to exercise authority within the province has obviously to be taken into account.

Before the Revolt, the stadhouder was the representative, or viceroy, of the sovereign within Holland. As such he was appointed by the crown, or rather by the governor-general of the

Netherlands as representative of the crown, from the ranks of the higher nobility. The stadhouder, therefore, exercised the powers of the sovereign within the province in his name. Willem of Orange had been stadhouder of Holland (as well as other provinces) before being forced to flee in 1567 and, although he had (not unnaturally) been replaced as governor by the Spanish authorities, he laid claim to the office immediately after the outbreak of the revolt in 1572 and this convenient claim was accepted by the rebel States of Holland. Until 1581 he led the revolt against Philip II in Philip's name, as his loyal stadhouder in Holland (and elsewhere). After the abjuration of the Spanish king, the office was not discontinued, partly perhaps because of the prospect of a new sovereign being recognized—in which case it would regain its constitutional *raison d'être*, and also be useful as a bulwark of the interests and privileges of the province against the new ruler.

After his assassination, Willem was replaced after a brief hiatus by his son Maurits in 1585, who was both very young and too concerned with military matters to make a great deal of use of the political potential of his office until after the turn of the seventeenth century. He was at first mostly content to accept the political tutelage of Oldenbarnevelt, and it was only during the Truce crisis that it became clear again just how important the office of stadhouder could be within Holland. The manner of Maurits's intervention at this time brings out both the ambivalence of his own position and some of the fundamental uncertainties of the constitutional situation in province and state. His arrest of Oldenbarnevelt and his associates, formally on the orders of the States General, was almost certainly illegal, but it was his ability to enforce the *wetsverzettingen* in the Holland towns which showed the powers of the stadhouder at their most bizarre, and yet most effective. He toured the voting towns dismissing magistrates and other regents and replacing or reappointing them according to his own judgement. This was the exercise of sovereign powers to change the town governments and through them the composition of the States of Holland, which had itself appeared to be sovereign since the Revolt. Thus Maurits, an appointed officer of the States, assumed powers which enabled him to change the personnel and policies of his paymaster, which seems a constitutional monstrosity—but in the peculiar circumstances of 1618 it worked. He got away with it because he could rely on the support not only of all

the other provinces, but also, and perhaps most importantly, of a
significant minority within the States led by Amsterdam. This set
an important precedent: although the stadhouder's right to change
the personnel of the town governments was never recognized in
any formal sense, in practice later stadhouders were able to institute *wetsverzettingen* from time to time, most spectacularly, as far
as the seventeenth century was concerned, in 1672. Maurits's success made it clear that the stadhouder was the only power in the
province which could take on the voting towns and win—in certain circumstances. It was a lesson the princes of Orange, and the
regents for that matter, never forgot.

From 1618 onwards, the formal position and powers of the stadhouder in Holland remained more or less the same, but the real
power of the office had been dramatically transformed; except during the first stadhouderless period, for the rest of the seventeenth
century the successive holders of the post were the political leaders
of the Republic, and the dominant figures in Holland as well. The
effectiveness with which this new-found power was wielded varied,
of course, with the character and ability of the incumbent, and
with the circumstances in which he had to operate. Frederik
Hendrik, Maurits's half-brother, built on the latter's legacy,
strengthened by a determination to act not as the leader of a party,
but as a moderating influence working towards the reconciliation
of political and religious rivalries within the province.[1] Part of his
success, however, stemmed from the lack of fundamental disagreements over policy between himself and the States of Holland.[2] In
retrospect, he appears to have been the stadhouder with the
smoothest relationship with the States before the eighteenth century. He even seems to have recognized the necessity of making
peace with Spain more readily than some historians—or indeed
contemporaries—have thought. While this political rapport is
partly the result of the influence he wielded on the States of
Holland through the effects on the voting towns of his sophisti-

[1] See J. J. Poelhekke, *Frederik Hendrik, Prins van Oranje* (Zutphen, 1978),
179–80.
[2] S. Groenveld, *Verlopend getij: De Nederlandse Republiek en de Engelse
Burgeroorlog 1640–1646* (Dieren, 1984), 108–10; *contra* P. Geyl, *Oranje en Stuart
1641–1672* (Utrecht, 1939), ch. 1. Poelhekke, *Frederik Hendrik*, 496 ff., suggests a
rather more fundamental disagreement over foreign policy with the majority in the
States of Holland in the prince's last ten years, but the whole tenor of the book is
to stress his essential moderation and concern to avoid political polarization.

cated patronage system, it is perhaps equally important to notice how sensitive he was to the real changes of opinion which took place during his period of office and his readiness to bow to the inevitable.

In sharp contrast his son and successor, Willem II, demonstrated what could go wrong when this delicate system of power and patronage was misused. As in 1618, the stadhouder relied on a dubious mandate from the States General to put pressure on Holland. In a weak rerun of Maurits's decisive action in that year, Willem toured the voting towns of the province to try to induce them to accept the military budget (*staat van oorlog*) drawn up by the Council of State. When this rather clumsy attempt at intimidation failed, he tried to use not the threat of, but actual, military force to achieve his ends. His arrest of six members of the States together with his attempted surprise attack on Amsterdam using Generality troops were both illegal and foolish; his resort to the use of military means was in itself already a confession of political failure. The failure of his attempt to bully the voting towns into changing their policies showed the impotence of the stadhouder when he was faced—unlike 1618—with a States of Holland which was united against him. A compromise solution was cobbled together to give a temporary resolution to the crisis, and this included face-saving elements for the prince, but while 1618 had revealed the latent strength of the stadhouder's position, 1650 showed its weakness when confronted by a united and determined States of Holland with Amsterdam at its head. There can be no mistaking the defeat which Willem suffered in the summer of 1650,[3] but whether he would have been able to reverse this decision in the following months or years must remain an open question because of his—perhaps fortunate—death before the end of the year. The damage which this episode caused to both his personal prestige and the office he held is impossible to measure, but it seems likely that the stadhouderless experiment would never have been tried had it not been for the backlash to Willem's actions in 1650. For the orangists 1618 demonstrated that a stadhouder could head off civil war; for the republicans 1650 showed that he could cause it.

[3] However, this is not the way that all historians have seen the matter: Rowen, for example, seems to regard the episode as a qualified success for the prince (Rowen, *The Princes of Orange*, 91).

For an analysis of the functions and importance of the stad-houder in Holland, the subsequent stadhouderless period is extremely enlightening. First, it showed that the province, if not the Republic, could be more than adequately governed without a stadhouder, even in wartime; but it also demonstrated that, given the sort of crisis which faced the Republic in the summer of 1672, restoration of the stadhoudership seemed a natural as well as a necessary move, even to a great part of the regent oligarchy. Moreover, the politics of the last few years of De Witt's period of dominance suggest that some position of importance would in any case have had to be found for the young prince of Orange. More generally, they seem to imply that only the absence of an adult prince allowed the stadhouderless experiment to take place at all.

The reaction to the French invasion brought Willem III to the offices and authority his father and grandfather had enjoyed. Another round of *wetsverzettingen*, which did not even require him to visit the towns involved, emphasized the renewed strength of his political position, a point which was underlined when the stad-houdership was made hereditary—something which not even Frederik Hendrik had achieved. Despite this propitious start, how-ever, Willem's power in Holland—in sharp contrast to some of the other provinces of the Republic—was under challenge within only a few years, and it soon became clear that in the most important province the stadhouder was still dependent on the co-operation of the voting towns, and had a distinctly limited ability to force them to comply with his policies.

At the centre of the complex of powers wielded by the stad-houder in Holland was the paradox that the office retained impor-tant powers which stemmed historically from the prerogatives of the counts of Holland, even though the king of Spain, as inheritor of those rights, had been repudiated. The count had been replaced as supreme political authority in the province by the States, and the stadhouder now no longer represented an absent sovereign, but was an appointed official of the States, and yet he was able to become its rival for political power. In principle, the continued exi-stence of this office made no sense after the take-over of power by the States of Holland in the course of the Revolt, except that the recognition of Willem of Orange as stadhouder helped both to pro-vide desperately needed leadership and to maintain the fiction that the rebels remained loyal to their sovereign. In the constitutional confusion following Willem's assassination in 1584 and during the governorship of the earl of Leicester (1585–8), their stadhouder became an important political weapon in the hands of the States of Holland, with Maurits being deployed as a counterweight to Leicester in both military and political affairs. So by the time Leicester left the Netherlands, the existence of the stadhoudership in Holland was an established fact and was gaining the authority of precedent. Moreover, the system worked: Oldenbarnevelt and Maurits co-operated effectively for almost twenty years, without the conflicts latent in the situation becoming appparent. It would probably have surprised contemporaries had they known that this was to be the only time in the history of the Republic when a politically dominant *landsadvocaat* (or *raadpensionaris*) would coexist with a stadhouder. The success of Maurits in 1618–19 established the stadhouder even more firmly as an integral part of the political system of Holland, and consequently when the stad-houderless period occurred it took on more the appearance of an innovation than the logical consequence of the supremacy of the States within the province; by 1650 it would seem that the 'author-ity', as Temple called it,[4] of the princes of Orange as stadhouder had been generally accepted as a necessary and proper part of the government of the province.

If the actual office made little sense, although it was perhaps a practical political necessity, some of the most important of the stadhouder's powers appear in retrospect even more curious. In particular, such powers as the right to appoint magistrates and even *raden* in the voting towns, giving an appointed official of the States the right to influence the composition of those very same States, were constitutional curiosities. Part of the reason for such anomalies was a refusal to admit that a revolution had taken place in the sixteenth century to establish the new regime: the Revolt was construed as the rescue of the proper and established political system from attempted subversion by the ruler. Thus, once Philip II had been disposed of, everything that remained was supposed to function as it had done before his attempted usurpation, and prece-dent remained the touchstone of political propriety—except, of course, in the case of the count, whose rights and privileges were systematically obfuscated by the official and unofficial propaganda

[4] Sir W. Temple, *Observations upon the United Provinces of the Netherlands*, ed. G. N. Clark (Cambridge, 1932), 80.

of the new regime. So the stadhouder's powers remained in detail basically what they had been before the Revolt: it would, after all, have been difficult to challenge the rights of the stadhouder as established by precedent without bringing into question political authority at all levels, which rested precisely on the same basis.

The stadhouder was *ex officio* president of the Court of Holland (see Chapter 3 of this Part), had access to the States of Holland (where he was also, but not *ex officio*, a member of the *ridderschap*), and had general responsibility for the maintenance of public order and justice within the province. One of the sovereign attributes of the office was the right of pardon. He was also considered to have an—ill-defined—duty to maintain the true religion within the province, though what this true religion was that he was supposed to protect was nowhere clearly formulated.

He had extensive powers of appointment to posts within the province, the most important politically being those concerning the magistrates and *vroedschappen* of the voting towns. In nearly all the towns, the yearly-changing magistrates, burgemeesters and *schepenen*, were appointed by the stadhouder choosing from a short-list supplied by the town government, and in some towns even vacant places in the *vroedschap* were filled in a similar way. However, in Amsterdam only the appointment of *schepenen* was subject to such influence from the stadhouder on its internal affairs.

It is difficult to assess just how important such powers were. On the one hand, the stadhouder's choice was strictly limited: in the case of the magistrates, lists containing twice the number of names required to fill the vacancies were submitted to the stadhouder, and he made the appointments from these names. In the case of the *vroedschappen*, triple lists were sent to him out of which he made the final choice. So, in form at least, the ability of the stadhouder to influence either the composition of the magistracy or of the regent group as a whole within a town was very limited. However, there is reason to suspect that in practice the influence of the stadhouders was much greater than appears on the surface. In the eighteenth century stadhouders occasionally made appointments outside the lists submitted to them; in the seventeenth century they seem to have done so only very rarely, but probably not because they were less powerful than their successors. It seems more likely that they did not need to do so. Most of these rights of appointment were either established or confirmed in the wake of Maurits's triumph in 1618, and in periods of stadhouderly dominance, local regent groups probably felt that it would have been neither proper nor prudent to alienate the stadhouder by submitting nominations which contained too few names congenial to him. One suspects that informal consultations beforehand ensured on most occasions that candidates acceptable to both sides were submitted—and appointed. In any case, the general powers of patronage together with the specific control of appointment to key posts in the towns ensured that the stadhouder could build up substantial bodies of supporters among the regents of the towns of Holland.

This influence on the choice of burgemeesters and *schepenen*—and to an extent over the appointment of *raden* as well—was clearly one of the ways in which the stadhouders were able to build up their support among the ruling groups in the voting towns, at least from about 1618 onwards. This is a process which is extremely difficult to follow, but from at least this point on there were orangist parties (or factions, according to taste) among the regents of most of the *stemhebbende* towns. Though their existence can partly be explained by conviction and partly by the internal political dynamics of the towns, it seems plausible to suggest that they gained a significant part of their strength from the support of the stadhouder. His influence on appointments within the towns was an important part of the stadhouder's patronage armoury, but he also had a wider range of places and *douceurs* in his gift which he could deploy to reward, encourage, and discipline his adherents in the towns. Admittedly, detailed studies of the workings of this patronage system are lacking, and we have to make do with patchy anecdotal material, but there is some rather harder, negative evidence. During the first stadhouderless period, when there was no significant outside support for the orangist regents but when on the contrary considerable patronage powers had come into the hands of De Witt and his supporters, the power of the orangist groups in the voting towns declined markedly and there was a slow but steady build-up of republican power in the towns. Overall it would seem that, in the absence of a stadhouder, and with the support of De Witt, the republicans had a distinct advantage in the internal conflicts of most of the towns in the province. After 1672, Willem III used—and possibly abused—his formal and informal powers to aid his supporters in the voting towns with greater ruthlessness perhaps than any of his predeces-sors. Concerned only to gain support in the States for a foreign policy which he regarded as a necessity for the survival of the state, he did not scruple to give his backing to such corrupt figures as the *baljuw* Van Zuylen van Nievelt in Rotterdam as long as they were able to deliver the goods in terms of voting support in the States. However, his failure to achieve control of the States in the end also illustrates the limitations of the stadhouders' power, particularly with regard to Amsterdam where they had no role in the appointment either of burgemeesters or of *raden*.

One area that was recognized as belonging to the duties of the stadhouder was the maintenance of the true religion. What this was was nowhere defined, of course, and the duty was possibly more in the nature of a pious admonition than intended as a direc-tive to specific action, but it did present the stadhouders with excellent propaganda opportunities, and at times did in fact lead to deeds. The most spectacular example of the exercise of this respon-sibility was Maurits's support for the contraremonstrants in 1617–19, and it enabled him to give a religious appearance to what was essentially a political *coup*. From this point in the century onwards it was possible for the stadhouders to play the Reformed card by posing as champions of the true religion against the urban regents in particular, who could easily be typecast as lukewarm supporters, or even enemies, of the Reformed Church. There was more to this part of the stadhouder's responsibilities than mere propaganda, however, as can be seen from Willem III's interven-tions in disputes within the Reformed Church later in the seven-teenth century, where his concern was clearly to prevent theological divisions from getting out of hand as they had done earlier. So, while the picture of Maurits as a defender of religious purity is more than faintly risible; Frederik Hendrik sympathized if anything with the remonstrants rather than the narrowly orthodox; Willem II was hardly convincing as a champion of the faith; and only Willem III can be plausibly be put forward as a true defender of the Reformed Church; nevertheless, exploitation of this area of responsibility was consistently a source of strength and popular support for the stadhouders.

In general, the traditional nature of the political system allowed the stadhouders to exploit a rich reservoir of precedent to extend their real powers. No clear distinction was ever made between before and after the Revolt, as in theory no significant change had taken place at that time. The rising against Spanish rule had supposedly restored the ancient constitution, not produced anything new. Thus, in the wake of the Revolt, the emphasis in the seventeenth century was always on the defence of the 'privileges' as the code term for the existing political and social system, but there could be no choosing between privileges—whatever was an established right was indeed right. However, the powers and privileges which the stadhouders had enjoyed before the Revolt were part of this concatenation of privileges which the Revolt had preserved, so a Revolt which had as its *raison d'être* the defence of existing rights had also to preserve those of the stadhouder. Lawyers usually had little difficulty in finding precedents to justify actions by the stadhouders—even those which, seen from a different perspective, look more like those of a sovereign prince than a servant of the States. The most spectacular of the powers which the stadhouders claimed, and one which they were able to exploit from time to time with dramatic effect, was the authority to 'change the law' or *wetsverzetting*. There can be no doubt that the power to intervene unilaterally to change the personnel of the town governments should logically have ended with the repudiation of the authority of the count; such intervention looks very much like an act of sovereignty, which the stadhouders did not possess. However, there were precedents for such acts, even after the Revolt, and in 1618 Maurits got away with it—largely, one suspects, because he was supported by Amsterdam and a number of other towns. The result would almost certainly have been different if the States of Holland had been united against him, but, as it was, the dramatic events of that year established such a clear and unambiguous precedent that it was easier for opponents of the stadhouder to argue for the abolition of the office itself than to claim that as it stood its powers did not include the right to 'change the law'.

In 1672 the changes in the town governments were carried out in a much more matter-of-fact way than in 1618. No formal visitation of the towns by the stadhouder backed by the hardly veiled threat of military force was required; by this time it had become accepted that under certain circumstances the stadhouder had the right and power to undertake *wetsverzettingen*, and in the aftermath of the murder of Johan and Cornelis de Witt there was little dispute that

such circumstances obtained in the late summer of 1672. Later
Willem III too was able to use this power in Rotterdam in 1692 to
unseat the regent group which had come to power in the aftermath
of the riots of 1690, and to bring back to power his creature Van
Zuylen van Nievelt and his faction. This event demonstrates again
that, if used sparingly and with discretion, the authority to 'change
the law' was one of the most effective weapons in the whole complex armoury of the stadhouders of Holland.

A vitally important factor in the effective power of the stadhouder in Holland was the political importance of the holder's
position in the Republic as a whole. Whatever the theoretical situation, and however much the States of Holland may have tried to
ignore the fact, the leading role which the princes of Orange
played in the Dutch state profoundly affected the way in which
they operated, and were allowed to operate, as stadhouders in
Holland. From the first weeks of the Revolt to the end of the
Republic, the only holders of the stadhoudership of Holland were
the successive princes of Orange.[5] Through their title, status, and
the history of their house in its relation to the Dutch state, the
princes of Orange were not as other men; moreover, the powers
they held in the other provinces and in the Generality strengthened
their position in Holland.

Of course, these circumstances did not effect the strict constitutional position in Holland itself—the princes remained formally
subordinate as stadhouder to the States of Holland—but in practice their authority was considerably enhanced. On the other hand,
this situation also stimulated opposition to the stadhouders within
the province; the very fact that they were in a position to exploit
the potential of the office to the full, because of their resources of
power and influence elsewhere, made them more feared and distrusted, and thus more carefully watched. Republican feeling
would not have been as strong as it was, if the stadhouders had
not possessed such authority that they seemed at times to represent
a threat to those very privileges which the regents believed the
Revolt had been fought to preserve.

The role played by the princes of Orange in the Republic as a
whole will be discussed in Part 3; here it is necessary to touch on

---

[5] Technically this is not completely true: unlike the other holders of the office,
Maurits was not prince of Orange until the very last years of his life because this
title was held by his elder brother (who remained under Spanish tutelage).

their position as commanders of the army and navy and stadhouder of a number of the other provinces only in so far as these
offices affected the way in which the stadhouders could act in
Holland. One important consequence of this multiple office-holding
was that they held a very large number of posts and positions
directly in their gift, and with regard to others their recommendation was usually decisive. This increased considerably the spoils
available to fuel the patronage system which they could employ to
strengthen their influence among the regents of Holland. The single
most prolific source of such patronage was probably the army of
the Republic, where the commander had influence over appointments at all levels, and in particular had the right to grant commissions to places falling vacant during a campaign—a very significant
consideration for Maurits and Frederik Hendrik in particular, as
they were on campaign almost every summer of their careers
(except during the Truce), and not unimportant for Willem III
either. It is possible, however, that the attraction of a commission
in the army was greater among the nobles of the land provinces
than among the regents of Holland. The enthusiasm for a military
career does not seem to have been great among the oligarchs of the
most prosperous province of the Republic; in the main, personal
and family fortunes were probably better served by staying at
home and paying attention to business—or politics.

In a distinctly less subtle way, their position as head of the army
also gave the princes of Orange a weapon which could be used
effectively in internal politics, but could also turn very awkwardly
in the wielder's hand. The army, composed of mercenaries and
containing a large element of non-Dutch troops, could be expected
to obey their commander's orders, and I know of no case of troops
refusing obedience for reasons 'of constitutional propriety.
However, a military *coup* was hardly an ever-present threat, even
though some republican propagandists chose to represent the situation as if it were. Willem II's ill-considered move in 1650 demonstrated the underlying weakness of the military option. The more
subtle tactics of Maurits in 1618 were effective partly because the
use of force was implicit rather than open, and partly because his
intervention tipped the balance of power between two parties
within the oligarchy rather than overtly challenging regent power
as such. It is, indeed, possible that Maurits would have won anyway, even without his display of veiled military force—but not

certain. The military power of the stadhouders was certainly taken seriously by their opponents, though their counter-measures were more impressive in theory than in practice. The employment of *waardgelders* by the towns in the last act of the Truce crisis[6] was never likely to provide an effective counter-balance to the army of the Republic; and the political measures taken in the aftermath of 1650 to subject the movement of troops to the control of the States of the relevant provinces were only likely to be effective when they were unnecessary. However, these measures do demonstrate that the control over the army exercised by the stadhouders was seen as a very real part of their powers by those most nearly concerned with the question.

The prestige attaching to the princes of Orange was a further advantage, though one that cannot be counted or measured. That the stadhouders of Holland were also sovereign princes in their own right, as independent rulers of the principality of Orange in the Rhône valley, was an incalculable but very significant advantage, and the princes, at least after the rather sober Maurits, did not hesitate to exploit it to the full. They expressed this qualitative superiority to their fellow countrymen physically in both dress and general style of living. Indeed, it may well be that for many, if not most, of the inhabitants of Holland it was not clear where the sovereign prince ended and the stadhouder who was a subordinate of the States began. The status of the princes, together with their exercise of anachronistic but recognized powers, tended to invest the stadhoudership with something of the appearance of sovereignty, and it was not always easy to distinguish this from the real thing. We know that foreign commentators found the constitutional position of the stadhouders difficult to understand, and perhaps many of the inhabitants of the province were in a similar state.

Moreover, orangist propaganda invested the house of Orange with an almost mystical identity as the personification of the state. In practical terms, the perceived services to the Republic of successive princes of Orange progressively strengthened their position. The role of the first Willem, the 'father of the fatherland', during the difficult early years of the Revolt formed the basis for an

---

[6] *Waardgelders* were troops hired by the individual towns for defence and the maintenance of internal order. They were subject to the orders of the town governments and not to the commander of the Republic's army.

enduring Orange myth, which was developed through the subsequent leadership of Maurits and Frederik Hendrik. The myth was tarnished by contact with the grubby reality of political life from time to time. Maurits's actions during the Truce crisis played the dual role of boosting the strength of the Orange myth for the believers on the one hand, and forming the basis of an anti-Orange myth on the other; the misdeeds of Willem II in 1650 unambiguously damaged the image of the princes of Orange; but the events of 1672 and especially the way they were represented in orangist propaganda restored the prestige of the house and brought the myth to an even greater splendour.

Inevitably, it was difficult to separate out the functions of the princes of Orange as stadhouders of Holland from their political and military position in the Republic as a whole. This circumstance affected contemporary perceptions as much as those of later historians. For example, the heated polemic over the stadhoudership which took place chiefly in the 1660s[7] was really about the position of the princes of Orange as leaders in the Republic, and did not primarily concern the stadhoudership of Holland itself. Yet in a sense the controversy has not been ill-named, as the stadhoudership of Holland was vital to the whole position of the princes of Orange—without this office they would have been unable to play a leading role in the Republic. Holland's decision in 1651 not to appoint the infant Willem III to the stadhoudership undermined the position of the house of Orange overall in the Republic; and his appointment to the office in 1672 was the vital step in his rise to power. Again, on his death, the failure of Holland to appoint a replacement meant not only the beginning of the second stadhouderless period, but also the second period of eclipse for the power of the house of Orange in the Republic. Willem IV inherited the princely title, but lacking the stadhoudership of Holland he could only play a rather minor part in the political life of the Republic in the early eighteenth century. Only when the upheavals of 1747 brought him this office could he take over the directing role in Dutch politics. Thus, while it is clear that the overall position of the princes of Orange within the Dutch state strengthened their situation in Holland, it is equally the case that the stadhoudership of Holland was the linchpin of their complex of powers. Take that

[7] P. Geyl, *Het stadhouderschap in de partij-literatuur onder De Witt* (The Hague, 1947).

away and all collapsed. It was possible for De Witt and his supporters to contemplate allowing the young prince a seat in the Council of State and command of the army, but the Eternal Edict (passed by the States of Holland in 1667) was designed to ensure that he never became stadhouder of Holland—or any other province. A prince of Orange as captain-general was seen as compatible with the rule of the 'True Freedom' as long as it was not joined to the stadhoudership of any province, but particularly not that of Holland. The reverse situation—a stadhouder without command of the army—was probably seen as almost a contradiction in terms; it was evidently plausible to hope to prevent a captain-general from becoming stadhouder, but not to prevent a stadhouder from becoming captain-general. In brief: while the stadhoudership of Holland was a provincial post, it was central to the position of power which the princes of Orange built up in the Dutch Republic.

3. Provincial Administration and Courts

This is a short chapter because, despite the importance of Holland in the Dutch Republic, and despite the fact that provincial autonomy meant that it very largely ran its own affairs, with the very minimum of delegation to or interference from the central government, the administrative machinery available to govern the province remained remarkably slight throughout the seventeenth century. The decentralized nature of the Dutch political system meant not only that the central government of the Republic was very limited in its powers, but also that there was a certain weakness at the centre of provincial government. The reason for this situation is that particularism favoured not just the province against the centre, but also the local against the provincial, and much of the weight of government was in practice devolved to the towns and even to the villages and country districts. This very general decentralization of both political power and administrative responsibilities stands in sharp contrast to the strengthening of central government and the burgeoning of bureaucracies in much of the rest of Europe during this century. Although the States of Holland were unquestionably supreme in political authority, they relied heavily on the towns for the execution of their decisions in legal and financial matters, and the administrative apparatus available for the government of the province remained distinctly rudimentary.

The most prominent organs of central control outside the States themselves were the provincial courts, and here there were some peculiar features, as both these courts served not just Holland but Zeeland as well, thus constituting a very unusual contravention of the normally watertight separation between the two provinces. These courts were partly the lineal descendants of the court of the counts of Holland and Zeeland, and partly a replacement for the *Grote Raad* (Great Council) at Mechelen as appeal court. The members of these courts were appointed by the stadhouder from nominations by the states of the two provinces (both bodies divided in a ratio of 3 : 1 in favour of Holland).

The *Hof van Holland* (Court of Holland) was the supreme legal instance in the province, and had lost nearly all its political functions by the seventeenth century. Its jurisdiction covered civil and some criminal matters, and brought it into seemingly endless jurisdictional conflicts with the towns. This sort of problem could easily slip over into the political, as it clearly did during the Truce crisis when the Court was dominated by contraremonstrants and attempted to intervene in the treatment of their co-religionists by remonstrant magistrates in the towns and elsewhere. However, even in less fraught times the towns were intrinsically jealous defenders of their jurisdictional autonomy and sought to minimize the effective authority of the Court over them. In such attempts the towns could usually—and naturally, given the membership of the States—rely on the support of the States of Holland. In the end, thus, the Court found it very difficult to assert its authority over the towns and over their local courts of law.

The *Hoge Raad* (High Council) acted as a court of appeal from the Court of Holland, but also had direct jurisdiction in some areas, such as over the local water-control administration (*waterschappen*). Its problems with the States and the towns were similar to those of the Court, and the affairs of both were further complicated by arcane and labyrinthine disputes over competence between the two courts, in ways characteristic of the *ancien régime* and not only in Holland.

Both bodies were staffed by trained jurists, or at least by men with law degrees and experience of practice in the courts. Membership of one or other of these courts became a career peak for many of the pensionaries of the voting towns. For such of the latter who were more lawyers and administrators than politicians, and this must probably have been the majority, a well-paid and prestigious seat in the *Hof* or *Hoge Raad* was an attractive post, particularly as the duties attached to these positions were apparently not very onerous. This was a career structure for those outside the regent élite, yet from families prosperous enough to be able to pay for a university education in law: some years of practice as an advocate before the *Hof*, then employment with one of the voting towns, or alternatively perhaps in a post with one of the admiralties, and finally the *Hof* or *Hoge Raad*. Certainly the members of these courts came from reasonably wealthy and necessarily well-connected families (otherwise they would never have been nominated), but in general not from regent families.[1]

There were also a number of chambers of account (*rekenkamers*)—for North Holland, South Holland, and for demesnes. The main chambers were concerned with the collection and accounting of provincial taxation, though their powers in these matters were limited, as might have been expected, by the thoroughgoing particularism of the towns, enforced through the States. In particular, the local receivers of taxes were in effect—certainly in the case of extraordinary taxation such as the 100th or 200th Penny—appointed at the local level, and were rather more under the control of their town governments than of the chambers. This close control of fiscal matters by the towns, and the relegation of the provincial chambers of account to an almost subordinate role, was wholly typical of the Holland (and indeed the Dutch) system, and allowed what one might politely call full expression of local interests.

Although the admiralties were Generality bodies, it is perhaps appropriate to deal with the three based in Holland here as, whatever the constitutional situation may have been, for the most part they acted like provincial rather than national bodies. In Holland they were based at Rotterdam (for the Maas), at Amsterdam, and at Hoorn/Enkhuizen (for the Northern Quarter). They were governed by boards of councillors (*raden*) appointed by the States General from the nominations of the various provincial states. In the admiralties within Holland, each of the boards had a majority of members from the home province. The competence of the admiralties included not only the building, fitting-out, and manning of warships, but also the collection of the 'convoys and licences' (*convooien en licenten*), import- and export-duties used to support the navy. Thus the admiralties were in the business of collecting and spending very large amounts of money, and it is, perhaps sadly, hardly surprising that corruption at all levels should have become notorious. The evidence comes from scandal and common belief rather than hard facts, but sufficient escaped into the light of day

---

[1] At least this seems to have been the case for the members coming from Holland; it may be that regents from the Zeeland towns found such appointments rather more attractive than their counterparts in Holland.

to suggest that common gossip was not so wrong.[2] A disproportionate number of these scandals erupted in Rotterdam, whether
because it was more corrupt than the others or only more unlucky
is not clear. What is clear is that a position as one of the *raden* of
an admiralty was much desired by the members of the regent élite
in Holland. Unlike the provincial courts, or the chambers of
account, the boards of the admiralties were staffed by regents, and
it is again notorious though unproven that few of them lost financially from the appointment. It does seem that the proximity of
large sums of money, together with a very large degree of autonomy, was far too great a temptation for the average public figure
in Holland. Cynically one might be inclined to conclude that the
notable lack of such corruption elsewhere in the political system
was a product of lack of opportunity rather than a high level of
probity among the regents.[3]

Much of the administration of the province was in fact carried
out on a shoestring by the *raadpensionaris* and his secretaries and
clerks, together with the *gecommitteerde raden* and their skeleton
secretariat. The way in which they carried out the work of government was determined not so much by principle and logic, as by a
complicated interplay of precedent and immediate practical necessity. Much has to be traced back to the dominant figure of Johan
van Oldenbarnevelt, who established the procedures for the
efficient governance of Holland round himself, his office, and those
bodies which he could most conveniently control. Although he was
eventually defeated in one sense, the system he had in a large measure created—in the Republic almost as much as in Holland—
survived more or less intact, and was to remain largely unchanged
for the rest of the history of the Republic. As with many aspects of
Dutch government, the central administration of Holland changed
and evolved rapidly out of existing institutions in the first two or
three decades after the beginning of the Revolt, but once a more or
less workable system had been established it became almost impossible to change it. This system was ultimately the result of a balance of forces between towns, States, and stadhouder, and any

---

[2] A. van der Capellen, *Gedenkschriften*, ed. R. J. van der Capellen (Utrecht,
1777–8), i. 382; Wagenaar, *Vaderlandsche historie*, xv. 326–31; Roorda, 'Een zwakke
stee'.

[3] See the remarks on political corruption and official venality in general in De
Bruin, *Geheimhouding en verraad*, 97–103.

change that would have benefited one at the expense of the others was naturally blocked by the potential losers. For much, if not all, of the seventeenth century this system worked reasonably well, at least by the standards of the time. However, when it began to reveal its inherent shortcomings in the following century it proved practically impossible to do anything to correct them. The system had lost its ability to respond to changing circumstances, and reform became impossible without a major change in the balance of political power. In particular, the power of vested interests at the local level would have to be effectively challenged either by stronger government from above, or by democratic reforms from below, or by both; such changes only became possible with the upheavals at the end of the eighteenth century.

4. Republicans and Orangists

Just as modern scholarship has tended to explain urban politics in terms of factional conflict rather party differences (see Part 1, Chapter 4), so recent interpretations of provincial politics in Holland in the seventeenth century have moved in a similar direction.[1] The dichotomy between republicans and orangists is being discarded as an unhelpful anachronism: faction operating at the provincial level, not party, is seen as the reality of the time. In contrast to this approach, my argument in this chapter is essentially that republicanism and orangism, or support for the States of Holland, on the one side, or for the stadhouders, on the other, were the two defining orientations of political life in the province of Holland, and similar polarities probably existed in the other provinces as well, though the latter question lies outside the scope of this discussion. They provided the conceptual vocabulary which shaped the possibilities not only for political thought but to a significant extent for political action as well, until at least the end of the seventeenth century. These competing but related ways of interpreting contemporary political reality demanded and commanded loyalty from individuals and families both within the regent group and in the population of the province more generally, certainly not in the same sense as a modern political party, but nevertheless shaping the loyalties and perceptions of political actors in fundamental ways.

However, it is important not to exaggerate the extent to which the two sides were in conflict. Republicanism and orangism were closely related in terms of both political theory and practice, and both were expressions of the interests of a narrow political élite. On a whole range of issues arising in the day-to-day business of politics there was no real difference between the two sides, or rather the differences that existed were not determined by conflicting ideologies. Even where real conflicts over policy existed—over the powers of the stadhouder and, most notably, over the direction

---

[1] See esp. Groenveld, *Evidente factïen*.

of foreign policy—they sprang from differences of emphasis rather than fundamentally opposed views of society and the nature of the state. The protagonists on either side came from the most privileged sections of society in the province and, despite obvious disagreements, had more in common with each other than with the politically unprivileged mass of the population. They shared a broadly similar educational and cultural background, and their views on the nature of the political process and who should be involved in it were essentially 'similar. Neither side, however much prepared from time to time to appeal to popular opinion and emotions for tactical reasons, had any intention of broadening out the political system by allowing the participation of non-regents.[2] The arguments between orangists and republicans concerned principally what was the best form of political leadership for the existing system, and what foreign and domestic policies were best suited to maintaining the economic and social *status quo*.

Nevertheless, although conflict was restricted to a relatively narrow band of issues, political strife could be remarkably fierce in a way that is possibly characteristic of intra-élite rivalries. Moreover, it might perhaps be a mistake to project this somewhat comfortable picture of underlying consensus on to the problems of the first decades of the seventeenth century. It may well be that what made the Truce crisis so dangerous was precisely the absence of that unquestioning social solidarity which became so characteristic of the political élite later in the century. Such an underlying confidence regarding the unity and stability of the political system had not yet developed in the first years of the century. The Republic was still a relatively new creation and was still exploring its own nature. Perhaps only with the resolution of this crisis did the basic stability and strength of the political and social system of Holland and the Republic really become clear to contemporaries.

When we look at the nature and practice of orangism, it is clear that, for the stadhouder and his supporters within the province, the fundamental practical problem was that they needed the backing of the States of Holland, and they could only achieve this by gaining support in the voting towns. It is easy to see why republicanism should have found strong support among the regent oligarchy, as it was the

---

[2] Though some theorists on the republican side, most notably Pieter de la Court, seem to have been prepared to argue for a move in this direction.

creation of their interests and gave theoretical backing to their political power, but it is not so clear why any significant number of regents should have supported orangism, which apparently promoted the interests of a dangerous political rival. In practice the situation was less unpromising than it appeared on the surface. First, orangism did not threaten the political and social domination of the oligarchies within their towns, but sought to put the prince of Orange at the head of the existing political system, where he would still have to work with and through the regents. In addition, the local regent oligarchies proved susceptible to manipulation by means of the extensive patronage system at the stadhouder's disposal; and the endemic divisions and rivalries within the town governments prevented them from always presenting a united front against such influences. There were very strong incentives for one or other of the local factions to strengthen, and perhaps legitimize, its position by linking into the stadhouder's system and taking on at least an orangist coloration. Moreover, the stadhouders in general could hope to be able to mobilize considerable popular support against the town governments when they needed to, by playing the patriotic card and exploiting the prestige and trust enjoyed by the house of Orange.

Orangism combined pragmatic considerations with the emotional appeal of the prestige of the house of Orange. On the practical side, it was argued that the Republic, especially because of its decentralized nature, needed the leadership of a person of authority who could stand above provincial rivalries. Such an 'eminent head' to give firm central direction was especially necessary in times of war; this was an important consideration for the Dutch, for whom warfare was a more normal condition than peace in the seventeenth century. Also, such an authority was needed to prevent internal differences and disputes from getting out of hand: after the Truce crisis, it was argued that only the intervention of Maurits had saved the country from civil war. On a more emotive level, the house of Orange—the only practicable source of such leadership in the Republic—appears to have aroused strong feelings of loyalty and even identification. The services of successive princes of Orange to the Republic not only deserved reward, but were guarantees of future reliability. In an uncertain world, many felt that the princes could be relied upon to serve the interests of the Republic as a whole, while regent politicians would always be suspected of putting their own province first.

There was also a significant religious component to orangist sentiment, if not theory. The alliance between the Reformed Church and the princes of Orange which was forged during the Truce crisis added to the popular appeal of orangism, and brought the support of an educated and highly articulate group, the ministers of the offical church. Not that all ministers were orangist, but the princes did come to be seen as the champions of orthodoxy against regents who were always likely to put material considerations before the word of God. The powerful strain of protestant thought which looked to the godly prince to protect and promote the true church could not but strengthen this link.

At two points during the seventeenth century the stadhouders were able to mobilize their support to particular effect: the *wetsverzettingen* of 1618 and 1672. Technically what happened on these occasions was that the stadhouder dismissed, or accepted the resignation of, the sitting town governments, then reappointed some of the former regents and brought in newcomers to replace the others. The scale of the changes varied from town to town but was sufficient on each occasion to ensure that the towns would support the stadhouder's policies in the States of Holland, at least in the short term. However, after neither 1618 nor 1672 did the orangist domination of the voting towns last for more than a few years; these spectacular assertions of the power of the stadhouder did not lead in most cases to a lasting orangist dominance within the local regent groups. Some towns were affected longer than others, but it is nevertheless clear that men brought into the oligarchy as orangists in 1618 or 1672 were likely to modify their positions when faced with the realities and possibilities of government. A sort of natural political drift set in which, if not combated by the various threats and inducements available to the stadhouders, tended to move the towns away from orangist positions towards the support of their own particular interests.

After 1618, despite the bitterness of the preceding conflict, this drift towards what might be seen as normality happened remarkably quickly, most notably in Amsterdam, which had led the contraremonstrants in the run-up to 1618 but by the mid-1620s was at best divided on the religious issue. Partly this was because this question, which had so divided opinion and consciences in 1618, was no longer a very immediate political issue except in the matter of the toleration of separate remonstrant churches. It was, moreover, hard to make this latter question a major source of political conflict as by then the new stadhouder, Frederik Hendrik, had made it pretty clear that he was in favour of toleration. This weakened the orthodox party, as they could no longer rely on the alliance with the stadhouder which had so strengthened their hand in the recent crisis; now it was the moderates who could hope to gain outside support for their policies.

However, this drift away from contraremonstrant orangism does not mean to say that the towns necessarily moved into opposition to the stadhouder or his policies, for Frederik Hendrik was attempting to free himself from too close an identification with the contraremonstrants, and to build up a broad measure of support for policies which were not, in the main, contentious—certainly not intentionally so. In the internal politics of the province, he was a strong proponent of reconciliation between the recently antagonistic groups, and on this issue his only opponents were the extreme contraremonstrants themselves, and these were much weakened precisely by the withdrawal of the stadhouder's support. In foreign policy there was a general consensus that the war against Spain had to continue until satisfactory peace terms could be achieved, and it was some time before real differences emerged concerning precisely what was acceptable. In general, the overall moderation of Frederik Hendrik's policies ensured that his period of office marked the domination of consensus and co-operation rather than conflict between stadhouder and States. It must be stressed, however, that this relative harmony was achieved through the pursuit of generally non-controversial policies—it was not a consequence of the *wetsverzetting* of 1618 producing a lasting orangism in the towns and thus a pliable States. Frederik Hendrik's strong position came from his own political skills, and his able manipulation of patronage: the towns were perhaps susceptible to cajoling and pressure, but they could no more be coerced after 1618 than they could be before. It is probably true, however, to say that the opposition between republicans and orangists, which had its origins essentially in the political divisions of the Truce crisis, was latent for much of Frederik Hendrik's stadhoudership as a direct result of his avoidance of confrontational tactics.

After 1672, the rapid change in the policies of the town governments is even more obvious, for in contrast to the broadly consensus policies of Frederik Hendrik, the unremittingly bellicose foreign policy of Willem III very soon aroused resistance from the towns of Holland, and in particular from Amsterdam. Even the most overtly orangist of councils began to question the wisdom of the prince's policy, and the whole panoply of devices at the stadhouder's disposal for influencing regent opinion had to be brought into action. In this case, the wholesale changes in the personnel of the town governments had had only very short-term effects, and the natural tendency of the regents to distrust expensive and dangerous foreign policies and to emphasize the needs of the economy came into its own.[3]

Direct intervention on the lines of the *wetsverzettingen* of 1618 and 1672, however, could only be attempted in emergencies, and for the rest of the century the stadhouders had to employ other means to build up and maintain support in the voting towns of the province. They normally had to accept that the very nature of the political system placed limitations on their power to influence events and carry through their policies. By judicious use of patronage and other powers, they could increase their influence within the system, and in emergencies they could, and did, intervene directly in the towns to beef up their support. They could not, however, change the system, and perhaps would not have done so if they could. The stadhouders in the main wanted more influence within the existing system; they probably did not think of subverting it. There was one exception, of course: but even in the case of Willem II, it may be endowing the prince's actions with rather more rationality than they in fact possessed to interpret his attempted *coup* in 1650 as part of a plan to change the constitution in his favour. He was being frustrated by the sustained opposition of the States of Holland to his cherished ambitions, and wished to bring them to heel. Whether he had thought through the long-term political implications of what he was trying to do is doubtful. In any case, he was very much an exception among the stadhouders, who in general were no more likely to want, or to be able, to destroy the power of the regents than contemporary monarchs were able to contemplate ruling without their nobilities. In Holland there was no alternative to rule with and through the regents, and from the stadhouders' point of view politics was about gaining control and influence over the regents, not destroying their power.

One curious element in the make-up of the orangist party that

[3] J. L. Price, 'William III, England and the Balance of Power in Europe', *Groniek*, 101 (1988).

deserves comment is that certain of the voting towns were consistent supporters of the stadhouder. Notably, Leiden and Haarlem gained, and largely deserved, a reputation for a staunch orangism which lasted for most of the rest of the century after their governments had been changed in the *wetsverzettingen* of 1618.[4] It is not at all clear why this should have been the case, unless it relates to rivalry between these manufacturing towns and the towns more dependent on commerce. Perhaps these textile towns felt the need of support from the stadhouder against the predominant influence of the trading towns within the States of Holland, and sought to buy this by extravagant orangism (see Chapter 5 of this Part). The industries of both towns were very heavily dependent on imported raw materials and half-finished goods, and equally they needed to be able to sell their cloths in foreign markets. This made them vulnerable and sensitive to fluctuating international conditions. Moreover, they were far more economically specialized than the trading towns, which meant that any downturn in textiles hit them with peculiar force. Perhaps also the greater social polarization within these manufacturing centres as compared to the socially more diversified trading towns made the regent élites less confident and more susceptible to pressure from the orangist masses. In any case, the stadhouders could thus usually rely on the support of some of the voting towns, including two of the bigger ones.

In the case of the republicans, their origins can probably be traced, if not to the beginning of the Revolt, then to the opposition in Holland to the power and policies of the earl of Leicester, or even perhaps to the resistance to the proposal a little earlier to elevate Willem of Orange to the countship of Holland. Willem died before the issue could come to a head, but the outcome of Leicester's defeat was the domination of the regent oligarchs of the towns of the province under the increasingly firm leadership of Oldenbarnevelt. After the fall of the Advocate and his supporters in 1618, the republicans remained the proponents of at the very least an alternative emphasis as regards the way in which the province should be governed and the policies it should pursue.

---

[4] In the case of Leiden, the town government's generally orangist attitude seems to have wavered by about 1675, when the town began to support a peace with France, and ended, more or less definitively, after a serious dispute over the nominations for *schepenen* in 1685. Subsequently, the stadhouder seems to have worked through the minority faction in the *raad,* led by Jacob van der Maas (*schout,* with a brief intermission, from 1687 to his death in 1696) (Prak, *Gezeten burgers,* 59–63).

While in the main the regents could work under the leadership of Frederik Hendrik, this did not preclude the development of a propagandist tradition which tended to demonize Maurits and the contraremonstrants and, implicitly at least, warn against overpowerful stadhouders. After the shock of the attempted *coup* by Willem II, the republicans returned to power during the first stadhouderless period under De Witt and reached their seventeenth-century apogee as the party of the *Ware Vrijheid* (True Freedom). Although defeated in 1672, under the leadership of Amsterdam they remained a powerful force in the politics of the province throughout Willem III's period of office.

Dutch republicanism developed a considerable body of theoretical writings, but what it meant for the majority of its supporters among the regents and elsewhere is less easy to say. Clearly, one important element was negative: opposition to the rule of a single person. The Revolt was seen as a struggle to defend the privileges of towns, nobles, and provinces against Spanish oppression. Here the concept of the privileges came to represent something like a constitution, but, as it was interpreted in favour of the regents alone, its popular appeal was somewhat limited by the seventeenth century. After the *coup* by Maurits in 1618, the princes of Orange became the focus of republican fears of the institution of a new tyranny, and the actions of Willem II in 1650 could only strengthen such suspicions. However, in practical terms, republicans were more concerned to preserve the existing political system than to weaken the position of the stadhouder, except in the particular circumstances which operated after 1650. The privileges were regarded as protecting life and property from princely depredations, but how far they were capable in practice of limiting regent absolutism is another matter.

On a more theoretical level, the republicans could link into the great European tradition of republican thought, though the degree to which they actually did so is disputed.[5] Certainly, the body of republican writing is more varied and impressive in quality than that of orangism, although it seems to have been rather slow to get started.[6] What is perhaps particularly characteristic of the Dutch is

---

[5] E. O. G. Haitsma Mulier, *The Myth of Venice and Dutch Republican Thought* (Assen, 1980), chs. iv and v.

[6] E. H. Kossmann, *Politieke theorie in het zeventiende-eeuwse Nederland* (Amsterdam, 1960), 7–10.

the high priority they tended to give to economic considerations. The true interest of the Dutch state lay in the pursuit not of honour, but of general prosperity, and only a republican government could be relied upon to concentrate on this end.

There was also a religious aspect to republican thought: it tended to favour a considerable measure of toleration and to distrust the influence in politics of the Reformed Church. Whether religious toleration was a good thing in itself or not—and there was more than a little ambiguity even in republican thinking on this point—religious persecution was believed to be demonstrably bad for trade. There was also a strong erastian streak in republicanism, as well as the faint beginnings of secularism, both of which cautioned against too close an identification of the state with the Reformed Church. In practice this meant a close control over the official church, and the toleration of moderate protestant dissent. The catholics were another matter: they were allowed a certain degree of freedom, not on principle but out of necessity.

It is easier than in the case of the orangists to see the sources of republican political support in the regent group of the province as a whole. The republicans found their natural head in the *raadpensionaris* or the burgemeesters of Amsterdam, or both. As a strong stadhouder could usually ensure the appointment of a reasonably amenable *raadpensionaris*, this meant that any opposition to Frederik Hendrik or to Willem III had to be led by Amsterdam, which meant the sitting burgemeesters and the *oudraad*. In the main, the active politicians (as opposed to the often more radical pamphleteers) of the republican group were not opposed in principle to the existence of a stadhouder, but were opposed to specific policies and, more generally, were concerned to ensure that the powers of the stadhouders were kept within the bounds which they felt to be acceptable. In normal times they were prepared to work with the stadhouder to achieve common ends, just as the stadhouders were normally prepared to work with them. The republican regents knew just as well as the stadhouders that such co-operation was essential if the political system in the province was to work at all.

It was precisely this inability of the majority of the towns of Holland to find a way of working with the stadhouder—and vice versa, of course—which constituted one of the most significant aspects of the Truce crisis: indeed, this was the element which perhaps more than anything else made it a crisis. In the event, the move by Oldenbarnevelt and his supporters which indicated both the depth of this division and the dangers which it threatened was the decision empowering the towns to recruit *waardgelders* for the maintenance of internal order. Whatever the practical justification of this act may have been—and the serious popular disturbances together with the unreliability of the *schutterijen* in the remonstrant-controlled towns was a real problem—in effect it was seen as such a far-reaching challenge to the authority of the stadhouder as to threaten civil war. His opponents claimed that this was Oldenbarnevelt's first step in an intended build-up of a military force to challenge the army of the Generality. At the very least, recruiting troops who would be responsible to the town governments and not to Maurits undermined the latter's authority in military matters and so was seen as a threat to his whole position within the political system—as indeed it was. This action by the States was, however, not as revolutionary in its implications at this time as such a move would have been later in the century, as Maurits's political role before the crisis, especially in Holland, had been much less important than that of the stadhouders after 1618. Indeed, it is probably misleading to imply that Oldenbarnevelt and his supporters were republicans in the sense that the term was to acquire later in the century. Only after Maurits's triumph in 1618 and the rise of the stadhouders to a dominant position within both province and Republic could republicanism as a defence of privileges against the power of the stadhouder have any meaning; before the crisis there had been no significant threat to Oldenbarnevelt's system of running Holland through the voting towns and the Republic through Holland. Nevertheless, it was this attack on Maurits's authority over the military and thus on his position within the political system which induced him to counterattack and challenge for power. Orangism and republicanism as opposed political ideologies arose out of the conflicts during the Truce, which revealed the stadhouder as a potential alternative to the regents of Holland as political leader of the province and the Republic.

After the relatively conciliatory period under Frederik Hendrik, an open challenge for dominance in the province was launched by Willem II. In contrast to the States' threat to the authority of the stadhouder which had sparked off the final round of the conflict in

1617–18, in 1650 it was the stadhouder who precipitated a crisis by attempting to subvert the control of the States of Holland over finances. Willem made the situation worse by attacking the autonomy of the towns through first embarking on a series of visitations with the aim of cowing them into obedience and, after that failed, by arresting six delegates to the States and sending troops against Amsterdam. What had provoked all this was entirely legitimate opposition by Holland to the size of the army that the prince, with support from the delegates of the other provinces in the States General, was trying to maintain. Only at the point where Holland began to pay off some of the troops assigned to its repartition could it be legitimately criticized on constitutional grounds. The States of Holland, led by Amsterdam, had attempted to reduce the size of the army, not only for reasons of economy but also as a way of blocking any renewal of the war with Spain. So again at the root of the matter was a failure of the States and stadhouder to find the necessary *modus vivendi* which would enable the system to work. Failing that, the stadhouder attempted to break the impasse by violent means, but only aggravated the situation. In the aftermath a compromise was reached which should have been attainable before, but how long this renewed co-operation would have lasted had the prince lived—given his temperament and apparently unchanged ambitions—is impossible to say, as the problem was solved by the death of the stadhouder before the end of the year.

The development of a more systematic and principled republicanism, which opposed the very existence of a stadhouder, was to a very large extent a reaction to the actions of Willem II in 1650. It is questionable whether this rigorous and rationalist approach to political questions made much more than a superficial impression on the essentially traditional and conservative ways of thinking characteristic of the regents of Holland. The evidence on this matter is thin, however, as is the case with too many important political questions in the seventeenth century, and we must make do with inferences from what actually happened. Unfortunately, the record is ambiguous. On the one hand the regents worked reasonably well with Maurits, Frederik Hendrik, and even Willem III, and there seems on this evidence to have been no fundamental or inevitable conflict between regent rule and leadership by the stadhouder. On the other hand, it can be argued that, up to the Truce crisis, Holland was governed under Oldenbarnevelt by an essentially republican system allowing only a rather minor political role for Maurits. If we add to this period the years 1650–72 and 1702–47 we can see that between 1585 and 1747 there were only about fifty-two years of domination by the stadhouders. Looked at in this way, the republican attitude begins to look more normal, and the toleration of a powerful stadhouder rather less so.

However, the suspicion lingers that by the middle years of the seventeenth century co-operation between the regents and a moderate and reasonable stadhouder had come to seem the normal and right way to run the province as far as most regents of Holland were concerned. The introduction of the stadhouderless system by Holland in 1651 was as much a pragmatic solution to an immediate problem as it was an act of republican principle. The double accident of the unexpected death of the prince leaving only a posthumous son meant that there was no obvious adult candidate for stadhouder, and, given the recent experiences of the leading politicians of the province, it is hardly surprising that they opted to return to what were perhaps increasingly seen as the great days of Oldenbarnevelt. The theoretical justifications of this decision came later; at the time a sense of relief seems to have been predominant. The death of Willem II resolved a conflict which had not been definitively ended by the compromise of the summer of 1650. It is understandable that the States of Holland jumped at the opportunity of ensuring that there would be no return to the extremely dangerous situation that they had just lived through.

Perhaps our uncertainty over the political attitudes of the regents is as much a reflection of the confused nature of the situation itself as of our ignorance. There can be little doubt that the basic political orientation of the regents was conservative, in the sense that they believed that the historically established way of doing things was right, because for them this is what right meant. They shared this characteristic with most of the ruling strata of the period; not abstract theory but custom and precedent determined what was proper. However, tradition was, or could be made to appear, ambiguous, and this was certainly true in the case of Holland. It was open to republicans and orangists at the mid-century to use history to argue for and against the stadhouder, and indeed they did so, but for the ordinary regents it probably seemed clear that the stadhoudership was part of the traditional system, and should be retained as long as its incumbent was prepared to stay within his proper sphere. If, however, he broke the restraints which the system placed on his powers—as Willem II had done, in a way which perhaps reminded contemporaries of the attempted usurpations of Philip II—then to dispense with a stadhouder was the lesser of two evils.

Those who argued in principle against the stadhoudership during the first stadhouderless period were a small group of often self-consciously radical men whose contemporary influence seems to have been very limited.[7] At once the most able and the least representative of the opinions of the political class were the brothers Johan and Pieter de la Court, whose uncompromising, indeed often deliberately outrageous, Cartesian-rationalist approach to politics was a far cry from the hidebound traditionalism of the time.[8] On the other hand, many of the writings of this group were polemical in intent and, stripped of their theoretical elements, the message they had to deliver was a simple and, in the circumstances, telling one—that stadhouders were a threat to Freedom. The contents of this particular usage of the term 'freedom' were peculiar, if not entirely unusual in this period, and consisted of the conflation of *vrijheid* with *vrijheden*, freedom with privileges. Freedom consisted of the maintenance of privileges, which in itself was a shorthand for the existing system in government and society. Maurits's actions in 1618, together with the execution of Oldenbarnevelt, were added to Willem II's in 1650 to demonstrate that the stadhouders were potentially as much a threat to the traditional political system—the 'privileges'—as Philip II had been.

Such themes seem to have gone underground after 1672, and the renewal of the stadhouderless system after the death of Willem III seems to have been as much an instinctive reaction to the prince's domineering almost-rule as a consequence of republican theory. In this case it was the lack of a direct descendant which presented the regents with their opportunity to end the stadhoudership. In general it would seem that the regents of Holland were not opposed to the stadhoudership in principle, but rather were sufficiently alienated from time to time by what some stadhouders actually did as to take advantage of fortuitous circumstances in the middle of the seventeenth century and at the beginning of the eighteenth to dispense with the office altogether.

[7] For a brief study of this literature, see Geyl, *Het stadhouderschap*, 6–16, 21–35.
[8] Van der Bijl, 'Pieter de la Court'; Van Tijn, 'Pieter de la Court'.

The first stadhouderless period demonstrated some of the less attractive aspects of republicanism: the unrestricted rule of the oligarchy, and the purely negative conception of Freedom which it embodied—that is, Freedom was the freedom of the regents from interference from above in their absolutist rule over their own political sphere. Yet it also showed that Holland did not need a stadhouder for it to be able to run its affairs efficiently, even in wartime. It is true that the military collapse of 1672 brought the regime down, but the system had survived and even triumphed in two previous wars since 1650.

Whether this would have been possible without the presence of Johan de Witt is another matter. Holland was extremely fortunate to be able to call on the services of such an able politician—a man who stands comparison with Oldenbarnevelt—just when they were most needed, but it must also be remarked that there must have been something right about a system which allowed such a man to rise to the top. De Witt was a singular combination of the politician, the administrator, and the statesman. Without considerable political skills he would never have reached the position he did, nor could he have achieved much once there. An able administrator was vital to the smooth running of the affairs of the province (and of the Republic), and there was no one other than the *raadpensionaris* who could do the job. Yet it is as a statesman that he is remembered, although it was in this part of the task that he ultimately failed—largely because of extremely difficult international circumstances, but at least in part through his own weaknesses.

In Holland, De Witt built up and maintained his power and influence through family connections and a system of political contacts throughout the province. In the first place there were his family roots in the regent oligarchy of Dordrecht, where his father had been a powerful figure before his arrest (as one of the 'six members') by Willem II in 1650. His brother, Cornelis, remained in Dordrecht as one of the most influential local regents—helped, of course, not a little by the position Johan had achieved in the politics of the province and the Republic—and also extended his family's connections by marrying into an important Rotterdam regent family. Johan carried on the good work by himself judiciously marrying into the most powerful regent family in Amsterdam. Besides these local power bases, De Witt maintained regular contacts with supporters and clients throughout the voting towns, the nature of which are at least partly revealed in his correspondence, though the short distances between most of the towns and The Hague meant that this is probably only the tip of the iceberg, as face-to-face contacts are likely to have been far more important than letters. The purpose of such contacts was to sound out opinion and exert pressure, in order to calculate both what could be got through the States of Holland and where influence needed to be exerted to change key votes.

Yet, had there been an adult prince of Orange to succeed Willem II all this would very likely never have happened. What made things worse for the orangists was that Willem did leave a son, but a posthumous one, and this led in the event to deep and debilitating conflicts within the orangist camp which weakened its ability to resist the policies of the republicans. Indeed, these divisions were quite possibly the decisive factor in the whole political situation: not only did the extreme youth of Willem III make it relatively easy for the republicans to deny him the offices and powers which his father had held, but his very existence prevented any other member of the family succeeding to them either. The infant prince also became the object of a three-way struggle for control and for leadership of the house of Orange. Not only was there conflict between the two widows—Amalia von Solms (widow of Frederik Hendrik) and the princess Mary—but also the stadhouder of Friesland, Willem Frederik, was apparently hoping to be able to step into Willem II's shoes and stand in for the young prince until he came of age. This honourable intention was distrusted by both Amalia and Mary, one of the very few issues on which it proved possible for them to reach an agreement. Thus, at the crucial period of the setting-up and consolidation of the new regime, the orangist camp was fatally divided. Had it been more united, it might well have been able to take advantage of the defeats in the first Anglo-Dutch war, or of the controversy that erupted over the Act of Seclusion[9] of 1654, to secure the stadhoudership for the young prince under some sort of regency arrangement. In the

---

[9] This act was passed by the States of Holland alone, and barred any member of the house of Orange, in effect, from the stadhoudership of the province. It was a condition, insisted upon by Cromwell, of relatively moderate peace terms from England. The orangists believed, or affected to believe, that the republicans had persuaded Cromwell to 'demand' this act: J. H. Kluiver, 'Zeeuwse reacties op de Acte van Seclusie', *Bijdragen en Mededelingen betreffende de Geschiedenis der Nederlanden*, 91 (1976).

event, it let the inexperienced De Witt and his uncertain regime off the hook.

However, the strength of the moderate orangist tradition became steadily more apparent as the years passed and it seemed more and more likely that the rather sickly young prince would in fact survive into manhood. In retrospect, it looks as if the whole stadhouderless system was only possible in the absence of an adult prince of Orange. Yet, it is just possible that without the disasters of 1672, the prince would have been contained within the republican system. It was clearly De Witt's intention to allow Willem honourable employment within the state, but without access to real political power—somewhat on the lines, perhaps, of Maurits's position before the Truce crisis, but with the added safeguard of keeping the prince out of the stadhoudership of Holland. Whether Willem and his supporters would have been satisfied for long with command of the army and session in the Council of State alone is doubtful, and the strength of the opposition to the Eternal Edict of 1667 (which made illegal the combination of the captain-generalcy with the stadhoudership of any province), especially outside Holland, gives an impression of the latent power of orangism.

Also, as the prince approached maturity he began to provide a focus for opposition to De Witt and his regime. This opposition came not from orangists alone—indeed, orangism seems to have been rather a protective colouring which De Witt's opponents put on when it suited them than their principal motivation—but rather from political rivals who found their own ambitions blocked by the long domination of De Witt. It must be remembered that he had only been 24 when he took office as *raadpensionaris* for the first time, so even by the late 1660s he was still relatively young and capable of continuing to dominate the political scene in Holland for another twenty years at least. The prince of Orange offered ambitious politicians an alternative to this rather dispiriting vision. However, this was not quite the equivalent of opposition politicians clustering round the heir to the throne: Fagel and his like were much too circumspect, De Witt too powerful, and, one suspects, Willem was not quite naïve enough to encourage anything of the sort. Such opposition was very restrained until the military débâcle of 1672 brought De Witt down. It is one of the more intriguing but frustrating aspects of seventeenth-century Dutch history that we cannot know what would have happened had it not been for the dramatic events of 1672 (just as we cannot know how the conflict between the States of Holland and Willem II would have developed after 1650). We can never know whether De Witt could have held on to power, would have been forced to share power with the prince, or would have been ousted by him. However, the drama of 1672 provides us with insights into the nature of politics in Holland which we otherwise might have lacked, which is a considerable compensation.

In retrospect, it seems that, more than the strength of republican feeling, it was the irresponsible actions of Willem II in 1650 which broke, albeit temporarily, the power of orangism within Holland. The comment supposedly found on a scrap of paper in a church collection-box in Amsterdam, 'No better news in eighty years' (*Geen blijder maer in tachtig jaer*), celebrating the death of the prince, may have come from an extreme republican, but such a comment even from such a quarter would hardly have been conceivable only three years beforehand. Certainly, the apparent threat of civil war brought by the prince's actions fatally undermined the orangist arguments regarding the security and unity which the princes of Orange brought to province and Republic. Conversely, the dire warnings of the republicans about the dangers inherent in the powers of the stadhouder had been overfulfilled, and even cast a shadow over the past. Maurits's actions in 1618, viewed from the perspective of 1650, looked a lot more sinister than they had done during the period of office of the relatively tactful Frederik Hendrik.

How this blow to orangist prestige affected local politics, and how important it was, is impossible to say with any precision. The immediate consequences of the States of Holland's decision not to appoint a stadhouder were more obviously important. In particular, the voting towns were now freed from stadhouderly interference with their internal affairs and the composition of their magistracies and governments. The appointment of yearly magistrates and new *vroedschappen* was now left to the towns alone, and one important aspect of this change was that the orangist parties in the towns were henceforward deprived of what was probably in many cases vital outside support. This seems to have led to a steady erosion of orangist strength within the oligarchy as a whole, and the progressive entrenchment of the power of the True Freedom. There was a marked build-up of republican power in the towns, a process that only began to move into reverse in the last years of the period. The scale of the *wetsverzettingen* in 1672 was in part an indication of the size of the problem from an orangist point of view.[10] This year, however, saw the new stadhouder being granted, spontaneously, all the powers over such appointments which his father had enjoyed, and the orangist parties installed in power in that year could be supported and maintained by means which were suddenly traditional again.

At the beginning of the seventeenth century the opposition between the regents and the stadhouder for political leadership in Holland was latent, and the domination of the States of Holland led by Oldenbarnevelt seemed unchallengeable. It was only with the fierce political conflicts of the Truce period that the pattern began to be set which would dominate the theory and practice of politics for the rest of the century. When Oldenbarnevelt seemed to be leading the country into civil war, Maurits emerged as the alternative pole of political power. His success ushered in a period of over thirty years of Orange direction of the politics of the province, but the fundamental challenge to the power of the States of Holland offered by Willem II in 1650 precipitated a violent swing to republican leadership and a temporary eclipse of the stadhouder's power. Yet when De Witt's government demonstrably failed with the French invasion of 1672, the pendulum naturally swung back to the only conceivable alternative leader, and Willem III came to power and stayed there for the rest of the century. In practice as well as in theory it seems that after 1618 either the States or the stadhouder had to dominate, and this fundamental structure was revealed again after Willem's death, when the States took over power and ushered in another stadhouderless period, which was to last until the middle of the eighteenth century.

[10] This build-up of republican strength certainly took place in Rotterdam (Price, 'Rotterdam Patriciate', 182–95, 216–25) and, although the evidence from the other voting towns is rather more impressionistic, voting patterns in the States of Holland support this interpretation of what was happening.

5. Urban Rivalry

The impression has perhaps been given that the regents of the voting towns acted as a monolithic political bloc within Holland, but this is far from the truth for, quite apart from rivalry between States and stadhouder, the political life of the province was deeply affected by conflict between the towns. Within a broad political consensus centring on the protection of the privileges—and thus the power—of the oligarchies, and support for the trading and manufacturing economy, there existed long-term, perhaps even structurally determined, tensions and conflicts of interest between the voting towns of Holland. Jealousy and mistrust marked the relations between the towns as much as co-operation; differences of interpretation of common political and economic interests as much as consensus. Unfortunately, the nature and effects of these rivalries have been very little investigated, though they were probably major factors in the politics of the province throughout the century, and may well have decisively affected the outcome of some of the most important political conflicts of the period.

Looming over all the tensions and rivalries between the towns was the problem of Amsterdam. The relative size and wealth of this town made it at one and the same time the obvious leader of the Holland towns and difficult to assimilate within a system based in principle on equality between the towns. Amsterdam habitually not only claimed leadership in the States of Holland but also demanded that its own opinions and interests be given special consideration. In the dynamic economic growth of the last decades of the sixteenth and the first half of the seventeenth century, Amsterdam established its overwhelming economic predominance within Holland and then maintained this lead, but the formal political system could give no recognition to this situation, and the pretensions of the town's representatives to special consideration tended to be met with mistrust and resistance by the other voting towns. Yet, in practice, the realism which was such a characteristic of the Dutch regents ensured that Amsterdam was accorded far more weight in the affairs of the province than its single vote in the States seemed to allow. The underlying problem of imbalance remained, however, and on occasion the town felt that its interests were not receiving proper consideration—and at such times the results of Amsterdam's discontent could be far-reaching.

As a general assessment of the underlying realities of political power in seventeenth-century Holland, it can be argued that when Amsterdam and the rest of the voting towns were united, the States of Holland could not be defeated; but that when there was a rift between the leading town and the majority in the States, then the whole of the latter's position became vulnerable. In this interpretation of Dutch politics, the move of Amsterdam into opposition to Oldenbarnevelt was an indispensable element in Maurits's victory in 1618, while one of the reasons why De Witt's position collapsed so quickly and completely in the summer of 1672 was the readiness of the dominant politicians in Amsterdam to bring him down. Conversely, again according to this interpretation, the failure of Willem II in 1650 demonstrates the ultimate impotence of a stadhouder faced by a united States of Holland led by Amsterdam. This latter point, of course, depends upon how the events of 1650 are interpreted: as a defeat for the prince, or as an unstable stalemate which might yet have been converted into victory by Willem had he lived. In any case, the prince's failure to enforce his will on Amsterdam, and to break the united front of the voting towns, was an enormous and quite possibly crippling blow to his prestige in Holland. To restore his position would have required the use of desperate shifts, such as the use of French troops to break the resistance of the States of Holland. That his death prevented the humiliated prince from any such dangerous move was probably as much a hidden blessing for the house of Orange as it was a cause of covert rejoicing for the republicans.

The influence of Amsterdam within the political system of Holland is seen most obviously in that town's role as leader and champion of the States against the stadhouder. The traditional view of the politics of the 1630s and 1640s portrays Amsterdam leading an ever-stronger peace-party in the States of Holland against a stadhouder more inclined to war, or even towards a dynastically oriented foreign policy.[1] If recent research has drastically revised this picture by showing that Frederik Hendrik was far

---

[1] Geyl, *Oranje en Stuart*, ch. 1.

more inclined to work with than against the States of Holland, and in the end prepared to recognize the strength of the movement favouring peace and to co-operate with it, this leaves—at least as yet—the role of Amsterdam as prime mover in the drive towards peace more or less intact.[2] Willem II, however, seems likely to continue to be seen as attempting first to delay the peace, then to renew the war, against the determined opposition in both matters of the States of Holland led by Amsterdam under the Bicker brothers, whose prominent role seems almost as clear now as it did to the frustrated prince at the time.[3] Similarly, Amsterdam's role in resisting Willem III's foreign policy has become a commonplace in historical writing, though perhaps more stress should be placed on the essential reasonableness and moderation of its position than is usually done.[4]

On the other hand, perhaps not enough emphasis or attention has been given to the less dramatic but probably at least as important co-operative role which the town often played, with its burgemeesters working in comparative harmony with stadhouder or *raadpensionaris*. Indeed, the smooth running of Holland's affairs required at least the grudging consent of Amsterdam's political leaders, and preferably their co-operation. It seems tolerably clear that the good understanding, carefully nurtured on both sides, between the leading town and Frederik Hendrik was the fundamental reason for the relatively trouble-free relations between stadhouder and States in the 1620s and 1630s, and the degree to which such comparative harmony persisted even into the 1640s has recently been stressed.[5]

It is even more clear that a vital prerequisite for the successes of De Witt in the 1650s and 1660s was his good relationship with Amsterdam. De Witt consulted the burgemeesters of the town, particularly in his early years as *raadpensionaris*, on a wide range of affairs as well as matters involving the specific interests of the town, in a manner that they must have found both gratifying and flattering.[6] His close alliance with the dominant party in the town was clearly one of the most important components of his system of

[2] Groenveld, *Verlopend getij*, 108–10.
[3] S. Groenveld, 'Willem II en de Stuarts', *Bijdragen en Mededelingen betreffende de Geschiedenis der Nederlanden*, 103 (1988).
[4] Price, 'William III'.   [5] Groenveld, *Verlopend getij*, 109 and *passim*.
[6] Rowen, *John de Witt, Grand Pensionary*, 345–8.

running the province. Again, towards the end of the century, the difficulties between Willem III and Amsterdam have perhaps tended to overshadow the extent to which the support of the town's leaders was necessary to the success of the prince's risky enterprise in 1688; it is hard to see how this expedition could have been successfully launched had it not been for the backing of those who mattered in Amsterdam. Moreover, after 1688 there seems again to have developed a greater harmony of views with regard to foreign policy between the town and the stadhouder, so much so that on the latter's death it was the burgemeesters of Amsterdam who helped to ensure that his anti-French policies would continue to be pursued by the new leaders of the Dutch Republic.[7]

The conventional historical accounts give rather less prominence to the role of Amsterdam as the opponent, and indeed destroyer, of over-mighty *raadpensionarissen* as well as stadhouders. On occasion, the town proved ready to move against its apparently natural ally in Holland, when the latter was seen to be standing in the way of the town's interests. It is hardly a coincidence that the two most prominent occasions when the town helped not just to defeat but to bring down a *raadpensionaris* came at times when first Oldenbarnevelt and then De Witt had built up what seemed to be an unassailable position in Holland. The explanation for the apparent paradox of the leading town attacking the two greatest champions of the power of the States should perhaps be sought in the consideration that, on each occasion, Amsterdam's political leaders felt that the *raadpensionarissen* had become too powerful. To put it more cynically, it seems plausible to suggest that Amsterdam turned against Oldenbarnevelt and De Witt when it thought that they had become too independent and ceased to give sufficient consideration to the opinions and interests of the town.

Amsterdam's decision to move against Oldenbarnevelt during the Truce crisis was, of course, in part the consequence of a shift in the balance of power within the local oligarchy,[8] but seen in a broader perspective this shift can be interpreted as a reflection of the underlying long-term interests of many politically powerful citizens of the town. On a range of issues, quite apart from the remonstrant question, Amsterdam had found itself thwarted by the

[7] A. Porta, *Joan en Gerrit Corver: De politieke macht van Amsterdam 1702–1748* (Assen and Amsterdam, 1975), 18–19.

[8] Elias, *Vroedschap*, i: liii–lvi.

policies and political skills of Oldenbarnevelt. Most notably in the negotiations for the Truce with Spain, and the consequent blocking of plans for the foundation of a West India Company, the dominant men in the Amsterdam government saw Oldenbarnevelt as sacrificing the specific interests of their town in the pursuit of his own ends, which they professed to see as not just wrong-headed but distinctly suspicious. Unfortunately for the States of Holland as a whole, rather than bringing the Advocate to heel, this move by Amsterdam into opposition deepened the divisions between the towns. Oldenbarnevelt was forced into greater dependence on an alliance of remonstrant towns, while Amsterdam gathered round itself a group of smaller allies. Perhaps more than anything else it was this disunity within the States which opened up the way for Maurits's victory. The structural problem here was that a powerful *Advocaat van den Lande*, firmly entrenched through well over two decades in office, with a formidable accumulation of knowledge and expertise, and supported by a substantial group of voting towns, was able to ensure that the majority in the States of Holland followed his lead despite Amsterdam's opposition, but by doing so he was contravening the unwritten law which guaranteed that town against such inappropriate treatment. The inability of the political system at this time to accommodate the needs of Amsterdam was an example of the way the crisis had upset normal perceptions and procedures—indeed, it was to a significant extent this failure which turned the internal disagreements of the time into a crisis.

Less dramatically, perhaps, but in an essentially similar way, Amsterdam moved away from De Witt into something like structural opposition in the late 1660s. The reasons for this political shift were complex in detail, and again involved a short-term convulsion in the town's internal balance of power, but one element was probably decisive, and that is the fact that the *raadpensionaris* had been in power for a decade and a half, had established his own power base, and was much more of an independent force in politics than he had been in his earliest years in office. The leading regents of Amsterdam seem to have become resentful of the dominant role which De Witt had come to play, and wished to dilute his power—hence the suggestion that Van Beuningen, an Amsterdam regent of course, should take over some portion of his multifarious duties as a sort of joint *raadpensionaris.*[9] Such a move was intended both to strengthen Amsterdam's direct influence on decision-making, and to take away a significant measure of De Witt's power.[10] In general, Amsterdam's leaders felt that, once again, their town's specific interests were not being given enough weight in the affairs of state. Amsterdam's opposition pushed De Witt into greater dependence on a group of south Holland towns rather than bringing him to heel.[11] The contest between the *raadpensionaris* and Amsterdam at this time was less vicious than during the Truce, but it certainly set up the situation for the very rapid disintegration of De Witt's whole political position in the summer of 1672.

Looking at the century as a whole, it begins to appear that, from the point of view of Amsterdam, too strong a *raadpensionaris* was almost as bad as an over-mighty stadhouder. In either case the town was liable to feel that its interests were not being properly deferred to by the leadership within Holland. To an extent this was an unavoidable problem, stemming from the disparity in size and wealth between Amsterdam and the rest of the voting towns, to some extent paralleling the position of the province of Holland within the Dutch Republic. Indeed, it was in some ways more difficult to accommodate Amsterdam within the political system of Holland than it was Holland within the Republic. Whereas Holland could appeal to the principle of provincial sovereignty to strengthen its hand in the States General, Amsterdam at the most could claim a high degree of autonomy and a veto in important matters but remained unavoidably an integral part of the province. In this way there developed a dangerous gap between the realities of power and wealth within Holland, and the insistence of the formal political system on equality between the towns; this could only be bridged if the weight of Amsterdam's contribution to the finances of the province were recognized in very practical ways in the running of Holland's affairs. It must be stressed, however, that normally this is indeed what happened: the problem could be contained more or less harmoniously by the power-broking processes essential to the smooth running of the province. Nevertheless, it

[9] M. A. M. Franken, *Coenraad van Beuningens politieke en diplomatieke aktiviteiten in de jaren 1667–84* (Groningen, 1966), 70.

[10] One reason for the poor relationship between De Witt and Amsterdam at this period was that the faction within the town's oligarchy which had been his great supporters—that led by De Graef van Zuidpolsbroeck—had lost power.

[11] Franken, *Coenraad van Beuningen*, 75–7.

remains true that the situation was a major potential weakness, and that the difficulty of balancing Amsterdam's pretensions against the rights and jealousies of the other towns built an element of inherent instability into the political system of Holland. Looked at from this angle, it is perhaps surprising, not that difficulties in fact arose from this imbalance from time to time, but that there were not more such conflicts.

More generally, differences in, or conflicts of, economic interests were also a fertile source of disputes between the voting towns. Although the subject has received far too little attention from historians, it is clear that, despite the general consensus of support for trade and manufactures there were frequent and lasting conflicts between the towns over how these common interests could best be served. Two obvious examples with very important implications for foreign policy were the widespread disagreements over the likely economic consequences of the Truce, which were all the more vehement because of their speculative character, and the disputes over the best reaction to Colbert's punitive tariffs on Dutch exports of 1667. The governments of the voting towns saw the preservation and pursuit of their town's economic interests as one of their prime duties, but this pursuit of prosperity was almost as likely to pit one town against another as it was to unite them against foreign threats. One of the main tasks of the States of Holland, and of the political system of the province in general, was to mediate between the competing interests of the various towns in order to achieve something like a coherent policy while minimizing internal conflict. It was not always possible to do both, and it sometimes seemed that neither was possible.

In the disputes between the towns of Holland over Oldenbarnevelt's plans for a truce with Spain, the flourishing ports of the Northern Quarter, Hoorn and Enkhuizen, were inclined to favour a continuation of the war at least in part because they felt that this would favour their colonial trade, though in the end they came over to the side of peace. Delft's opposition to the truce was more determined, and has similarly been attributed to its considerable interest in the VOC.[12] In so far as these towns opposed the Truce, they were lined up alongside Amsterdam, which suffered a major defeat on this issue, for which it was to exact a harsh revenge.

[12] J. I. Israel, *The Dutch Republic and the Hispanic World 1606–1661* (Oxford, 1982), 31, 41.

This temporary defeat is a reminder that Amsterdam's interests did not always coincide with those of the rest of the towns of Holland, and that this disparity was one of the most important causes of conflict within the province. Amsterdam's economy was wide-ranging and flexible, while most of the other towns were more limited or specialized, particularly as regards the areas or type of trade in which they were involved. This basic difference of economic orientation meant that Amsterdam was likely to take a significantly distinct line on specific issues, especially as it was probably rather more resilient economically than the other towns of Holland. One example of a major policy clash arising out of such differences came in the reaction to the French tariffs of 1667. All the towns agreed, of course, that the new customs were a serious threat to Dutch prosperity and that something had to be done about them, but it was less easy to reach an agreement in the States as to what that should be. Amsterdam pushed strongly for reprisals in the form of bans on the import of French goods into the Republic, while Rotterdam favoured a much less rigid position. Given the very broad basis of Amsterdam's trade, it could perhaps afford to deprive itself of the link with France for some time, but Rotterdam had a very heavy involvement in trade with France and in particular had a near monopoly of the trade in French wine to the Republic and northern Europe, and so could not afford to be so aggressive.

An even sharper distinction in fundamental economic interests existed between the towns whose prosperity was based on trade and commerce, led by Amsterdam and including all the ports, and those heavily dependent on manufactures. The outstanding instances of the latter were Leiden and Haarlem, the great centres of textile production. Of course, these manufacturing towns were integrated into the trading economy of Holland, particularly as they were dependent on imports for the raw materials and half-finished cloths on which they worked, as well as needing access to foreign markets for their finished products. However, their over-whelming dependence on wool and linen textiles tied their prosperity very closely to good relations with both the areas supplying their materials and those providing their markets. There is evidence to suggest that the changed conditions of international trade in textiles during the Truce caused difficulties for the industries of both Haarlem and Leiden, and that the consequent discontent among the artisan population made these two towns particularly volatile politically at this time.[13] Subsequently, these towns were strong supporters of the continuation of the war in the late 1620s and the 1630s, along with Gouda, another town which was heavily dependent on manufactures. This determined opposition to peace or a renewed truce has been attributed to the strength of contraremonstrant feeling in these towns, but their perception of their own economic interests may have been quite as important.[14]

This basic difference in economic orientation may help to explain why the political experience of these towns in the seventeenth century was rather different from that of the other voting towns, which in general were much less specialized economically. It has been noted that both textile towns were consistently orangist for a long period after 1618 (in Leiden's case until it turned against Willem III's war policy after about 1675), and it is often suggested that the governments of both towns tended towards orangism out of consideration for the volatility of the textile workers who composed such a high proportion of their populations. It is true that the social polarization between employers and workers in these textile towns was much starker than in the rest of Holland, and it is nearly as clear that emotional orangism was strong among the textile workers, but it has not yet been convincingly demonstrated that it was this situation which produced the peculiar political orientation of the oligarchies of these towns. (This is not to deny that popular violence or the threat of it had considerable influence on the governments of these towns, particularly in troubled times.) An alternative, or complementary, explanation would start with the specifically different economic interests of Haarlem and Leiden: they were faced in the States of Holland with a large and permanent majority for the ports and trading towns, led moreover by the powerful Amsterdam; in such circumstances, it may well be that the textile towns turned to the stadhouder as a counterbalance to the influence of the trading towns. They may have hoped to win the support of the stadhouder for their economic interests in return for steady political support.

Apart from the differences of interest between primarily trading and manufacturing towns, there were a range of other matters

---

[13] Ibid., 59 ff.
[14] Ibid. 231–2, 289.

which could bring the voting towns of Holland into conflict. Dordrecht's determination to protect its long-standing staple rights, for example, was a constant source of conflict with Rotterdam in particular, and led to violent clashes between the two towns between 1618 and 1620 when Dordrecht attempted to extend the staple to French wines. A compromise was finally reached on this issue, but disputes over what was legitimately covered by the staple continued for the rest of the century.[15] Similarly, the determination of Gouda and Haarlem to protect their toll privileges hindered the development of the new canal network for passenger barges, and ensured that the new waterways were in the end designed to be unsuitable for freight. Gouda also blocked Delft and Leiden's plans to replace the dam on the Vliet by a sluice, again in order to prevent traffic from being diverted away from its toll.[16] Thus individual towns could and did protect their own privileges, even if it was at the expense of the economic welfare of Holland as a whole; all the *stemhebbende* towns were fierce and often effective defenders of their own corner. Such attitudes are neither surprising nor particularly reprehensible, but one of the chief weaknesses of the political system in Holland was that it could not deal very effectively with such conflicts of interest: the considerable degree of autonomy which the towns enjoyed, and which was fundamental to the system, made it almost impossible to override the perceived interest of an individual town for the good of the province. If the towns in dispute could not reach an agreement, there was little that could be done.

The relationships between the voting towns of Holland were also affected by their very different economic experiences during the course of the seventeenth century. In very general terms, it may be said that all the towns shared in the economic growth of Holland in the late sixteenth and the early decades of the seventeenth century, but that subsequently the situation changed dramatically, with the smaller towns beginning to falter while the larger towns continued to expand until about the last quarter of the century, when they too began to experience serious difficulties. In the south of Holland, Rotterdam began to overshadow formerly prominent towns like Delft and Dordrecht, not to mention the smaller towns of the region, from the second or third decade of the

[15] H. C. Hazewinkel, *Geschiedenis van Rotterdam* (Rotterdam, 1940), ii. 120–1.
[16] De Vries, *Barges and Capitalism*, 19, 31–2.

century; and, in the north, Amsterdam eclipsed the towns of the Northern Quarter, including even Enkhuizen, which, after a period of explosive economic growth, started to have serious problems from about the end of the 1620s.[17] The political effects of these differences in economic experience over the century are unclear, both in general and in detail, but such disparities in fortune are a likely source of resentment and tensions between the towns. For example, it may be that Hoorn and Enkhuizen, unlike most of the trading towns, were pro-war in the 1620s and 1630s because they were already in decline and faced the prospect of peace with less confidence than their rivals. It is important to take into account such differences between the towns in order to avoid misleadingly simplistic interpretations of their economic interests. While it is true to say that the voting towns of Holland were united in the priority they gave to the concerns of trade and manufactures, there were significant differences between them as to the specific policies which would serve those interests, reflecting the different economic orientations, prosperity, and experiences of the various towns in the course of the seventeenth century.

[17] R. Willemsen, *Enkhuizen tijdens de Republiek* (Hilversum, 1988), 91–2.

6. Religion and Politics in Holland

Of all the factors affecting the way in which politics operated in Holland in the seventeenth century, the religious environment, if not necessarily the most important, is perhaps the one that is most difficult to evaluate and to understand. It is a truism to say that religion and politics could not be separated in seventeenth-century Europe, but one of the most interesting aspects of the history of Holland during this century is the extent to which a significant change in this respect was already becoming apparent. While religious matters still played an important—and sometimes vitally important—role in the political life of the province, there can also clearly be seen the beginnings of that process by which a separate political sphere with its own priorities and values, largely distinct from those of religion, was created. In short, the process of secularization was beginning, but within an overall situation in which the influence of religion was still strong. Religion retained an important influence on political life in Holland, but by the end of the century it was no longer quite so difficult to distinguish religious and political priorities as it had been in the late sixteenth century.

Again, when assessing the role of religion in the political life of Holland in this period, it is not enough to look merely at the Reformed Church, for the religious diversity and relatively high degree of toleration that existed within the province were just as important in their political ramifications, though perhaps in less obvious ways. Such diversity and toleration were both a cause and a consequence of the hesitant secularization of the period. Equally, it needs to be explained both why the political system allowed or even promoted such diversity, and what the effects on the political life of the province of this relative toleration were. However, it is important not to exaggerate the degree of religious toleration that existed in seventeenth-century Holland: if, on the one hand, the practical circumstances of the time propelled the regent oligarchy towards a wide measure of toleration for dissident protestants, on the other hand there were distinct limits, equally determined by the contemporary situation, on how far that toleration could go—not only with regard to catholics but also to the more radical of the protestants.

The Reformed Church was the official church in Holland, as it was in the Republic as a whole, but its position was weaker than that of the state churches elsewhere in Europe at this time, in particular because it had no religious monopoly. There was, in other words, no duty of either membership of, or attendance at, this church imposed by the civil authorities on the population at large. In contrast to nearly all contemporary theories of church–state relations, the political and religious communities were not coextensive; citizenship was not tied to church membership. Yet there was a clear link between the state and the Reformed Church. All public figures, including the regents in general and administrators at town or provincial level, were supposed to be supporters of the Reformed Church, and it was almost universally recognized that one of the chief duties of the civil authorities was the maintenance of the 'true religion'. In practice, of course, problems were likely to arise, particularly over this latter duty, as it was always a matter of dispute what precisely the 'true' religion was and who was entitled to define it. The civil authorities in the main were reluctant simply to bow to the church's dictation on this question, or indeed any question. Although the leaders of church and state were both in theory and practice members of the same church, nevertheless they were in almost permanent tension over the degree to which the views of the official church should determine at least the main lines of public policy.

In general, it can be suggested that the regent oligarchy at both local and provincial level was marked by an ambivalent attitude to the Reformed Church throughout the seventeenth century. On the one hand, the importance of the church as a unifying force in political and social terms was recognized, and all of the regents were in principle members of this church; in return, the church recognized the duty of all Christians to obey the magistrate which God had placed over them. However, in practice, there were fundamental problems affecting the relationship between the civil authorities and the official church, arising partly from the membership and attitudes of the local oligarchies, but also stemming from the highly independent stance taken by the church itself. The magistrate had far less direct control over the church than in almost any other protestant, or indeed catholic, country at this time: the regents were concerned to minimize this independence, the leaders of the church to maintain it unblemished.

One cause of friction between church and magistrate was that, in the early years of the century, the town oligarchies of Holland continued to include a considerable number of catholics and crypto-catholics, as well as protestants whose relationship to the official church was at best uncertain. Even later in the century, when catholics and open nonconformists had been forced out of the town governments, the situation was still not entirely unambiguous. In at least some towns the condition of full membership of the Reformed Church could not be enforced on the regents, and they could only be required to be supporters of the church in rather vague terms. Such evasive forms of words may have been used especially in towns where the oligarchy had strong remonstrant sympathies, even after the defeat of 1618.

One especially prominent characteristic of the regent group as a whole was determined resistance to any attempts by the church to influence political affairs. The town governments of Holland were united in their rejection of any such interference, and this attitude was expressed not just at the local but also at the provincial level: the States of Holland were just as determined to prevent the church from intervening in politics, and used both formal and informal means to achieve this end. In one important way the provincial authorities exercised effective control over the church: they paid the salaries of its ministers. Withholding pay was a sanction which threatened any minister who seriously displeased the secular power. The concern of the regents to control the activities of the church so as to limit its potential political role is also shown by the institution of *commissarissen politiek* (political delegates) representing the States at the meetings of the synods of north and south Holland.[1] The task of these representatives was to ensure that the discussions of these bodies remained within limits acceptable to the States, and did not trespass into political areas which the States felt to be none of their business.

The regents were not, of course, opposed to religion as such,

---

[1] There were no synods for Holland as a whole: north and south Holland were separate provinces of the Reformed Church. Whatever the reason for this, it weakened the potential political voice of the church in the province in a way that was particularly convenient for the regents.

and there is no reason to doubt that the great majority of them were as sincere in their loyalty to the beliefs of the Reformed Church as any other church members. Their objection was to the interference of the church as an institution, particularly through its ministers, in matters which they felt belonged properly to the civil authorities. They were especially sensitive to political affairs being dealt with in sermons, for this laid questions which they believed to be the province of the regents alone before the whole of the church-going public. The political demonology of the regent oligarchy was peopled, amongst others, by unruly ministers who stirred up their congregations to riot and revolt. One example of this that had become standard by the seventeenth century was the calvinist take-over of the towns of Flanders and Brabant after the Pacification of Ghent: these upheavals were seen as the root cause of the loss of the southern Netherlands to the Spanish—notably by Oldenbarnevelt.[2] It was asserted that these militants had forced the political leadership of the southern provinces into the hands of the Spanish by threatening not only the security of catholicism but also the established political and social order. The calvinist radicals who had supported the earl of Leicester against the States of Holland were seen in a similar light; only their defeat, it was argued, had saved the Revolt in the northern provinces. By the middle of the seventeenth century, the actions of the contraremonstrants were being fitted into this lineage of dangers to an ordered political society, at least by republicans, being represented as an example of the dangers to the peace and stability of the state of allowing the ministers of the Reformed Church to meddle in matters which were not their concern.

The church, in sharp contrast and in part as a reaction to the perceived lack of support from the regents, from the early years of the century cast the princes of Orange, as stadhouders of the province, in the role of its protectors—protectors, moreover, it increasingly came to appear, of its interests against a regent oligarchy which was seen as being at best dangerously liberal in religious matters and at worst positively hostile to the church. This religious role of the princes was built on the part which the propagandists of the church imputed had been played by Willem of Orange in support of the church during the Revolt, although to see

² Gerlach, *Het proces tegen Oldenbarnevelt*, 115–16.

this notably *politique* prince as a champion of orthodoxy was carrying freedom of historical interpretation a little far.[3] This vision was immensely strengthened by Maurits's decision to back the contraremonstrants during the Truce crisis, which set the stage for the alignment of orthodoxy with orangism. It survived the more than somewhat liberal reputation of Frederik Hendrik and the dubious character of Willem II to strengthen Willem III's hand in 1672, and in turn the myth was not a little improved by the latter's own policies in defence of European protestantism. Although there was an unmistakable element of wishful thinking in all this—as the church was in dire need of a powerful symbol of the religious identity and providential purpose of the Dutch state—nevertheless there was also an important sense in which the wish was fulfilled. The stadhouders did, indeed, act to a significant extent as the champions the church wished them to be. As the support of the church, or rather its members, became increasingly important for the stadhouders, so the latter were encouraged to maintain this support by at the very least making some appearance of promoting the interests of the Reformed Church in return.

It is particularly noticeable that popular orangism, as far as we can understand this somewhat elusive phenomenon, appears to have been inextricably entwined with Reformed orthodoxy from at least the period of the Truce crisis onwards. This is not, of course, to say that all orangists were orthodox or vice versa, but that the emotional power of orangism seems to have come to a significant extent from the identification of the princes of Orange with the interests of the Reformed Church, which in turn carried a heavy emotional charge because of the widespread tendency to confuse and conflate religious orthodoxy and patriotism. This confusion was seen most clearly during the Truce crisis, when, paralleling perhaps the early years of the Revolt, the orthodox calvinists came to be seen as the only group which could be absolutely relied upon not to sell out to Spain, as their own survival depended on the continuation of Dutch independence. During this period, it was entirely typical that the remonstrants should have been accused not only of horrible heresies, but of a secret plot to return the country to the Roman obedience, just as Oldenbarnevelt was accused of

[3] E. O. G. Haitsma Mulier, 'Willem van Oranje in de historiografie van de zeventiende eeuw', in Haitsma Mulier and A. E. M. Janssen, *Willem van Oranje in de historie 1584–1984* (Utrecht, 1984), 32–3.

deliberately weakening the Republic so as to be able to deliver it into the hands of the Spanish. The orthodox, however, could be suspected of no such treacherous intent, and Maurits by throwing his hand in with them was proclaiming himself in effect a true patriot as well as a defender of orthodoxy. This connection in the popular mind, and not only there, of orthodoxy with patriotism was to endure throughout the century (and much later too, of course), perhaps in part because of the relative weakness of the church's position. For in the early years of the century there were large numbers of dissenting protestants and, even more disturbingly, an unknown amount of catholics, and both groups could be seen as a real threat to the still precarious position of the Reformed Church. These circumstances may have created a sense of insecurity among many which pushed them to an even closer reliance on the guaranteed loyalty to the Dutch state which only the orthodox seemed to offer. Certainly, the conflation occurred again during the paranoia of the summer of 1672, when again remonstrants were *ipso facto* suspect, and religious orthodoxy as much as orangism was the criterion by which regents and would-be regents were judged in the popular estimation. In such an atmosphere the elevation of Willem III to the stadhoudership, and his success in leading the country out of the dire straits of 1672, were greeted with a fervour in which patriotic and religious motives were again inextricable. Willem as Moses casting down the golden idol as well as leading his people out of Egypt would seem a not inapt image.

Although the Reformed Church as an institution was limited in its political role, with town governments keeping an eye on local church councils and the political commissioners on the synods of the province, individual ministers of the church were able to play an important part in the production of orangist propaganda through sermons and publications. As has been argued, the regents of the Holland towns were always apprehensive of the potential political influence of the preaching in the Reformed Church, and the measures that were taken to control the appointment of ministers, to guard against politically inconvenient sermons, and to punish transgressors, are evidence of how seriously the matter was taken. Equally, the fact that ministers continued to preach in ways that gave more or less serious offence to their political masters is an indication that such controls were far from being perfectly effective. Rotterdam seems to have had particular difficulties with its ministers towards the end of the first stadhouderless period: the subversive sermons of Ds. Ridderus during the second Anglo-Dutch war have already been mentioned, and two other ministers of the Reformed Church in this town are reported to have played a major role in stirring up the popular disturbances against the town government in 1672. Similar subversive activities by ministers of the public church in that year are reported for The Hague, Delft, Dordrecht, Amsterdam, Haarlem, and Monnickendam as well.[4]

Probably more important than sermons, however, not least because much less easily controlled, was the printed propaganda produced in book and pamphlet form by the ministers of the official church. It may be that historians have a tendency to exaggerate the importance of the printed word, as it leaves the sort of tangible evidence behind that is often lacking for other types of propaganda, but it is nevertheless true that a great deal of polemical literature was produced in the seventeenth century, much of it in a form calculated to appeal to a popular audience. Moreover, it must be remembered that Holland as a whole had perhaps the highest literacy rate of all Europe at this time, and therefore such material could be expected to reach a broad public. The part played by ministers of the public church in the production of this orangist literature has perhaps been exaggerated somewhat, because of an assumption that publications with a certain religious tone and language must have been their work, which is begging a lot of questions. Nevertheless, the ministers of the church were an interest group with the education, leisure, and motivation to produce such orangist literature in quantities, and they almost certainly did. There seems little doubt that, in so far as the church had any significant political influence at all, it was exercised in favour of the stadhouders in Holland. Not all ministers of the Reformed Church were orangist[5]—the regents after all did have an important say in the appointment of ministers to the churches within their towns, and reliable republican sentiments might well have proved a considerable career advantage at times during the century—but most do seem to have recognized a providential purpose for the Dutch Republic, and to have regarded the princes of

[4] Geyl, *Democratische tendenties*, 8; Roorda, *Partij en factie*, 107 n. 4, 133 n. 4.
[5] Uit den Bogaard, *De Gereformeerde en Oranje*, 149–50, 193.

Orange as instruments of that purpose—which says a great deal for the strength of their faith but rather less for their realism.

In practical terms, the Reformed Church had already suffered a strategic defeat by the beginning of the seventeenth century, and was never able to reverse this. In the years immediately after the Revolt the calvinists had achieved the take-over of the existing church buildings for their own worship, gained the financial support of the new state, and procured the offical banning of catholic services, but as it turned out this was the limit of their success in using the civil authorities to give them a privileged position in the province. Attempts by the church and its champions to bring about an effective ban on the services of the various dissident protestants failed, and so did all attempts to make catholicism itself illegal. In principle, nonconformists were excluded from public office, and catholic worship was banned, but otherwise both dissenters and catholics were tolerated. However, the Reformed Church continued throughout the seventeenth century to put pressure on the political authorities within the province to try to ensure that radical protestants were curbed and the existing laws against catholics enforced.

Despite their failure to persuade the States of Holland of the necessity of banning public worship by the mennonites and other protestant sects, the paladins of the Reformed Church continued their vigilance, and were ever ready to respond with outrage to the activities of those they regarded as radicals. Their pressure on the civil authorities in Holland was frequently, but not always, disappointed, but they persevered. One major defeat they were forced to swallow was the toleration of the remonstrants once the latter had accepted their position as a separate church. However, it would be a mistake to assume that such pressures were ineffective. They created an atmosphere in which it was necessary for radicals to act with a certain circumspection, particularly as far as publishing was concerned, and pressure from the church often led to the States of Holland passing edicts restricting the activities of such groups.[6] The socinians were the favourite targets for much of the century— though the term was used very loosely as a catch-all for unacceptable opinions in general rather than for any precisely defined set of

---

[6] S. Groenveld, 'The Mecca of Authors? States Assemblies and Censorship in the Seventeenth-Century Dutch Republic', in A. C. Duke and C. A. Tamse (eds.), *Too Mighty to be Free* (Zutphen, 1987); Enno van Gelder, *Getemperde vrijheid*, 154–7, 160–2.

beliefs—but quakers and other received their share of attention. There hangs a major question-mark over the extent to which such legislation was ever enforced, or intended to be, in practice; nevertheless, the magistrates could not always ignore the law, and arrests were made, prosecutions carried through, and heavy—even harsh—punishments inflicted on nonconformists, particularly those who had published too openly or created a public scandal. Even in Holland the heterodox thinker was well advised to keep his head down, and publish anonymously or, preferably, posthumously. The vigilance of the authorities never satisfied the church, but it ensured that Holland was not quite as tolerant of religious radicalism as is sometimes suggested.

The situation with regard to the catholics was different: although being a catholic was not against the law, worshipping as one was. A combination of pressure from the Reformed Church and very general anti-catholic prejudices among the regents ensured that the *plakkaten* against catholic worship remained in force throughout the century, and were even strengthened at times. However, the influence of the Reformed Church was not sufficient to ensure that the *plakkaten* were enforced with any rigour, particularly by the second half of the century when the association of catholicism and potential treason had lost much of its persuasiveness. In practice, catholic worship was allowed in return for sweeteners paid to local police officials; despite the laws, the catholics had achieved *de facto* freedom of worship in the course of the century, although perhaps not full membership of the national community.

In general, the Reformed Church saw as one of the main duties of the civil authorities the maintenance of unity and doctrinal purity within the public church, and it did not hesitate to call upon the secular arm to act against the heterodox. The most serious case of this sort was, of course, the controversy over the remonstrants, but other movements of opinion within the church later in the century also brought calls for the suppression of what were claimed to be heterodox doctrines. In general, both the stadhouder and the States were primarily concerned to maintain peace within the church rather than support pure doctrine; the first instinct of both was to attempt to sweep such problems under the carpet and, failing that, to move against the weaker party to bring as rapid a return to calm as possible. It was the failure of Oldenbarnevelt to react in this way which materially contributed to the severity of the Truce crisis.

This general picture of a society which was unusually tolerant for the time—though rather less so than might at first appear—is put in question by the severity of the problems which developed round the remonstrants. Not only did this movement within the Reformed Church lead to a situation when civil war seemed imminent and the break-up of the Republic possible, but even after their defeat in 1619 the remonstrants were subject to a degree of persecution which hardly fits in with the overall picture of moderation in religious matters. For a number of years after their victory at the synod of Dordt (i.e. Dordrecht, 1619), the orthodox calvinists pursued their remonstrant opponents, whose beliefs were not so very different from their own (in the eyes of uncommitted outsiders at least), with a greater tenacity than they did the catholics, although on the surface the latter seem to have been a much more serious challenge to protestantism. To the adherents of 'ie beliefs declared orthodox by Dordt, this very similarity was p ecisely the danger, as it could deceive innocent believers into failing to see the way in which remonstrant teachings undermined the whole structure of the true faith. In their eyes the differences may have been small, but they were vital.

The crisis within the Dutch state, and particularly within Holland, which arose out of the remonstrant movement in the first instance, demonstrated in a dramatic fashion some of the weaknesses of the Dutch political system; but equally the eventual peaceful assimilation of the remonstrants showed some of its strengths. In brief, as long as the remonstrants were trying to secure a place for themselves within the Reformed Church, they set up tensions which the Dutch state was peculiarly ill-equipped to handle, but as soon as they were prepared to regard themselves as a completely separate church they ceased to be a real problem. The crux of the dilemma posed by the remonstrants was not simply that they were regarded as holding heterodox views by the dominant group within the Reformed Church, but that they were inside the church and constituted a real threat to orthodoxy because they enjoyed considerable political support, within Holland at least. The remonstrants and their opponents were rivals for the soul of the Reformed Church, and as long as this contest within the church lasted there could be no toleration. Once the remonstrants accepted their position as a separate church, however, they became eligible for the relatively favourable treatment which was accorded to all respectable protestant sects.

As a movement of any great importance, the remonstrants were limited to Holland, where they originated in the theological speculations of the Amsterdam minister and later professor of theology at the university of Leiden, Jacobus Arminius (Jacob Harmensz.). There does not seem to have been anything particularly new about his ideas,[7] but in the circumstances obtaining in Holland in the first decade of the seventeenth century they began to have a remarkably powerful set of effects, both gaining considerable support and stirring up passionate opposition. The arminians found support among students and candidates for the ministry, but also politically powerful backing in the ranks of the oligarchies of the Holland towns.

There seem to have been good, or at least superficially attractive, reasons why many of the regents favoured the remonstrants. Oldenbarnevelt, for example, although his own theological position appears to have been closer to that of the contraremonstrants,[8] hoped to be able to move the Reformed Church in the direction of greater comprehension in order to embrace a larger proportion of the population than seemed likely to be drawn in by a theologically narrow church, and so promote political unity. A latitudinarian church seemed more likely to prove an effective unifying force than the existing Reformed Church, whose urge to acquire converts was always balanced by its fundamental exclusivism. Moreover, another attraction of the new movement was that a broad and moderate church might be expected to be more amenable to control by the magistrate than the church had been so far. In looking for a firmer subordination of the official church, the regents were aspiring to no more than the civil authorities possessed in most contemporary protestant states.

Thus, the readiness of the remonstrant leaders to elaborate a specifically erastian political theory was well judged to increase the support they received from Oldenbarnevelt, the States of Holland, and the governments of the voting towns. The degree of opposition the remonstrants faced within the ranks of the Reformed Church

---

[7] Cf. W. Nijenhuis, 'Varianten binnen het Nederlands calvinisme in de 16e eeuw', *Tijdschrift voor Geschiedenis*, 89 (1976).

[8] Den Tex, *Oldenbarnevelt*, iii, ch. 1.

forced them to look to the town governments and the States for support and protection, and in return they acknowledged the ultimate authority of the civil power in church affairs. Although it would obviously be a mistake to ignore the degree to which the moderate, even eirenic, views of the remonstrants were attractive in themselves to the regent oligarchy, the political advantages which such a church seemed to offer both at town and provincial level were an important element in the movement's appeal. The fact that the regents were attracted by a mixture of genuine conviction and political expediency both broadened the appeal of the movement and brought a depth of commitment from at least some which political opportunism alone could not have provided.

Equally, the degree of fanatical opposition which it aroused on the part of the 'orthodox' can only be explained by a similar combination of religious and political motives. For the remonstrants were seen by their enemies not only as threatening the purity of the church, but also the survival of the state. The intensity of this hostility is surprising only perhaps to those unfamiliar with the history of theological disputes within the Christian church, but, while the readiness of theologians to damn each other over the placing of a comma is easily understandable in terms of their own systems of value, it is not immediately obvious why such a dispute should have stirred up the passions of more than a handful of theologians and ministers.

One particularly dynamic element in the whole situation was the deep mistrust which the orthodox felt towards the remonstrants. It was not just that the doctrines professed openly by the arminians were anathema to hard-line calvinists, but that these were believed to be only the tip of a crypto-catholic iceberg. It seems to have been felt that there was no secure middle ground, but that the first step away from the pure doctrine of the Confession and Heidelberg catechism started a spiritual journey that inevitably led to Rome. The remonstrants were, indeed, accused of teaching much more extreme doctrines in private than they would ever admit to in public, but the underlying fear was that they were secret romanizers, all the more dangerous for the deceitful and insidious way in which they went about their task.

The strategic location of the remonstrants also aroused deep fears for the future of the Reformed Church. In 1603 Arminius became a professor of theology at Leiden, which was the only university in Holland and vitally important for the training of future ministers of the church, as well as being the most prestigious theological centre in the Republic. Even more significantly, perhaps, by the early years of the century the States College at this university had come under remonstrant control: this institution had been founded to train students from economically modest backgrounds, supported by various bursaries, for the ministry, and was of great importance for a church still very short of well-qualified *predikanten*. So, in the eyes of the orthodox, the very well-springs supplying much-needed new ministers were being poisoned by the remonstrants, who thus seemed capable of undermining the doctrine of the whole church within a generation through the influence of the products of this arminian education.

Such fears were all too likely to trouble a church whose position in Holland, let alone the Republic as a whole, was far from secure. Precise figures for the membership of the Reformed Church in the first two decades of the seventeenth century do not exist, and they might well be misleading in any case because of the existence of large numbers of people who were regular attenders but not full members of the church.[9] There seems little doubt as to the general picture, however: only a minority of the population of the province were committed adherents of the public church in these years; the rest were either members of one or other of the protestant sects, were more or less catholic, or religiously indifferent or disoriented. Many of the latter were, if anything, traditional in their religious instincts and would be attracted back into the catholic fold once the old church got itself organized. Indeed, one of the reasons for political support for the remonstrants was the hope that a more liberal church would prove attractive to this mass of floating religious voters.[10] In these circumstances, the intransigence of the champions of Reformed orthodoxy sprang not from strength but from weakness; it was the perceived vulnerability of the church which made its defenders so desperate.

In this highly charged atmosphere, disagreements over foreign policy added a further element of distrust and suspicion. Oldenbarnevelt's attempts to arrive at a negotiated settlement with

[9] Van Deursen, *Bavianen en slijkgeuzen*, 128–31.
[10] It is intriguing to note the figures on church membership in Haarlem around the end of the second decade of the century in Spaans, *Haarlem*, 104, which seem to suggest that over half the population of the town had no firm religious affiliation.

Spain, and his forcing-through of the Truce in 1609 against considerable opposition, most notably from Maurits, aroused doubts not only about his judgement but about his patriotism. The Truce was seen by its opponents as a respite for the Spanish in which they could rebuild their strength before inevitably attacking the Republic again with renewed vigour. Moreover, as the war against Spain was seen as one of the few things holding the Dutch provinces together, the Truce was also seen as a threat to the survival of the Union. Thus Oldenbarnevelt's policy was seen as weakening the international position of the Republic at the same time as it undermined its unity. When the Advocate's support for the remonstrants, which was regarded as weakening the church, was also brought into the consideration, then the result began to take on a particularly sinister appearance, as the Reformed Church was another of the few important common bonds holding the provinces together. When the supposed romanizing tendencies of the remonstrants were added to the picture, then it began to make a paranoid form of sense: Oldenbarnevelt could be seen as having sold out to the Spanish, and his policies were designed to weaken the Republic so as to make its reconquest easier. It is difficult to accept that many contemporaries genuinely believed this sort of nonsense, but such scepticism is probably a profound misunderstanding. After all, matters of state were considered to be the province of the regents alone, and thus were a closed book to the mass of the Dutch population. The latter lacked any basis of reliable information against which they could measure rumour and misinformation. In such circumstances, Oldenbarnevelt's preference for an alliance with catholic France rather than protestant England, while making a great deal of sense to the informed—though apparently not to the vindictive Van Aerssen[11]—looked distinctly suspicious to the uninitiated.

After Maurits's coup in 1618 and the execution of Oldenbarnevelt, the synod of Dordt condemned the remonstrants' teachings and presented the 'orthodox' with a complete victory within the Reformed Church. Subsequently, the remonstrants suffered serious persecution from local and provincial authorities—the town governments of Holland having been purged of men of

---

[11] François van Aerssen had been Dutch ambassador to the French court before falling out with Oldenbarnevelt and being recalled in 1614. He subsequently became one of the Advocate's bitterest enemies.

remonstrant sympathies and packed by the (genuine or oppor-
tunist) orthodox—for a number of years, but by the 1630s they
were opening their own churches in the towns of Holland, despite
impassioned protests from the public church. This new church
never achieved a mass following, but could be influential as it contained a disproportionate number of wealthy and highly educated
members. There remained a sort of elective affinity between the
remonstrants and republicanism: not all republicans were remonstrants by any means, though they seem to have been sympathetic
in general to liberal protestantism, but remonstrants on the whole
tended to be republicans, if only because of the close link between
the stadhouders and Reformed orthodoxy. In general, while the
Remonstrant Church could not really be called the States-party at
prayer, nevertheless membership was closely associated in the
minds of contemporaries with a republican orientation. In the summer of 1672, the popular movements which swept through the
towns of Holland attacked those with remonstrant sympathies with
almost as much fervour as they did the followers of De Witt, and
not without reason.

The defeat of the remonstrants did not signal the end of disputes
within the Reformed Church, but such internal conflicts were never
again allowed to spill over into a major threat to civil peace let
alone the survival of the state. Such effective containment seems to
have been less a function of the nature of the disagreements themselves—to the protagonists they may well have seemed quite as
serious as the issues raised in the earlier conflict—than of the political context in which they occurred. The drive for a 'further
Reformation' (*nadere Reformatie*), the rigorism of such influential
church leaders as Jacob Voet (Voetius), the reaction against the
theological innovations of Cocceius,[12] were all potentially explosive. Indeed, the church in the second half of the century saw a
divide between voetians and cocceians which to some extent paral-
leled that between gomarists and arminians. Moreover, such disputes continued to be capable of having significant political
implications, as was the case in Zeeland.[13] Yet such matters were

---

[12] After establishing his reputation at the university of Franeker in Friesland,
Johannes Cocceius was a professor at Leiden from 1650 to 1669. His general theological approach was viewed with mistrust by the rigorists, and controversy finally
erupted over his approach to the question of sabbatarianism.

[13] Van der Bijl, *Idee en Interest*, ch. 7.

never again allowed to get out of hand; both regents and stadhouders—most notably Willem III—were primarily concerned to maintain control over the situation, and they succeeded.

The protestant nonconformists, the group the remonstrants effectively joined after their expulsion from the Reformed Church, were in an enviable situation for a dissenting group, certainly by seventeenth-century standards. Already by the first years of the century it was clearly established in practice that the efforts of the Reformed Church to restrict their freedom of worship had failed. The States of Holland together with the governments of the towns of the province had made it plain from at least the mid-1580s that they were averse in principle and certainly in practice to the persecution of fellow protestants. Such toleration, however, did not mean either complete equality for nonconformists or total freedom of religious belief and practice. In the political arena, nonconformists were, in principle, excluded from participation in government and public employment in general. This rule was only slowly and imperfectly applied, but by the middle of the seventeenth century at the latest nearly all politicians from town governments upwards were members of the Reformed Church, though some remonstrant sympathizers remained. How effectively nonconformists were excluded from other public offices is unclear, but even if there were exceptions to the Reformed monopoly of such positions, baptists and remonstrants were clearly at a disadvantage in the pursuit of public careers. On the other hand, for many if not all of the baptists—by far the majority among the nonconformists—this was of no real significance as they would have refused public office on principle anyway.[14]

A more dangerous restriction on religious freedom was the possibility of extreme views, or at least their expression, being persecuted by the civil authorities. There was no clear definition of what was unacceptable, and there were persistent disagreements between the Reformed Church and town governments in particular over what should or should not be permitted. In general, problems only arose over the public expression, by preaching or publication, of

---

[14] However, it is interesting to note the presence of baptists in local government at the village level in the late eighteenth century (G. J. Schutte, *Een Hollandse dorpssamenleving in de late achttiende eeuw: De banne Graft 1770–1810* (Franeker, 1989). Is this evidence of laxer standards among baptists at this time, or of a hitherto hidden degree of nonconformist involvement in local administration?

extreme views; opinions which were kept private were ignored by the magistrate. The ministers of the Reformed Church kept indefatigable watch for dangerous ideas, usually branded imprecisely but damningly as socinian, and rarely tired of calling on the civil authorities for action, but the latter seem to have held to one chief guideline only—the maintenance of public order. Mostly they found that peace and quiet was best served by turning a blind eye to the activities of religious extremists—but the magistrates were quite prepared to act when it suited their interests to do so.

Politically, it may well be that the nonconformists provided some sort of background support for the republicans, as they were dependent on regent control of public life to retain a tolerated space for themselves in Dutch society. The close association of orangism with orthodox calvinism, together with the unmistakable instinct for persecution shown by the leaders of the Reformed Church, made it seem likely that any major shift in the balance of power towards the stadhouder might well result sooner or later in a worsening of the situation of nonconformists. However, the periods in office of Frederik Hendrik and Willem III—in contrast to Maurits's support for orthodoxy—must have done much to reduce such anxieties, in so far as they were to any degree widespread. Although both had shown themselves willing to make concessions to the orthodox in order to minimize conflict, this was no more than most regents were prepared to do. In any case, as the dissenters were excluded from active and open participation in public life, it is not entirely clear how they could influence political developments in favour of the republicans. At the town level, their presence possibly meant that there was some measure of popular support for the regents to act as a counterweight to the influence of Reformed orthodoxy and orangism. Perhaps their greatest effect was less tangible, but far-reaching: their very existence, as a group whose toleration very evidently presented no threat to either state or society, provided a practical demonstration of the error of those political theories which equated religious dissent with rebellion, and thus initiated a fundamental shift in European perceptions of the nature of the political community.

The same could hardly be said for the catholics, who were generally regarded with distrust by non-catholics, a distrust which varied in intensity according to the international situation. Their position was not helped by the fact that the main enemies of the

Republic—the Spanish in the first half of the century and the French after 1672—were not just catholic powers but identified themselves as champions of aggressive and intolerant catholicism. The sheer size of the catholic group in the Republic was a problem: throughout the century, catholics constituted too large a proportion of the population even in Holland to be treated lightly. Like the protestant dissenters, the catholics had freedom of conscience, but unlike them not of worship. In practice, of course, the catholics did have churches—their hidden or *schuilkerken*—and did worship in them, but they were expected to be unobtrusive and were often constrained to pay protection money to local police officials.

One of the problems was that the catholics were regarded as a potential fifth-column by their protestant fellow-citizens, particularly during the Eighty Years War with Spain but to some extent again in the early years of the wars with the France of Louis XIV. Such suspicions do not seem to have led to persecution of catholic lay people, and even priests were largely left in peace. One reason for this relatively tolerant practice was the international situation of the Republic for most of the century, for if the Republic's chief enemies were catholic so were some of its most important allies— France against Spain, and then Austria against France. This diplomatic miscegenation meant that the political leaders of Holland were reluctant to risk the sort of problems with allies that clumsy handling of the catholics at home might create.

On the other hand, pressure from spokesmen of the Reformed Church continued throughout the century for measures to restrict and discourage the catholics. This pressure combined with the anti-catholic prejudices which marked even the most liberal of protestants in this period to ensure that *plakkaten* and other measures against catholic practices continued to be passed by the States and the various local authorities throughout the century. Enforcement, however, was an entirely different matter: while the civil authorities could be induced to inveigh against papist 'naughtinesses', in practice they did the minimum they could get away with.

The relatively tolerant attitude of the civil authorities within Holland towards protestant dissenters and catholics was most unusual for seventeenth-century Europe, and was much remarked upon by contemporaries—mostly, let it be said, with disapproval. The reasons for this almost anachronistically tolerant policy of the regents in Holland can be sought in their dominant ideology; their strongly Erasmian humanism, it is argued, fostered an extreme distaste on moral grounds of religious persecution in itself, unless public order was threatened. Yet it is not clear that the culture and education of the dominant social groups in Holland at this time was fundamentally different from that of the ruling groups of much of Western and Central Europe, where the persecution of religious dissidents remained not only a self-evident political necessity but also a moral imperative. The very different practice of the regents of Holland must be traced, not to the principles imbued by their education and culture, but to the peculiar religious situation they had to deal with. The same set of social and political attitudes, more or less, which elsewhere in seventeenth-century Europe could be used to justify religious exclusivism, led in Holland to a big step being taken in the direction of religious toleration on principle. The ideology of toleration in Holland was not a necessary consequence of the pervasive influence of Erasmian humanism, but the creation of the peculiar religious history of the Republic, which from its very foundation had to live with the reality of very widespread dissent from the official church. However, just as the circumstances faced by the regents demanded a certain degee of toleration, so they also imposed distinct limitations on the extent of that toleration.

In this context, it is possibly of relevance that Holland also ceased the persecution of suspected witches at the very beginning of the seventeenth century, when the European witch-craze still had a considerable and bloody history ahead of it. A woman was condemned to death for witchcraft in Gorinchem in 1608, but this sentence was probably commuted on appeal. Subsequently, the courts of the province practically ceased to proceed with cases of alleged witchcraft; in the seventeenth century they were much more likely to be dealing with cases of slander against those who made such accusations.[15] The reasons for deviation from the common European pattern are far from clear as yet, but one or two points are worthy of comment. First, the attitude of the Reformed Church was more cautious than might have been expected: while church

---

[15] H. de Waardt, 'Vervolging of verweer: Mogelijke procedures na een beschuldiging van toverij in het gewest Holland voor het jaar 1800', in M. Gijswijt Hofstra and W. Frijhoff (eds.), *Nederland betoverd: Toverij en hekserij van de veertiende tot in de twintigste eeuw* (Amsterdam, 1987).

councils made public calls for firmer action against witchcraft, a recent study of the disciplinary activities of the Amsterdam consistory suggests that the chief concerns were to admonish and correct rather than to punish—there appears to have been little or no desire to start burning people for the faith.[16] Secondly, the situation with regard to witchcraft prosecutions in this century varied enormously from province to province throughout the Republic, with Zeeland almost completely free from such cases, while elsewhere they continued into the second half of the century.[17] What is clear is that witchcraft beliefs and accusations continued in Holland as elsewhere, but that in the seventeenth century the courts were no longer willing to act in this area—except to punish slander.

In the religious history of Holland at this time, the curious position of the Reformed Church was of vital importance. On the one hand it was the official church of province and state and an important component of Dutch national identity—a fragile thing early in the century, though rather more robust later—yet its hold on the loyalty of the population of Holland, let alone of the Republic as a whole, was uncertain. Especially in the early decades of the century, the Reformed community in Holland displayed the characteristics of an embattled minority rather than those of a dominant church. In a century when established churches all too often displayed paranoid fears of minorities—or even conjured up enemies to fear, such as witches—the Reformed Church had good reason for its own paranoia: it was indeed threatened by the rival claims of catholics and dissident protestants. If the latter produced the greatest ideological challenge to the hegemony of Reformed orthodoxy, the former were the bigger practical problem and seemed to pose the more serious threat.

In these circumstances, even if the regents of Holland had been inclined to extend full toleration to catholics they would probably have been unable to do so. The Reformed Church had sufficient influence, especially within the upper reaches of Dutch society, to prevent any open toleration of catholicism. The regents could minimize persecution as long as the whole panoply of legal discrimina-

---

[16] H. Roodenburg, '"Een soort van duivelsche afgoderije": De bestrijding van toverij door de gereformeerde kerkeraad te Amsterdam, 1580–1700', in Gijswijt-Hofstra and Frijhoff (eds.), *Nederland betoverd*.

[17] Gijswijt-Hofstra and Frijhoff (eds.), *Nederland betoverd*.

tion was kept in place. A laudable hypocrisy was the necessary cover for what was in practice a moderately lenient policy. Quite apart from the pressure of the Reformed Church as an institution, it must be remembered that the regents themselves were members of the church, and most of them probably shared the view that the Catholic Church was a force for evil in human affairs, and also that they regarded that church—quite rightly—as itself inherently intolerant at this time, and thus likely to become a threat to the relative toleration of the Dutch system if it were allowed to gain too much influence. The regents were prepared to extent a limited toleration to catholics if only because the alternative—a serious attempt to root them out—was both impracticable and would have been unacceptably disruptive in social and economic terms. The regents could not extirpate catholicism, but neither could they tolerate it fully; their ambivalent position on this vital matter demonstrates clearly the practical and ideological limitations under which they laboured.

The problems stemming from the rise of the remonstrants dramatically illustrated the very real restrictions on the extent to which the civil authorities could regard religious matters as politically neutral. The response of the orthodox—within the church in Holland and the other provinces, and even among the regents of Holland themselves—showed that the power of those who believed that the integrity of the Reformed Church was essential for the preservation of the Dutch state was too great to be ignored or repressed. As long as the remonstrants seemed a threat to the survival of the church, as defined by the orthodox, from inside, their suppression appeared necessary for the re-establishment of political unity within Holland as much as in the Republic as a whole. However, when they proved ready to accept their expulsion from the public church and set themselves up as a separate body, they too could be more or less smoothly assimilated into the Dutch system.

Equally, the religious heterogeneity of Holland made a considerable degree of toleration a political imperative as well. If the attitude of the protestants, and especially of the Reformed Church, made full toleration of the catholics impossible, so their numbers made effective suppression politically impracticable. Similarly, although the protestant dissenters were a numerically less formidable group, any real attempt to persecute them (apart from a

handful of radicals) would have very quickly run up against powerful resistance and obstruction at all levels of society in Holland.
Most notably, very few regents in the province showed much
enthusiasm for acting against fellow protestants, if their presence
was no threat to public order. Put rather simplistically, the Revolt
had not been fought in order to carry on burning peaceful mennonites. In this case a principled protestant eirenicism reinforced
practical considerations to ensure a wide degree of toleration in
practice.

In the case of the catholics, it would seem that practical considerations were more important: the decentralized Dutch state simply
did not have the power to take on such a large minority of the
population. Even in Holland, where the catholic problem was less
acute, certainly in the towns, than in a number of the other
provinces, from the point of view of the regents the game was not
worth the candle. Clearly, up to the peace with Spain in 1648, the
social and economic disruption that would have attended any
attempt to root out catholicism was too great a risk, and even
after this point there seemed little to be gained from alienating a
section of the population which had demonstrated its political loyalty during the war. Although a fundamental hostility towards the
Catholic Church could be presumed among the regents—in a way
that it could not with regard to protestant dissenters—the will to
take risks in a potentially explosive situation could not. The civil
authorities lacked the coercive power to be sure of maintaining
control of the situation if they attacked the catholics, and they certainly had no intention of taking the risk.[18]

The religious situation in Holland had a complex effect on the
politics of the province because of the combination of considerable
religious diversity with the clearly felt need to maintain a privileged public church for reasons of political necessity as much as to
ensure the proper worship of God. Although catholics and protestant dissenters were tolerated to a significant extent, partly from
expediency and partly from principle, it was nevertheless felt that a
common religion was needed to hold the political community
together. Lack of religious uniformity fostered the beginnings of a
secularized conception of politics in Holland, but its progress
remained uncertain and ambivalent even at the end of the seven-

---

[18] Van Deursen, *Het kopergeld*, iv. 81.

teenth century. Moreover, it is evident that the relationship of religion to politics cannot be properly understood if the situation in
Holland is seen only in isolation: one of the reasons why the
Reformed Church had to retain its role as a symbol of political
unity was its importance in the politics of the Republic as a whole,
as will be argued in Part 3.

III

Holland and the Politics
of the Dutch Republic

The central government of the Dutch state was limited in both size and power, but it held the Republic together for over two centuries. One of the main arguments of this Part is that only such a severely limited set of central institutions could have served this purpose: any attempt to impose stronger leadership on the 'united' provinces would have broken the Union apart. Two apparently contradictory principles appear to have been basic to the constitution of the new state which emerged from the Revolt: provincial sovereignty on the one hand, and the union between the provinces on the other. Perhaps, however, these two ideas are only incompatible from the perspective of essentially modern perceptions of the absolute and indivisible nature of sovereignty, which are not necessarily applicable to the political institutions of the Dutch state. There is a strong case for arguing that discussion of the Dutch political system in terms of sovereignty can be seriously misleading, and that other concepts are more appropriate.

How the relationship between province and Generality was to work had been more or less firmly established by the end of the sixteenth century, before the new theories concerning the nature of the state (which can be conveniently associated with Bodin) had had time to effect the political perceptions of more than a small minority of theorists. So, rather than being described in terms of modern theories of the state, the Dutch Republic is perhaps better understood in the light of older conceptions which regarded the political community as a collection of individuals and groups, each with their proper rights and duties, and with all of these rights having equal political and moral weight—the prerogatives of a king were of the same nature as the meagre rights of a peasant, the former simply had far more of them. In such a polity the coexistence of a high degree of provincial autonomy with an ill-defined but crucial authority for the central institutions of the state was not seen as especially anomalous; both the province and the Generality had rights or privileges, and both these sets of rights had precisely the same status in law and morality. To an important extent, the Revolt had been fought to preserve and promote just such an interpretation of the proper nature of politics in the Netherlands, so a central authority which could override the rights and privileges of the provinces would have been a contradiction of one of its basic aims: the protection and preservation of the privileges. While it has to be admitted that the lack of a clearly defined and generally accepted central and final authority in the Dutch Republic could and did prove a problem on occasion in the seventeenth century, it can be argued that such difficulties were no more, and perhaps less, serious than those caused in other countries in this period by the presence of such a theoretically absolute sovereign. The existence of an undisputed sovereign could be as troublesome as its absence, despite what contemporary wisdom, with its overwhelming fear of the breakdown of order, might have said on the subject.

1. The States General and the Generality

The States General had direct control, formally at least, of certain important matters: foreign relations, the armed forces, and the administration of the Generality lands.[1] They sent out ambassadors and received the representatives of foreign powers; foreign policy and particularly matters of peace and war were decided in this assembly. Similarly, they were ultimately responsible for the direction and financing of the armed forces. The powers of the States General were probably somewhat greater in practice than in theory; the precise constitutional position was never absolutely clear and what was possible in practice seems to have varied considerably from time to time.

The States General consisted of the delegations from seven provinces: Gelderland, Zeeland, Utrecht, Overijssel, Friesland, and Groningen as well as Holland. Drente, although it was regarded as an autonomous province, was not allowed membership of the States, basically because it was so poor and small that the other provinces were not willing to give it equal representation, and there was no middle ground between that and no representation at all. Similarly, the Generality lands were excluded, despite persistent efforts to gain admission, especially from the towns of that part of Brabant controlled by the Republic.[2] The assembly was in permanent session, unlike the provincial states, which only convened occasionally (Holland more often than the others), and met in The Hague, physically close to both the meeting-place of the States of Holland and the quarters of the stadhouder of this province. The meeting-place of the States General was in great part the result of

---

[1] These were the areas of Flanders, Brabant, and Limburg which were part of the Republic, but had no representation in the States General. Largely catholic, they were ruled in effect as conquered territories by the Generality, unlike Drente, which was also not represented in the States General but had a more or less fully autonomous provincial government.

[2] M. P. Christ, *De Brabantsche Saeck: Het vergeefse streven naar een gewestelijke status voor Staats-Brabant 1585–1675* (Tilburg, 1984).

historical accident—for the first years of the Republic's existence no place outside Holland (or Zeeland) was safe from the Spanish armies—but it was also wholly appropriate to the peculiar relationship that both the States of Holland and the princes of Orange had with it.

Voting in the assembly of the States General was, of course, by province not by head, with each having a single vote; the provinces maintained delegations of varying sizes, chosen by methods peculiar to each. Holland's delegation, for example, normally had a representative from the nobility as well as delegates from the towns and always included the *raadpensionaris*. The presidency of the assembly changed every week, being held by a representative of each province in turn. The delegates of the provinces other than Holland were often long-serving, were relatively far-removed from their principals, and were also less easy for their formal political superiors to keep under strict control because of the infrequency with which their provincial states met. In contrast, the Holland delegation could be easily and tightly controlled, as the States of Holland not only met nearby, but were also far more frequently in session. In principle, the delegations were strictly bound by their instructions and had to refer new matters or modifications of old proposals back to their principals before they could give any valid opinion. For obvious reasons, this worked in practice as well as theory for the delegation from Holland, but equally obviously it was not so easy to carry out for some of the other delegations. For Friesland, but perhaps particularly for Gelderland and Overijssel, whose internal constitutions were especially unwieldy, it was difficult for the states to keep any effective control over their delegations, and they became vulnerable to influence in The Hague, most notably from the princes of Orange, in the course of the seventeenth century. Under Frederik Hendrik first, and later under both Willem II and *a fortiori* Willem III, this ability of the princes to influence very strongly, to say the least, the votes of the land provinces in the States General became a significant characteristic of the workings of the political system.

It has been remarked that the States General was more a conference of ambassadors from separate countries than a parliament).[3] In so far as there was a constitution, it was the Union of Utrecht

³ Fruin, *Staatsinstellingen*, 179.

of 1579, but this had much more the character of an offensive and defensive alliance for the prosecution of the war with Spain than that of the founding charter of a new state. It was clear that in principle unanimity was necessary in all important matters, but what exactly these matters were was a source of frequent dispute. In practice, this requirement of unanimity was disregarded from time to time when necessity drove. In 1618, Holland's veto in the States General was evaded to provide Maurits with an appearance of legal justification for his intervention to resolve the conflicts in the Republic—and particularly in Holland. Similarly, Willem II's actions in 1650, even in so far as they were warranted by the terms of his commission from the States General, were strictly illegal as the resolution had been passed despite the opposition of Holland's delegation. In the first instance, legitimacy was provided by success, while in the second Willem's failure exposed the all-too-uncertain constitutional basis for his actions. The requirement of unanimity was not only disregarded in order to act against Holland: on other occasions it was also bypassed in order to circumvent the opposition of one or more of the weaker provinces to a policy being driven on by Holland. The Treaty of Münster was signed, for example, despite the abstention of the delegate from Utrecht, and was ratified by the States General despite the refusal of Zeeland to assent to the treaty.

What the precise extent and nature of the States General's powers were is not something that can be answered properly in formal terms: what mattered was what it could effectively do in given circumstances—which is perhaps the only realistic test of political power. Certainly, if the principle of provincial sovereignty is accepted, then its independent power was nil; according to any strict interpretation of this constitutional position, the States General was simply the arena where equal and independent allies reached mutually acceptable decisions. From this perspective, the States General had no power to coerce, or in any way interfere in the internal affairs of, the sovereign provinces. However, this is an area where the use of the concept of sovereignty is misleading, and suggests a fundamental opposition between province and Generality that sheds little light on the practical politics of the seventeenth century. Although the habitually legalistic accounts of contemporaries stressed the inalienability of the rights and privileges of the provinces in a way which seems to make the absolute autonomy of these provinces clear, the matter is not so unambiguous if we look at the way in which things worked, and at the assumptions which equally clearly underlay this practice. First, from the legal point of view, there was an important hangover from the Habsburg period. Just as the stadhouders of the provinces were able to enjoy certain quasi-sovereign powers, which were in strict terms inconsistent with their position as appointed officials of the provincial states, so the central institutions of the Dutch Republic benefited from the practical precedents set before independence. It is important to remember that the fiction was always maintained that the political system was being preserved just as it always had been, except that a ruler who had attempted to subvert the system had been removed—thus, pre-Revolt precedents retained their force afterwards. However, this attitude of mind was not particularly beneficial to the States General, which had never played a directing role in government before the Revolt: rather, it tended to give an ill-defined yet significant access of authority to the princes of Orange and institutions such as the Council of State.

More important as far as the States General was concerned was the very general recognition that the Union was in fact something more than a mere alliance of fully independent powers. Whatever the more formalist commentators might say, there was no realistic dissent from the proposition that the Dutch Republic constituted a separate polity of some sort, and that the principle of Union in some sense overrode that of provincial autonomy. If this statement seems vague, it reflects the fact that this central question was never precisely resolved because it was in the provinces' interest to assert both the indissolubility of the Union and the autonomy of its members at the same time. The practical problems which this inconsistency at the centre of the political system entailed could only be dealt with in practice, they could not be resolved theoretically— certainly not in terms of sovereignty. The general recognition of the primacy of the Union led to the assertion when necessary of sovereign powers for the States General and other central institutions. The most spectacular example of this was, of course, the arrest and trial of Oldenbarnevelt and his associates in 1618–19. According to any strict interpretation of the principle of provincial sovereignty, both the arrests and the trials were totally illegal. Oldenbarnevelt, to take the most important case, was an official of the States of Holland, was subject only to the laws and jurisdiction of that province, and all his acts as Advocate had been meticulously covered by acts of indemnity passed by the States. Yet he was arrested by Maurits, apparently acting on the instructions of the States General rather than as stadhouder of Holland, and was tried and condemned by a special court set up by the States General for the purpose. Note that it had to be an *ad hoc* court, for there was no central court of justice for the Republic as a whole, either before or after this trial. However, it is not the patent illegality of this arrest and trial which is most striking, but rather that it worked. For a brief period, and for a specific purpose, the States General was able to exercise powers that were unambiguously sovereign, but as soon as the emergency was over, the principle of provincial sovereignty was once again able to assert itself in the political practice of the Republic.

A similar attempt to assert the primacy of the Union over the autonomy of the provinces was made by Willem II in 1650 at the expense of Holland. In this case the immediate result was a standoff, with a compromise being reached on the practical issue of the size of the army, but with Holland's autonomy essentially unbroken. However, the extent to which this attempted *coup* by the prince had stirred up constitutional uncertainties is revealed by Holland's decision to call the *Grote Vergadering* (see Chapter 6 below) as soon as Willem died. The purpose was essentially one of reassurance: Holland was in effect declaring that its defence of its own autonomy was compatible with continued and complete loyalty to the Union. The union between the provinces was in practice much stronger than strict theory would suggest; but the cost of combining the preservation of the Union and the autonomy of the provinces was a prevailing uncertainty as to just where final authority lay at any given time in the Dutch Republic.

The Council of State (*Raad van State*) can be seen either as the prime example of the failure of the Dutch Republic to develop viable organs of central government, thus as a poignant lost opportunity for a truly national body free from provincial egoism, or on the contrary as a triumph of pragmatism, of the ability of the political system of the Republic to make good use of the least promising materials. In either case, it is incontestable that the Council ended up as something very different from anything that had been planned or intended.

The Council can be seen as deriving ultimately from the body of the same name in the Habsburg system after the reorganization of 1530,[4] a body of nobles and senior jurists to advise the governor-general of the Netherlands on overall policy. More immediately, it derived from the successive councils appointed after the Revolt to advise Willem of Orange, and from the council set up after the prince's death in 1584 to assume responsibility for the government of the country. Most closely, however, it stemmed from the council through which Leicester attempted to govern the Netherlands, and one of its early weaknesses comes from this unfortunate period (1585–8). From this time until 1627, the Council contained one or more foreign members, originally the commander of the English troops in the Netherlands, the English ambassador, and one other. Only after the departure of Dudley Carleton, the English ambassador, in that year did the Council become a totally Dutch body. This foreign presence in itself might be considered to have prevented the Council from becoming the central governing body in the Republic which it was clearly intended to be, at least in 1584. However, it surely makes rather more sense to say that the English presence was allowed to continue for so long only because the Council had been largely bypassed, for other reasons, as a major force in the running of national affairs.

In the seventeenth century, the membership of the Council (apart from the English intrusion) consisted of the stadhouders (i.e. including the stadhouder of Friesland), and twelve representatives of the provinces—three from Holland, two from Zeeland, Friesland, and Gelderland (reduced for the last named to one from 1674), and one each from Utrecht, Overijssel, and Groningen (increased for the last to two from 1674)—and voting was by head rather than by province. Thus, although Holland had a slightly greater representation than any other province, this was far from sufficient to ensure its dominance on the Council, and it is here that the reason for the Council's failure to become the executive body of the Dutch government must be sought. The States General, with its possibility of a veto for Holland in important matters, was a much more effective vehicle for the promotion and protection of that province's interests than the Council could ever

---

[4] M. Baelde, *De collaterale raden onder Karel V en Filips II (1531–1578)* (Brussels, 1965).

be. So the body which had been intended to govern the Republic, checked only by the power of the States General, particularly in financial matters, became in practice an administrative organ of the central States, reduced to supervising certain areas of its responsibilities, while the States General itself moved to the centre of the stage as the real government of the country.

In effect, the Council of State in the seventeenth century had responsibility for the army and its finances. It drew up the annual military budget (*staat van oorlog*), and in general administered the land forces. It also had important administrative functions with regard to the Generality lands, in particular for the collection of taxes, and exercised certain judicial functions chiefly concerning the Generality and its functionaries. Less obviously, but in some ways perhaps almost as important, the Council became a pool of suitable men for employment by the state for a wide variety of *ad hoc* commissions.[5] Although by the very nature of things there were bound to be conflicts of competence and jurisdiction between the Council and the States General, these should probably not be taken too seriously. Since many of the provincial representatives on the Council would themselves have served for a period as delegates to the States General before their appointment, and all of them came from the same political élites which controlled the provincial estates and their delegations to the States General, the members of the Council of State cannot be seen as representing a separate constituency or interest. In the main the system worked well, because the States General was a more suitable body for the performance of the central executive functions originally mapped out for the Council of State, while the latter was found a useful and necessary role, but one which underlined its subordinate position. Thus the existence of the Council did not in fact further complicate the issue as to who really ran the country, which was just as well considering the already competing theoretical claims of the States General and the provincial states.

The *Generaliteits-Rekenkamer* (exchequer of the Generality) was set up in 1602, not to collect revenues but to provide a general accounting organ to supervise receipts and expenditure relating to

[5] A. Th. van Deursen, 'De Raad van State en de Generaliteit, 1590–1606', *Bijdragen voor de Geschiedenis der Nederlanden*, 19 (1964).

the affairs of the central government. It was made up of two representatives from each province, and was able to win a reputation
for effectiveness and honesty. This was just as well, as the lack of
a central treasury highlighted the need for an institution to oversee
the financial affairs of the state. There were two chief posts in the
financial sector of the Generality: the *thesaurier-generaal* (treasurer-
general) and the *ontvanger-generaal* (receiver-general). The former
had a seat in the Council of State, and general responsibility for
the expenditure of the central government; the latter supervised the
receipts and actually handled the money—one of the reasons why
the post could be particularly rewarding.[6]

The admiralties were a curious mixture of the central and the
provincial: formally they were Generality institutions but in practice they were controlled at the provincial, and in Holland even at
the sub-provincial, level. In a striking demonstration of the decen-
tralizing tendencies of the Republic, even in a matter as important
as the navy was for the Dutch—and in notably sharp contrast to
the army—there were five admiralties: three in Holland (for the
Maas in Rotterdam; in Amsterdam; and for the Northern Quarter
in Hoorn and Enkhuizen alternatively), and one each in Zeeland
and Friesland. They were headed by boards of councillors (*raden*),
appointed not only by the province in which they were situated,
but also by other provinces. They were responsible for the administration of their section of the fleet, and the two main admiralties
(at Amsterdam and Rotterdam) had large-scale facilities for the
building and repair of ships. The navy was commanded by the
admiral-general (usually the prince of Orange) and the senior
officers were appointed by the States General, emphasizing its formal control, but on the recommendation of the local admiralties.
These latter also had responsibility in fixed areas of the country for
the collection of the convoys and licences (originally taxes to pay
for the cost of convoying merchant ships, and payments for
licences to trade with the enemy), by the seventeenth century more
or less import and export duties for the support of the navy. This,
in effect, localized control, together with the large amounts of
money and the great number of jobs at their disposal, led to the
admiralties being the scene of widespread corrupt practices, from
straightforward peculation to evasion of the convoys and licences

[6] See e.g. De Muinck, *Een regentenhuishouding.*

to an unknown degree. Quite how serious this corruption was is impossible to say, but a number of scandalous cases in the course of the seventeenth century give the impression that they were exceptional only in being exposed, and that the general level of behaviour was not much better. Certainly, appointment as a member of one of these boards was highly sought after, notably by the regents of the voting towns of Holland, and was not a public service in which people expected to make a loss.

Perhaps the great chartered trading companies, the East and West India Companies, should be included as Generality institutions, as they received their charters from the States General and acted outside Europe very much as an arm of the Dutch state. On the other hand, both were divided into local chambers which had a considerable degree of autonomy, and even the central boards of direction of each—the *Heeren XVII* and the *Heeren XIX*—were based in Amsterdam and acted much more like an institution of the province of Holland than of the Generality.

A post with considerable political potential, though not always realized, was that of *griffier* to the States General, whose formal relationship to this body was somewhat analogous to that of the *raadpensionaris* to the States of Holland. He attended the meetings of the States General as secretary, and handled its correspondence—this, plus his membership of the relevant committee, gave him a potentially important role in foreign policy. In practice, one of the best-developed aspects of this particular office appears to have been the opportunities it gave for both official and unofficial monetary gain. The appointment was in principle for life.

In general, what is perhaps most striking about the central governing and bureaucratic institutions of the Dutch Republic is that there were not many of them. In a period of seemingly inexorable bureaucratic growth in the other major states of Europe, the central government apparatus of the Republic was by comparison tiny. That in these circumstances it was nevertheless able to do its job remarkably well is partly a compliment to the efficiency of these bodies, but largely reminds us that the real weight of government and administration lay elsewhere. It would be misleading to suggest that the weight of government in the Dutch Republic was light—it is just that it did not press down from the Generality. The inhabitants of the Dutch Republic were heavily taxed and much governed, but the weight of both came at provincial level, or even at the level of the town or rural district. Perhaps it would be best to regard the central institutions of the Dutch state as having not so much a governing as a co-ordinating function.

2. The Not-So-United Provinces

The nearest thing the Dutch had to a constitution or founding charter was the Union of Utrecht, and whatever may have been read into this document by later politicians and jurists, it was in origin and intention an alliance to improve the prosecution of the war against Spain. This was one of the reasons why the signing of the Truce in 1609 caused so much apprehension: many seem to have feared that once the war was ended the alliance would also collapse and with it the Union. What else, it was asked, held the provinces together other than the necessity of union for mutual defence? In retrospect, this fear can too easily be dismissed as chimerical; the advantage of hindsight can make it difficult to understand the fears of contemporaries, at various times during the century, of the possible break-up of the Republic. Perhaps even more importantly, if we take for granted the survival of the Union and the development of the allied provinces into something at least resembling a nation-state, then we can fail to see the importance of asking what it was that held the Union together, and why contemporary fears of political disintegration during the Truce and perhaps also in 1650–1 were not realized.

For there was no obvious or natural unity between the seven (or eight, with Drente) provinces, never mind between them and the Generality lands. The provinces commonly referred to each other in official documents and elsewhere as the *bondgenoten* (allies), and this terminology, together with the stress on the importance of the preservation of provincial autonomy, can be taken as a symbol of the rather limited sense of common identity possessed by the inhabitants of the Republic, at least at first. The various provinces did not have a history of living in the same political community; they had only even shared the same ruler for about a quarter of a century from the Habsburg take-over of Gelderland in 1543 to the Revolt, and their traditions were of mutual conflict rather than of co-operation. Only the experience of having to work together during the last decades of the sixteenth and the whole of the seventeenth century began to create a strong sense of Dutch unity.

Economically, too, it is not clear that the interests of the various provinces coincided even approximately; and even where language and culture were concerned, unity was not entirely self-evident.

Indeed, with regard to economic and social development and structure there were very sharp differences between Holland and the rest. The starkness of this opposition must be modified by admitting that Zeeland and Friesland to some extent shared in the economic development of the leading province, but not so much as to preclude deep jealousies, even perhaps hostility, on the part of the permanently economically outgunned Zeeland. The land provinces—Gelderland, Overijssel, and Utrecht—and even Groningen provide a sharp contrast to the dynamism, innovation, and wealth of Holland.

Holland was the locus of the Dutch economic miracle: Zeeland and Friesland were far behind, and the rest not even placed. This single province contained by around 1680 over 40 per cent of the population of the Republic, and probably more than half of its wealth. The growth of the towns of the province was a measure of this economic development: by the middle of the seventeenth century, Holland was the most highly urbanized area in Europe, and it was the trade and manufactures of the towns which were the most obvious forms of the province's economic success. However, it must not be forgotten that an equally important transformation had taken place in the countryside of Holland, producing a modernized, market-oriented agricultural sector closely integrated with the urban economy.[1] Indeed, it may well be that the changes in the farming economy were even more fundamental than those in the towns—where the late sixteenth- and seventeenth-century developments were an intensification of trading and manufacturing patterns already well established in the late Middle Ages—and that without them the boom in the other areas of the economy could not have taken place, or at least not to the same extent. Already by the first years of the seventeenth century, Holland had become the most economically advanced region in Europe, where the forces of commercial capitalism dominated both town and countryside as nowhere else, and its trade and manufactures continued to boom for much of the rest of the century, joined by an increasingly important capital market. This commercial economy found both its

[1] J. de Vries, *The Dutch Rural Economy in the Golden Age 1500–1700* (New Haven, Conn., 1974).

raw materials and markets very largely outside the boundaries of the Republic, so its interests and orientation were international.

The social face of this economic transformation was the growth of the broader bourgeoisie—merchants, petty traders, shopkeeper-traders, skilled artisans, together with the lawyers, doctors, notaries, teachers, and the like of the service sector—in the towns, and the establishment of the independent capitalist farmer with supporting services in the countryside. The class which lost out was the nobility: it may have retained much of its social prestige, but whatever economic power it had enjoyed in the past was now definitively over. The dominant force in the agricultural sector was the free-holding farmer, not the landlord, noble or otherwise. On the other hand, although the expansion in the size of the bourgeoisie, and especially of its richer elements, increased competition for places in the urban oligarchies, the dominance of the regent élite as the virtual representatives of the bourgeoisie as a whole went very largely unchallenged. Economic growth and change strengthened the position of the regents, but undermined that of the nobility of the province.

The economic growth characteristic of Holland in the sixteenth and seventeenth centuries was shared to some extent by Zeeland, Friesland,[2] and perhaps Utrecht and the town of Groningen. The situation in outline is most clear in Zeeland (though the details of its economic development are somewhat obscure), where the domination of the towns and the concentration on trade and industry, backed by a modern and commercialized agriculture, provide a weak version of Holland's experience. For, by the first decades of the seventeenth century it was becoming clear that the Zeeland towns could not compete effectively with those of Holland, and for much of the century this province revealed distinctly different economic interests to those of its dominant neighbour. It seems to be in part at least because of this relative economic weakness that Zeeland was keener on the predatory opportunities, especially privateering of various sorts, provided by the war with Spain and thus less enthusiastic for both the truce in 1609 and the peace in 1648, and much less confident of its ability to benefit from the end of hostilities and an open market than was Holland. Whether its opposition to the Truce and later to the Treaty of Münster was a

[2] J. A. Faber, *Drie eeuwen Friesland: Economische en sociale ontwikkelingen van 1500 tot 1800* (Wageningen, 1972).

true reflection of the economic interests of the province as a whole, or rather stemmed from the heavy involvement of the province's political élite in privateering and the WIC, is far from clear. In either case, however, it is a sign of a less well-developed and far less self-confident economy than Holland's.

In Friesland, the situation seems to have been more complicated, but the province clearly participated to a significant extent in the economic development exemplified by Holland. In agriculture, it is included by De Vries as part of the modernizing, market-oriented western region of the Republic,[3] while the towns, although they did not boom to the same extent as in Holland, were able to benefit considerably by providing shipping and other services to the leading economy. Socially, these developments led to a strengthening of the independent farming sector in the countryside and the middling groups in the towns, but probably to a lesser extent than in Holland. What there was of a nobility was certainly not strengthened by these economic changes, but the beneficiaries—in the countryside as in the towns—were a peculiarly Frisian oligarchy, with some of the characteristics of a nobility married to some of those of the urban regents. In any case, Friesland's economy was not so much a rival to Holland's as linked into its economic structures, and thus at least to some extent sharing its interests.

Although it would be an over-simplification to see the rest of the Republic—Overijssel, Gelderland, the countryside of Utrecht and Groningen, Drente—as totally traditional and untouched by the economic changes which were taking place in the more advanced areas in this period, nevertheless the contrast between these two broad regions is great. In this eastern or inland area of the Republic the balance, for example, between town and countryside remained much as it had been in the early sixteenth century. Indeed, not only did the towns in this region fail to emulate the dynamic expansion of those in the west, some of them—specifically the former Hansa towns, such as Deventer and Zutphen—declined in this period, certainly as centres of more than local significance. The demography of this region shows a slow but steady growth, entirely lacking the explosive increase of Holland, and the population of the towns grew, if at all, only enough to keep up with the

---

[3] De Vries, *Dutch Rural Economy*, pp. xiv, 121–7.

expansion within the rural sector. In particular, the economies of these provinces were much more in-turned, much less linked into international trade than those of the more developed regions. In brief, these provinces were much less dependent on trade and manufactures than Holland, and their reliance on imports of raw materials and semi-finished goods and on exports to foreign markets was similarly much less. Their agriculture was relatively more important, but also less capitalist and market-oriented. The smallholding peasant, often poor and rather more subsistence- than market-oriented, in an economy which found it difficult to deal with population growth except by morcellization of landholdings, was the basis of a very different rural society than that of Holland. In these circumstances it is hardly surprising that the nobility maintained its economic position far better than in the west. To put it briefly, while Holland had entered decisively into an entirely new phase in European economic and social history, the land provinces remained a part of that older world from which the more advanced areas had emerged.[4]

However, the very existence of Holland with its large urban markets for food and other agricultural products could not help but have a powerful effect on these regions. Although the influence of Holland could not of itself modernize the economies of the land provinces, it changed them in significant ways. Its uncomfortable proximity, providing both opportunities and problems for the agriculture of the poorer areas, was a major and not always welcome element in the lives of both urban and rural people in the seventeenth century.[5]

These economic differences between the various provinces which made up the Dutch Republic, and in particular the contrast between Holland and the rest, had inevitable and important effects on the politics of the Union. Partly this was because such economic disparities led to rather different emphases in foreign policy, but also because the very different social structures of the provinces led to quite distinctive political systems. In particular, whereas the changes during the sixteenth and early seventeenth centuries had enabled the urban oligarchies to establish an almost unchallenged

---

[4] See esp. B. H. Slicher van Bath, *Samenleving onder spanning* (Assen, 1957) for Overijssel.

[5] See J. Bieleman, *Boeren op het Drentse zand 1600–1910* (Wageningen, 1987), 364–6.

control of the politics of Holland (and Zeeland), elsewhere the
nobility remained a much more powerful element in the power
structure, with important consequences for policy formation and
execution. When attempting to understand inter-provincial tensions
in the seventeenth-century Republic, it is important to remember
that not only were the economic interests of the land provinces
very different from those of Holland, but that the social groups
controlling the politics of the land provinces were also significantly
different from the Holland regents.

The political power of the towns is perhaps a useful indicator of
such differences. Outside Holland, only Zeeland was similarly
dominated by its towns (and even here two of these were strongly
influenced by the prince of Orange as lord of Vlissingen and marquis of Veere): in the rest of the Republic the influence of the
towns was effectively matched, and sometimes overshadowed, by
that of the nobility. In Gelderland, the political system carefully
balanced the power of the nobility and of the towns, and the capi-
tals of each of the three quarters into which the province was
divided were favoured above the lesser towns. In practice, the
influence of the nobility as a whole was greater than this might
suggest, as nobles could, and did, take an important part in the
governing bodies of the towns, and their social pull also gained
them more than equal representation in the central institutions of
the province. Similarly, in Overijssel the influence of the three
major towns—Deventer, Zwolle, and Kampen—was balanced by
that of the nobility. In the province of Utrecht, the balance
between the two estates—the nobility, and the town of Utrecht
together with the lesser towns—was held by the peculiar institution
of the 'elected', chosen from the members of the secularized chap-
ters of the five chief churches of the provincial capital. The nobility
were well represented among these latter. With regard to the
towns, there was little of the formal equality so characteristic of
Holland: Utrecht was dominant, while Amersfoort was as powerful
as the rest of the towns taken together. The States of Groningen
were composed of two members, the town Groningen and the
Ommelanden (literally, the land around), and these two con-
stituents tended to act as separate provinces rather than as a true
unity. The town government represented Groningen in the provincial States, while the representatives of the Ommelanden were not
exclusively noble. Indeed, it was possible for the town to

strengthen its position in the province as a whole through the purchase by its citizens of land in the Ommelanden, which gave them
political influence.[6]

The political system in Friesland was very different, both from
that of Holland and from those of the land provinces, but,
although emerging from a sort of peasant self-rule, proved just as
susceptible to the growth of the influence of a closed oligarchy as
the rest of the Republic. The States consisted of four 'quarters': the
three rural quarters proper (Oostergo, Westergo, and Zevenwolden) and the eleven towns. The representation of the rural
quarters involved a surprisingly large number of voters electing delegates, half of whom were supposed to be noble. The more powerful landowners, noble and non-noble, used a fertile and complex
combination of bribery and other electoral malpractices to
influence elections. A peculiarity of the Frisian system was that the
votes in the countryside were attached to pieces of property rather
than persons, and in the course of the seventeenth century the ruling groups in the province adopted a policy of systematically buying up these vote-endowing properties, thus strengthening their
position at the expense of the remnants of peasant autonomy.[7] It is
clear that in this system the nobles and other large landowners had
great influence, but the towns seem to have been more powerful
than their formal position in the States would suggest, and it is
also open to doubt whether corrupt practices were ever able to
eradicate the need for the representatives of the rural areas to bear
in mind the opinions of their electors.

Out of this complex of varied but not totally dissimilar political
systems, a few points emerge with reasonable clarity. First, the
power of the nobility, so attenuated in Holland, was still considerable in a majority of provinces, certainly in Gelderland, Overijssel,
and Utrecht, but also in Groningen and Friesland—though there
remains the feeling that the nobility in these last two provinces was
rather *sui generis* and not entirely comparable to that elsewhere.
Secondly, the influence of the rural sector, whether represented by
the nobility or not, was everywhere (except Zeeland) far greater
than in Holland. Thus, whether we look at the question in class

[6] The system was complex and thus difficult to summarize in a few words, but it
was comparable to the situation in rural Friesland: see the following paragraph.
[7] J. A. Faber, 'De oligarchisering van Friesland in de tweede helft van de zeventiende eeuw', *Afdeling Agrarische Geschedenis Bijdragen*, 15 (1970).

terms—as nobility versus bourgeois-regent—or in terms purely of economic interest—trading and manufacturing towns versus a more traditional countryside—we can see that the States of the other provinces represented a very different mix of social and economic interests from those in Holland or Zeeland. This situation made the determination and pursuit of common policies for the Republic as a whole no easy matter.

One obvious consequence of this disparity of interests between the provinces was that the single-minded pursuit of mercantilist policies which was so characteristic of Holland was lacking elsewhere. Even Zeeland tended to be suspicious of its overbearing neighbour and to fear that the latter's economic policies were designed to benefit, in the main if not exclusively, itself alone. The distinctly weaker economy of Zeeland might have benefited from a rather different mix of economic policies than the broadly free-trade ones pursued by Holland. Above all, however, it was the priority given by Holland to economic concerns that caused difficulties between the provinces. Throughout the seventeenth century, Holland pressed whenever possible for a foreign policy for the Republic designed largely, if not solely, to support and protect its foreign trade. Although such policies were presented as being in the national interest, they tended to be viewed by those outside that province as a particular rather than a general concern. After all, the benefits of the burgeoning international trade of the Dutch Republic in this century were largely confined to Holland, with only lesser profits or spin-off rewards reaching the rest of the country. So, although it can be argued that the phenomenal expansion of Holland's economy benefited the rest of the Republic in a variety of ways, both direct and indirect, the persistent attempts by the regents of Holland to gear the foreign policy of the state to the economic interests of their province were, understandably enough, frequently seen as an expression of provincial egotism. The readiness of the Holland regents to make sacrifices for economic gain was notorious; the objections came when it was felt that the sacrifices were to be made by the other provinces and the gains to be enjoyed by Holland alone.

The general orientation of foreign policy to support the economic interests of Holland was also questioned by the lesser provinces for reasons other than their different economic needs. The strategic situation of the Republic brought with it further sharp clashes of interest. Put briefly, the land provinces were much more vulnerable to invasion than Holland (let alone Zeeland), and therefore were much more immediately concerned to strengthen the landward defences of the Republic by diplomatic and military means. In contrast, Holland was inclined to concentrate on the needs of trade, and on the preservation of a strong navy to protect Dutch merchant shipping. This attitude was evident even during the long war with Spain when the necessity of maintaining a strong army was not in dispute; after 1648 Holland's leaders tended to neglect the army in the belief that money could produce sufficient troops at the last minute whenever necessary. It was just such a policy that came unstuck in 1672, when an ineffective army and disastrously neglected fortifications combined with unusually low water levels in the rivers of the east to expose the land provinces to invasion. All of the Republic except the more easily defended Zeeland, Holland, and Friesland was occupied by the French (or by the troops of the bishop of Münster)—a sharp reminder of which provinces were vulnerable and which not. Cynically, it might be added that even on this occasion Holland's calculation worked: it did prove possible to scramble together an effective defence of the Republic's heartlands (as seen by Holland), from the basis of which the rest could be fairly rapidly regained.

However, it is understandable that the land provinces found it difficult to share Holland's coolly calculating point of view. The experiences of the inner-ring provinces—Holland, Zeeland, Friesland—and the rest in both the Revolt and much of the seventeenth century were very different. On the one hand, Holland, whatever its difficulties and even sufferings in the course of the Revolt and the Eighty Years War, was spared the presence of enemy troops on its soil after the Pacification of Ghent in 1576 (or, more precisely, from the surrender of Amsterdam to the rebels in 1578). From that point onwards, with the minor exception of the occasional raid, no hostile armies were able to penetrate Holland's defences. In stark contrast, Gelderland, Overijssel, and Groningen were for years on end the places where the war with the Spanish was actually fought; armies marched and counter-marched over their countryside, and their towns were fortresses possessed by one side and besieged by the other. Even in more peaceful times, the presence in strategic towns of permanent garrisons was a very visible reminder of the reality of war for the people of these provinces.

In these circumstances, it is hardly surprising that Holland's foreign policy stance of emphasizing economic over narrowly military
interests was often interpreted as a readiness to sacrifice the other
provinces' interests to its own. Holland was accused of regarding
the land provinces as little more than a useful barrier to slow
down any invasion and thus allow Holland time to build up its
own defences.

For much of the first half of the century such differences in
strategic vision were disguised by the circumstances of the war
with Spain, which required a permanent major military effort on
land and provided very little in the way of naval problems, though
the Dunkirk privateers were something more than a nuisance.
Thus, during this period there was no fundamental opposition
between a maritime and a land orientation in military affairs.
However, the controversy over the Truce of 1609 must have been
influenced by the different strategic priorities of the provinces.
Clearly, the majority in the States of Holland were willing to take
the risk that the Truce might, in one way or another, turn in
Spain's favour, in order to relieve the strain on the province's
finances and to give what was hoped would be a significant boost
to its economy. On the other hand, the land provinces could not
hope for the same sort of economic benefit from the Truce that
Holland expected, and were understandably more concerned that
the cessation of hostilities might leave them in time more exposed
to a renewed and possibly more powerful Spanish attack. The
movement of Spanish troops into the Rhineland during the Jülich-
Kleve succession dispute (1609–14), thus practically on the very
borders of the Republic, can only have exacerbated such unease,
strengthened opinion against the Truce, and increased the suspicion
attached to those who had driven it through.

After the Peace of Westphalia, the conflict between a foreign
policy geared to Holland's maritime concerns and the interest of
many of the other provinces in maintaining both a stronger army
and a closer watch on possible threats by land, became more obvious if not clearly more acute. This underlying clash of interests
was all the more difficult to resolve because the strategic dilemma
was quite probably insoluble. It was not just that the Republic
found it almost impossible to bear the financial strain of maintaining both a large army and navy, though this was problem enough.
In the war against Spain, the major effort could be reserved for the

army as the Spanish posed no great naval threat. Subsequently, until the rude awakening of 1672, Holland pursued a policy of concentrating on the navy to meet the English threat, while hoping to avoid a significant challenge on land. After 1672, the Dutch Republic had to maintain a large army to deal with the direct menace to the state's survival presented by Louis XIV's France, but at the same time had to retain a major fleet to deal not only with the French naval challenge but also with the ever-present possibility that the English would attack it again. Only Willem III's capture of the English state in 1688 allowed the Dutch to ease up on their naval expenditure.

This situation was a problem in itself, but on top of that came the even more basic problem of war and the Dutch economy. Put crudely, the Dutch had to fight to maintain their independence, but constant warfare weakened their economy and consequently undermined their ability to fight. This dilemma was not present in any acute, or possibly even serious, form during the long war with Spain; while the war at this time might not actually have helped the economy, it certainly did not prevent it from continuing to grow.[8] However, the wars with England in the mid-century, and with France later, produced all sorts of problems for Dutch trade. In particular, the long period of hot and cold war between the Republic and France presented the Dutch with a major dilemma. France was clearly a direct threat to the Republic and had to be checked, but constant war with France weakened the economy and hence the financial capacity to resist the French. Thus, very soon after 1672 Holland was pressing for a more circumspect policy with regard to France, in opposition to Willem III's single-minded policy of blocking French expansion wherever and whenever possible. Holland hoped to minimize economic losses so as to be as strong as possible when it became absolutely necessary to face France again, while Willem, supported by the land provinces, argued that such a policy would allow the French to strengthen their position and knock out potential allies of the Dutch, and was thus too dangerous.[9] The greater vulnerability of the land provinces, together with their memories of the recent French invasion and occupation, inclined them to side with the prince, the more so as their economies were much less seriously affected by

---

[8] Israel, *Dutch Primacy*, ch. 5.   [9] Price, 'William III'.

warfare than was that of Holland. Of course, the enhanced power which Willem enjoyed in these provinces was also a significant factor (see Chapter 4 below), but it is important to recognize that to a great degree he was rowing with the tide.

An aspect of the differences between the provinces which is much more difficult to assess is whether real cultural disparities existed which would have made the achievement of common policies even more problematical. This area of possible division in the Dutch Republic has not received much attention, and it is indeed extremely difficult to pin down with any clarity, let alone precision. Yet some suggestions arise directly out of the matters that have just been discussed, and may well indicate important areas of misunderstanding and antagonism which have remained largely unremarked until recent years. While the influence of the nobility in Holland may not have been so negligible as has been commonly assumed, nevertheless Holland was ruled by an urban élite with a markedly bourgeois-capitalist *Weltanschauung*, still bearing the stamp of the trading and manufacturing circles from which it had risen and within which it still very largely lived. That the triumph of bourgeois culture and capitalist values may have been incomplete in important ways[10] is less important in the present context than the fact of their relative success. It seems obvious that matters must have been significantly different in the other provinces, where the economic changes of the sixteenth and early seventeenth centuries had been less profound. Particularly in Gelderland and Overijssel— and perhaps Utrecht also—the towns were much less and the nobles much more powerful than in Holland and Zeeland. (Friesland and Groningen can perhaps be seen as transitional areas in this respect.) It seems likely that in these regions the values associated with the noble-dominated *ancien régime* elsewhere in Europe would still have been highly influential. The predilection of the nobles of the land provinces for service in the army, and their tendency to be drawn easily into the seductive nets of princely patronage, are perhaps not simply to be explained by the material rewards available, but must also be understood as the expression of a set of social and political

---

[10] Sadly, S. Schama, *The Embarrassment of Riches* (New York, 1987), esp. 6–7, 568–9, although he touches on the question as to whether Dutch culture was bourgeois or not, confines himself to ill-considered polemic and obfuscatory rhetoric, and thus fails to contribute anything of value to the discussion of this important question.

values more akin to those of nobles outside the Republic than to. those of the regents of Holland. This is a fascinating area, and one which would repay further study, but it would be a mistake to put too much weight on this aspect of inter-provincial differences with- out much more convincing evidence than we possess at present. It may well be that the above argument seriously underestimates the cultural influence of the dominant province on the rest of the Republic. Just as Holland's booming economy profoundly affected the other provinces, though not necessarily pulling them into a sim- ilar development, so the ideas and assumptions of capitalist Holland may have affected the values of even the Dutch nobles more than might at first be expected. After all, was not even Willem III a very bourgeois prince, at least to non-Dutch eyes?

In any case, it seems clear that there was a serious problem in finding common ground and purposes among such disparate provinces. The difficulty facing Dutch politicians in the seventeenth century was how to keep the 'United' Provinces together despite their different interests and, perhaps, values. Their success in deal- ing with this task should not be allowed to obscure the fact that it was a real problem and that failure was a distinct possibility. Moreover, it needs to be added that a further problem was that it was not always clear that the seven provinces, plus appendages, were the final form of the Dutch state. In the first decades of the seventeenth century, there were still hopes—and these were not entirely unrealistic, perhaps—that the whole of the Netherlands could yet be freed from Spanish rule and be united as an indepen- dent state. So what were the Dutch to be loyal to? The 'seventeen' Netherlands[11] were slipping away as a political idea capable of realization, and the Dutch-speaking area does not seem to have been as aware of its essential unity as some modern historians. There was no obvious geographical or ethnic, or even cultural, unity to the somewhat chance agglomeration of territories which formed the Dutch Republic. In these circumstances, it is hardly sur- prising that a sense of identity with, and loyalty to, the new Dutch state was slow to develop. Primary loyalties were rather to the province, or perhaps were even more localized.[12]

---

[11] The 'Seventeen Netherlands' was the usual contemporary term for the whole of the Habsburg territories in the Low Countries, though quite how that precise number of provinces was arrived at is far from clear.

[12] Groenveld, *Verlopend getij*, ch. 1.

The differences which existed between the provinces in terms of their political systems, social structures, and economic development meant that there was a real question about the viability of this new state. Indeed, to what extent—given the frequent stress on provincial autonomy—did it constitute a state at all? The fears of contemporaries that the ending of the war with Spain would lead to the disintegration of the Union were in the event proved false, but there were good reasons for such apprehensions. Moreover, the alert reader will no doubt have noticed that religious differences between the provinces have not yet been brought into the discussion, although there are grounds for arguing that this was the most divisive area of all, and one that brought the Republic the nearest it ever came to civil war during the seventeenth century. On a more prosaic level, these divisions within the Republic, even if they did not tear it apart, certainly made the generation of viable and consistent national policies a problematic business. The central government—if it deserves such a name—of the Republic had throughout its history a reputation for the slowness of its decision-making processes, because of the seemingly endless consultations which were vital to the political system. However, it is at least equally valid to see the Dutch Republic, with all its weaknesses, as one of the most successful states in seventeenth-century Europe. The rest of this Part is devoted to an attempt to see how this cumbersome and apparently ramshackle union was made to work so remarkably well in practice.

3. The Influence of Holland

Although the province of Holland had only a single vote in the States General, like any other province, its effective power within the Republic was much greater than this formal position might suggest. The size of its population, its wealth, and perhaps also its internal cohesion, gave Holland a predominance in the seventeenth century which partly justified the tendency of foreigners to confuse the part with the whole, and refer to the Republic as Holland. The seat of government, for reasons of history and possibly inertia, was also in Holland, but this was also a reflection of the importance of easy communications between the States General and the States of Holland for the government of the country to work at all smoothly. Most strikingly, the Advocate or *raadpensionaris* of Holland was for long periods the effective head of the government of the Republic (under Oldenbarnevelt and De Witt, and then again for most of the first half of the eighteenth century), and even during the times of political dominance by the princes of Orange remained necessarily a major figure in national politics. Through the manipulation of its financial strength, Holland was able to become, not the one province among many which was all that the formal political system allowed, and not even *primus inter pares*, but a directing force—sometimes indeed overbearing—challenged only by the alternative leadership and focus of loyalty provided by the princes of Orange.

The financial supremacy of Holland within the Dutch Republic is shown clearly by the official quota-system drawn up by the States General to determine the share of Generality expenditure to be borne by each province. Because of the exigencies of war, only four provinces contributed at all up to 1594 (Holland, Zeeland, Utrecht, and Friesland), then first Groningen and, in 1608, Gelderland and Overijssel were brought into the system. In 1612 the costs of common expenditure were divided roughly in the following percentages: Gelderland 5.5; Holland 57.2; Zeeland 11.00; Utrecht 5.7; Friesland 11.4; Overijssel 3.5; Groningen 5.7. There were some subsequent minor modifications, and from 1634 the division of the financial burden was firmly fixed as shown (again, the figures are percentages).

Gelderland	5.6
Holland	58.3
Zeeland	9.2
Utrecht	5.8
Friesland	11.7
Overijssel	3.6
Groningen	5.8

To a considerable extent, these figures explain both why Holland was able to exercise the influence it did, and why the formal insistence on equality between the provinces could not in practice work. Holland's enormously greater share of the costs of communal action—more than all the other provinces put together—meant that it could not be treated as just another province, whatever the formal rules of the political game may have said.

Moreover, the financial viability of the state was closely tied to Holland in another way as well. Much of the immediate income of the Dutch Republic, like any other seventeenth-century state, came from loans, especially to meet extraordinary wartime expenditure —which in the Dutch case was more nearly ordinary expenditure, given the preponderance of years in which it was involved in wars during the seventeenth century. However, the body which contracted the bulk of the loans raised by the Dutch in this century was not the States General but the States of Holland. The Revolt and the war against Spain, as well as the later conflicts, were primarily fought on the basis of the credit of the province of Holland, not of the Dutch state.

The effect of all this was that the Dutch Republic could not embark on any policy unless it could be sure that Holland would pay its share. One or more of the lesser provinces could default without too much damage, but if Holland held back its contribution nothing could be done. Thus, in effect, Holland's financial supremacy, plus the voting system in the States General which required unanimity for important matters, together with the practical impossibility of coercing Holland into paying for a policy it objected to, gave it an extraordinarily powerful bargaining position within the Union. At the least, this meant that Holland could exercise something very like an effective, rather than a formal, veto in the States General; if Holland was not prepared to support a measure then it was, for all practical purposes, lost. The dilemma for the prince and the other provinces was that they had to ensure, by one means or another, that Holland would provide financial support for the policies they favoured.

One of the most concrete ways in which this financial strength of Holland was exercised was in the method used to pay the army of the Republic. The army was subject ultimately to the States General, was commanded (usually) by the prince of Orange, and administered by the Council of State, but this centralized control and direction was more than a little modified by the 'repartition' system used to finance it. Each province was assigned a number of units of the army in proportion to its quota of Generality expenditure, and it paid these units directly from its own resources, with only the accounts being dealt with at the centre. Thus Holland had nearly 60 per cent of the whole army directly in its pay. On the whole this does not seem to have caused trouble, and proved a reasonably efficient system (at least for the troops under Holland's repartition—other units might not have been paid quite so regularly), but there were clearly possibilities here for clashes of loyalty between commander and paymaster. When a serious problem did arise in 1650, however, the repartition system was employed by Holland in a rather different manner to put weight behind its arguments, and in so doing revealed the degree to which the smooth workings of the Dutch political system required constant modifications to the formal constitutional position in order to accommodate Holland's particular situation. When the dispute over the size of the army reached a deadlock in the States General, with the majority of provinces following the lead of Willem II and insisting on a military budget which maintained a rather larger army establishment than Holland was willing to support, the latter found itself in a difficult position. On the one hand, it was clearly against the spirit of the law for Holland to be forced to pay for more troops than it had voted for in the States General—for consent was required in financial matters—but on the other hand the repartition system allocated certain units of the army to be paid by the province, and it was not empowered to change this unilaterally. The States of Holland broke the impasse by paying off some of the troops assigned to their repartition—in effect dismissing them, although this was the prerogative of the Council of State acting on the orders of the States General. While this action by Holland was technically illegal, and it would have certainly led to a chaotic situation in the army if all the provinces started to dismiss part of the troops in their pay whenever they felt like it, there was in effect not a lot the States General could do about it. This was the situation which led Willem II into his near-disastrous attempted *coup*: coercion, if necessary by armed force, seemed the only way to break the constitutional deadlock—the only alternative being for the majority in the States General to concede that 42 per cent could not, or should not, override 58 per cent.

This breakdown of the normally effective negotiation processes at the centre of Dutch government reminds us forcibly that what normally happened was that the financial supremacy of Holland was accorded what this province no doubt regarded as its due. In other words, Holland had an effective veto on all important decisions in the States General and, more positively, its willingness to pay for a particular policy was a long step towards its adoption. While the refusal of one of the smaller provinces could be overridden—and this occurred not infrequently—as its refusal to contribute financially would not be a serious problem, the same could not be said of Holland: some vetoes were more equal than others. Moreover, Holland could use its wealth to encourage other provinces to support the policies it espoused. It used a wide range of measures, including loans and other financial help, to back up its statesmen's forensic abilities. As most of the other provinces were more or less permanently in difficulties trying to meet their financial obligations to the Generality, such aid was more than a minor persuasive force.

Thus, in practice, the principle of provincial autonomy—or perhaps sovereignty, though this is a term from a rather different political philosophy than that which governed most of Dutch political practice—worked in such a way as to ensure the domination of Holland within the political system. This was the essential characteristic of the system created by Oldenbarnevelt in the decade or so after 1588. In the aftermath of the internal near-anarchy which followed Willem of Orange's death in 1584 and, even more directly, of the failure of Leicester's regime, it must have seemed clear to Oldenbarnevelt that the Dutch Republic could only become a viable polity if Holland's peculiar interests and needs were given their proper weight. Attempting to coerce Holland into supporting policies which were felt to be in the general interest, although they clashed with the perceived interests of the province itself, had failed decisively under Leicester, not least because of the activities of Oldenbarnevelt himself. While the principle of equal representation in the States General for every province regardless of wealth or the size of its financial contribution remained inviolable, the principle of provincial autonomy could be used not only to protect Holland from being outvoted and subjected to the will of the smaller provinces, but in practice to impose Holland's will on the rest. In brief, provincial independence gave the lesser provinces protection from their powerful ally, and at the same time allowed Holland to mould the policies of the new state in accordance with its own wishes and needs. The necessity for some such solution to the internal political problems of the late 1580s was particularly clear, as at this time only four provinces were paying anything at all into the central coffers, and the proportion paid by Holland was even greater than it was to be later. So the Council of State was pushed aside and the States General became the centre of the new and surprisingly effective political system which Oldenbarnevelt created out of the ruins of Leicester's, for in the States General Holland's single voice could be the dominant force through the positive weight of its financial contributions and the negative effect of its veto. This system was to remain essentially unchanged throughout the remainder of the history of the Republic; even the domination of the Orange princes at times in the seventeenth century and later could not alter the basic fact that the system as set up by Oldenbarnevelt gave Holland a decisive influence in the affairs of state.

The reality of Holland's effective power in the Republic was somewhat obscured between 1618 and 1650, when Maurits, Frederik Hendrik, and Willem II successively provided the leadership and co-ordination which had previously come from Oldenbarnevelt and the States of Holland. Even during this period of apparent eclipse, however, it remained true that what the princes needed above all was the co-operation of Holland; their power lay to a significant extent, not in their more obvious ability to command the support of the other provinces, but rather in their capacity to coerce, cajole, persuade, or manipulate the States of Holland. If Holland refused to agree to a policy, that policy was lost in the end.

The sudden removal of Willem II at the end of 1650 revealed the underlying shape of Dutch politics to be essentially the same as it had been in the years of Oldenbarnevelt's domination, and the methods subsequently used by De Witt to ensure Holland's leadership and control of the Republic did not differ in essentials from those used by his illustrious predecessor. In some ways, however, the control which Holland was able to exert during the first stadhouderless period was even greater than at the time of Oldenbarnevelt. First, and most obviously, the young prince of Orange was excluded from all the offices which his father had held, and thus the political counterweight to Holland which had centred on Maurits even before the beginning of his rift with the Advocate was totally absent. The stadhouder of Friesland, Willem Frederik, could not take over this role, nor could anyone else from the house of Orange. In consequence, not only was an alternative source of leadership in the Republic removed, but De Witt could also manipulate a good part of the patronage which the princes had formerly used to build up their political strength in the Republic, both as stadhouders of Holland and as captains-general of the army.[1] Not only could he deploy the patronage resources which flowed from his position as effective leader of Holland, but his position as the most important politician in the whole country gave him an even greater capacity to influence the flow of favours.

The elevation of Willem III brought a return to the situation which had obtained in 1618–50, as he could rely on the support of the land provinces—even more than his predecessors, in fact—but still needed the co-operation of Holland for the prosecution of his bold foreign policies. Just as the *wetsverzettingen* of 1618 had only ensured Holland's compliance for a few years, so those of 1672 failed to produce a regent group which was ready to follow the prince's lead without question. It is not so much that Holland put up an effective and consistent opposition to the policies of Willem III, as that the latter had to hammer out arrangements with, and make concessions to, that province. The prince had been powerful enough, however, to ensure that the institution of a second stadhouderless period after his death came as almost a natural reaction. Clearly, the regents of Holland were not overly confident of their ability always to keep a stadhouder/captain-general in check.

[1] Here the fact that Holland paid the costs of nearly 60 per cent of the army could begin to make itself felt directly in terms of patronage.

Yet, looking at the seventeenth century as a whole, certain points about the power of Holland within the Dutch system as it worked in practice, rather than in the formal distribution of authority, do seem to emerge fairly unambiguously. First, when Holland was united, or rather when the voting towns of the province were united, it was never clearly defeated. Even when the princes of Orange were at their most powerful, they had to make crucial concessions to the States of Holland. This was seen most obviously perhaps in the 1640s, when Frederik Hendrik and Willem II were forced to lead the Republic towards peace with Spain, whatever their own wishes may have been (and Willem II was profoundly hostile to the treaty). Again, Willem III was forced into making peace with Louis XIV at Nijmegen in 1678 despite his wishes and better judgement, and was then blocked in all his moves against France in the early 1680s. The princes of Orange could only take on Holland and win when the province was divided against itself. The classic example of the consequences of political divisions within the province came during the Truce crisis: whatever importance we attribute to the decision of Maurits to back the contraremonstrants, it can be argued that the crucial circumstance was the lack of unity in Holland. The fact that the opposition to Oldenbarnevelt and the majority of towns was led by Amsterdam seems to have been decisive. It was a difficult enough task for Oldenbarnevelt to check Maurits and the rest of the provinces without a fully united Holland behind him, but with Amsterdam and a number of smaller towns actually opposing him the position became entirely hopeless—though it is understandable that contemporaries could not see matters with quite this dispassionate clarity.

Subsequently, the persistent ideological and factional divisions within the regent oligarchy of Holland allowed first Maurits and then Frederik Hendrik, in their very different ways, to exploit the lack of consensus over aims as well as methods, and so entrench their political power. In many towns the contraremonstrant parties established in power in 1618 needed continued aid from the stadhouder to preserve their positions, and other differences between the towns also played into the stadhouders' hands. However, by the late 1630s and even more markedly by the 1640s there was a growing consensus within the oligarchy of the province concerning the need to reach a satisfactory settlement with Spain, and most importantly this consensus was led by the increasingly wealthy and influential Amsterdam. The combination of firm leadership from this town with a considerable degree of unanimity and no strong opposition among the other towns made the triumph of Holland's policy virtually inevitable, a reality that was recognized and accepted with some grace by Frederik Hendrik,[2] but to which Willem II remained stubbornly blind.

The persistent efforts of Willem II to lead the country in a very different direction from that desired by the regents of Holland reveal two important truths about the Dutch political system at this point, and most likely for the whole of the century also: that the Republic could not be run in opposition to the perceived interests of a united Holland, and that if a prince of Orange refused to recognize this fact the whole system was put in jeopardy. When Willem failed to get the Holland delegation in the States General to approve the *staat van oorlog* in 1650, then, unless some sort of compromise could be reached, there was practically nothing that he could properly do to further his policies. The issue became important at this point, not because of its intrinsic significance—for by this time the difference between the number of troops proposed by the Council of State and those which Holland was prepared to accept was not very great—but because of its implications for the future course of the foreign policy of the Republic. If Holland could succeed in checking the prince on the issue of the size of the army, then a precedent would be set for the blocking of the whole of his ambitious policy (which seems to have been aimed at renewing the war with Spain, and possibly also intervening in the civil strife in England in favour of his Stuart relatives[3]). Thus the apparently minor dispute over the precise size of the army in peacetime became in effect a power-struggle over who was to control the future policy of the Republic, the prince or the regents of Holland.

In the event, the outcome of the struggle was not entirely clear; on the one hand, the prince failed abysmally in his attempt to coerce Holland, but on the other hand his considerable powers within the Republic had not been broken, though his prestige had

[2] Groenveld, *Verlopend getij*, 223.

[3] Willem had married a daughter of Charles I, Mary, in 1641, the start of an intermingling of the histories of the two houses with important consequences for both Britain and the Dutch Republic (cf. Geyl, *Oranje en Stuart*).

probably suffered considerably. In a series of actions which awakened not entirely happy memories of 1618, Willem first tried to intimidate the voting towns of Holland by a series of formal visitations, accompanied by a considerable retinue. Although a number of towns proved less than totally resolute in the face of this mixture of moral and implied physical force, the visits failed in their chief purpose of effecting a significant change in the voting in the States of Holland. While this visitation had been of dubious legality—it was argued that the States General had no right to interfere in the internal affairs of any province, and some of the towns were prepared only to receive the prince in his capacity as stadhouder and not as emissary of the States General—the next move by the prince was both wildly illegal and extremely dangerous: he arrested six members of the States of Holland and sent a strong detachment of troops against Amsterdam. The second part of this plan failed under almost comic-opera circumstances, but the situation remained tense, with troops before Amsterdam, the six members in prison, yet the town defiant and the States of Holland, after initial vacillation, beginning to regain their collective nerve and unite against the prince. In the event the situation was defused by concessions from Amsterdam, letting Willem off the hook and allowing him to withdraw his troops and release the six members (on condition that they withdrew from politics) with some semblance of dignity. A compromise was swiftly reached on the question of the number of troops to be kept in service. The prince had not succeeded, but the result was not a clear-cut victory for Holland, more of a power stand-off. It was clear that the prince could not govern the Republic in opposition to Holland, but his powers, especially over the votes of the land provinces in the States General, meant that Holland could certainly not take over the leadership of the state without his co-operation. While Holland could block Willem's policies, it seems certain that he could do the same to Holland's. A minimum of co-operation and compromise between the prince and the States of Holland was needed for the Dutch political system to work at all effectively; whether a stable working relationship was possible after the trauma of the summer of 1650 was uncertain. The death of Willem in November resolved what might well have proved a lasting and corrosive political dilemma.

During the first stadhouderless period there was, of course, no effective focus of opposition to the dominance of the States of Holland under the leadership of its *raadpensionaris*, Johan de Witt; and the weakening of De Witt's position in his later years came not from the other provinces, nor from the young prince—though his very existence both stimulated and shaped the nature of this opposition—but from within Holland itself. Again, as in the lead-up to the defeat of Oldenbarnevelt, the main role was played by Amsterdam, partly at least because of its feeling that De Witt was becoming too powerful and too little responsive to the town's peculiar interests. There seems a recognizable pattern here: just as Oldenbarnevelt had been in a position of apparently increasing authority for almost thirty years when he was brought down by a combination of forces in 1618, so by 1672 De Witt had been leading Holland and the Republic for almost twenty years, with his expertise and authority growing almost year by year. In De Witt's case, the expression of the resentment and rivalries which his position caused was the less inhibited because of the lack of any immediate challenge to Holland's leadership in the Republic, thus weakening the need for provincial solidarity. Consequently, when things started to go drastically wrong in 1672, De Witt's position collapsed very quickly, allowing not only the young prince, but also a group of politicians who had been discreetly working against him for a number of years,[4] to gain power.

With the restoration of the stadhoudership of Holland and Zeeland and, in principle, all the other powers and positions which his father had enjoyed, to Willem III in 1672, the situation was distinctly similar to that in the years immediately after 1618. Again, wide-ranging *wetsverzettingen* had produced new governments in the voting towns of Holland which would be, initially at least, much more compliant supporters of the prince's policies than would normally have been the case. Moreover, in the aftermath of the near annihilation of the Republic by the French in 1672, the policy options open to the Dutch were somewhat limited: they had to clear the French troops from their territory and, diplomatically, gain as many effective allies as they could to help defeat France or at least fight it to a standstill. It was only when these objectives had been more or less satisfactorily achieved that the Dutch could again allow themselves the luxury of disputes over foreign policy.

[4] Franken, *Coenraad van Beuningen*, 76–7.

The fundamental power of Holland soon reasserted itself, however. Despite the trauma of the upheavals within the governments of the voting towns in 1672, which might have been expected to produce a compliant States of Holland for a decade or more, opposition to Willem's belligerent policy grew rapidly in the province once the immediate future of the Republic seemed reasonably secure. The Treaty of Nijmegen (1678) can be regarded as a triumph of Holland over the prince, who had wanted to carry on fighting France, or at least not to make peace without the inclusion of the Republic's chief allies. For the rest of the century, the Republic's foreign policy, although normally presented by historians in terms of the plans and views of Willem III, is as much a creation of Holland as of the prince, for nothing could be done without that province's consent. The States of Holland blocked Willem's attempts at further active opposition to France in the early 1680s, but the Enterprise of England in 1688, and the subsequent reopening of the war with France, could only have taken place with Holland's consent, though in the case of the expedition to England not necessarily in formal terms. Something like a consensus over foreign policy seems to have emerged after the middle of the 1680s, and, indeed, after Willem's death and the institution of a second stadhouderless period, the States of Holland led the Republic in a determined continuation of the late prince's policy of opposition to the ambitions of the French king. It does not seem, then, that either the power of Holland within the Republic or its capacity to act independently had been fundamentally damaged by the events of 1672. However, it is true that Willem III was in a better position than any of his predecessors to put pressure on town governments in the province to support his policies through their delegations in the States of Holland. While it would be misleading to exaggerate the extent of his ability to control local political developments, the evidence, fragmentary as it is, does suggest that his fostering of local political bosses was a considerable success. It did not make Holland anything like as subservient as the land provinces, but it did increase his influence within the province considerably.

Throughout the seventeenth century the States of Holland were the vital element in the determination of the policies of the Dutch Republic, specifically with regard to foreign policy. Before 1618 and from 1650 to 1672 they took the lead, under the guidance of

Oldenbarnevelt and De Witt, and even when the princes of Orange were the directing hand, Holland retained the power to block any policy that it disliked. Policy had to be made with the consent of the premier province, it could not be coerced. Only when it was seriously divided could it be beaten: Holland only lost when it defeated itself.

4. The Power of the Princes of Orange

The princes of Orange have to be brought into any consideration of the role of the province of Holland in the politics of the Dutch Republic because they, not any or all of the other provinces, were its main rivals for the leadership of the state throughout the seventeenth century and, indeed, throughout the whole history of the Republic. What makes this structural opposition particularly intriguing is that, while Holland's power and influence were based on distinctly mundane sources, primarily economic strength, the princes derived their peculiar place within the Republic's political system from a complex and sometimes even bizarre combination of specific powers and offices, together with an indispensable charismatic element. The way in which the princes were able to wield power as stadhouders in Holland has already been considered (Part 2, Chapter 2, above). This chapter is concerned with their political influence in the Republic as a whole.

For over half of the seventeenth century, the successive princes of Orange played a quasi-monarchical role in the Dutch Republic.[1] They were stadhouders of the majority of provinces (Holland, Zeeland, Utrecht, Gelderland, Overijssel, and sometimes Groningen as well) and commanded both the army and the navy. They also had the prestige which attached to sovereign princes, though the principality of Orange in the Rhône valley did not amount to much and, later in the century, was occupied by Louis XIV in a fit of small-minded pique all too typical of the Sun King. Moreover, they enjoyed a special status within the Dutch state, almost mystical, certainly charismatic, in its nature, as symbols of Dutch unity and common purpose, stemming from the close association of the house of Orange with the Revolt and the founding of the Republic. Beginning with the role of Willem of Orange in the first years of

---

[1] However, Maurits was not properly prince of Orange but only count of Nassau, until the death of his elder brother in 1619 allowed him to inherit the superior title.

the Revolt, which was presented by various writers after his death in such a way that he could become a symbol for all despite the frequently contentious nature of his actual policies,[2] the Orange myth became ever stronger in the course of the seventeenth century, although it was not unchallenged. In a country which had many nobles but was distinctly short of noblemen of any eminence after the Revolt, the princes of Orange had a unique position and were able not only to achieve great political power in the new state, but in a curious way came symbolically to embody Dutch identity and unity better than any other person or institution. The States General, the States of Holland, the *raadpensionaris*, the abstract idea of the Union, these could gain rational acceptance of their authority; but only the princes of Orange could inspire that passionate, irrational, and unreflecting loyalty that is the essential quality of national identity.

The unique prestige which the princes of Orange came to enjoy in the Dutch Republic, and which was one of the principal elements in their political armoury, is difficult to pin down with any precision, as it derived both from their social status and from the cumulative effect of the particular role successive princes played in the young Dutch state. Their social status as princes of Orange and/or counts of Nassau was unique within the Republic; no other noble family came near to matching their social eminence, and only the Frisian branch of the family could begin to approach it. This high ranking within the conventional social hierarchy of contemporary Europe gave the princes' peculiar position in the Republic the sanction of a set of political and social values which were recognized by the rest of European society. The value system of the *ancien régime*, which gave the princes their status, was being implicitly challenged by the burgeoning bourgeois culture of Holland, but the rest of the Republic still lived to a large extent within the old noble-dominated culture, and even Holland itself was far from emancipating itself completely from the norms which still held the rest of Europe in thrall.

The history of the connection of the house of Orange with the Republic added an extra force and particularity to this prestige. The chief titles held by the Orange-Nassau princes were, of course, foreign, but the role of Willem of Orange and his descendants tied the

[2] Haitsma Mulier and Janssen (eds.), *Willem van Oranje*, chs. 1 and 2.

house inextricably to the Dutch state and gave it an essentially Dutch identity. This history also encouraged the idea that the Orange family had a providential purpose: the princes were seen by many as the champions of Reformed protestantism, and to an influential section of the Dutch population the princes and the Reformed Church were intimately associated as tools of God's purpose for the Dutch people and polity. Given the policies and characters of most of the princes, this interpretation seems almost heroically implausible, but it was nevertheless an important aspect of the charisma of the family. More readily understandable, perhaps, is the way in which the special position of the princes was built up historically by the cumulative effect of their successive careers. The actions and achievements of each prince were both important in themselves and were also transformed almost instantly into a component of an increasingly important Orange myth, which added an extra lustre to the prestige of the house. Basic to the whole mythology of the conflation of the house of Orange and the Dutch polity was the reputation of Willem of Orange as the Father of the Fatherland, whose actual historical role, vital as it was, became less important to later generations than the use to which his name could be put as a symbol of the Union and religious orthodoxy—the latter element being particularly ironic given the markedly *politique* nature of the prince's own attitudes towards religion. The image of the house was strengthened in one way by the highly successful military careers of Maurits and Frederik Hendrik, which made them legitimate national heroes of the Eighty Years War, but Maurits's resolution of the Truce crisis left a much more ambivalent legacy. In terms of the Orange myth he had rescued the Republic from civil war and possible disintegration, and had saved the true Reformed religion from pernicious dilution; to others, however, he bore the ultimate responsibility for the judicial murder of Oldenbarnevelt—from this point on, the idea of the house of Orange had a divisive as well as an integrating potential. However, Frederik Hendrik, besides being a successful military leader, was able with considerable success to play a conciliatory role between the hostile tendencies in Dutch internal politics, in part by giving the impression of being above the party strife through the adoption of a quasi-monarchical style of life. Whereas Maurits's way of life had remained almost ostentatiously modest, his half-brother and his successors lived, literally, like princes, which in a period when action and essence were difficult to

distinguish was tantamount to being such. Indeed, it has been suggested that many Dutch contemporaries may have believed that the
princes were their country's rulers. While not necessarily going so
far as this, it is easy to understand that not all contemporaries can
have had a very precise notion of the nature and limitations of the
princes' authority, given their combination of very real powers and a
life-style which effectively expressed their pre-eminence in Dutch
society.[3]

One of the things the princes of Orange could offer to the Dutch
was leadership. They could act as symbols of national unity, and
more practically could provide in their own persons a single centre
of authority for the Republic. The term *Eminente Hoofd* (Eminent
Head) came to be used to express both these elements in the political role of the princes of Orange. According to this way of thinking, they were necessary both as a focus of loyalty and as a source
of effective action in difficult times, especially necessary given the
slowness and indecisiveness of the States General when left to
itself. The princes could act as more effective symbols of Dutch
national identity than institutions like the States General and ever-
changing and anonymous delegates, none of whom formally had a
personal, but only a representative, role. Put simply, the States
General could not ride around on a horse and wave to the crowds.
Moreover, the princes could lay claim, with some plausibility, to
impartiality with regard to the conflicting and competing aims and
interests of the various provinces, and thus could be regarded as
the effective representatives of the Union as a whole, while, for
example, the *raadpensionaris* was unavoidably associated with
Holland's interests, however much he might try to develop a truly
national policy. The fact that reality may have been rather different, or that at least some of the princes of Orange may have
tended to confuse the national interest with that of their dynasty, is
in this context beside the point.[4]

---

[3] It has recently been argued that, by about the middle of the seventeenth century, the princes had come to be seen by many, if not most, contemporaries as having something approaching a sovereign position in the Republic (Van der Plaat,
'Lieuwe van Aitzema's kijk op het stadhouderschap').

[4] The argument advanced by Geyl, *Oranje en Stuart*, concerning the role of
dynastic concerns in the foreign policy of the princes of Orange has been weakened
with respect to Frederik Hendrik by Groenveld, *Verlopend getij*, esp. 108–10, but it
remains a real issue as far as Willem II is concerned, and might well be more relevant for Willem III than the existing literature suggests.

In practical terms, the princes could, and did, provide an alternative to the States of Holland as head and director of the political system. Until his arrest in 1618, Oldenbarnevelt was the effective political leader of the Dutch Republic, acting as the embodiment of the power and authority of the States of Holland; from the last days of 1650 until the summer of 1672, Holland similarly dominated the state, for most of the time under the direction of De Witt; but for the rest of the century it was the four successive princes of Orange who led the country—thus for about sixty years. This role of leader and as focus of national loyalty is best exemplified by Willem III in 1672 and the immediately following years; the importance of his practical and inspirational leadership in helping to rescue the Republic from the disasters of the *rampjaar* have perhaps been exaggerated in orangist propaganda and historiography, but it would be equally misleading to underestimate it. The achievements of the prince in these early years had a truly heroic aspect which cannot be denied, even if it can now be seen that the situation of the Republic at the time he took over was not as weak as it seemed to be, and that the Dutch state would in all probability have survived without the prince's intervention. The fact remained that it was Willem III who accepted the task of leading the Dutch out of the valley of the shadow of death, and that he succeeded.

The distinctly more ambivalent aspect of the leadership role of the princes is best illustrated perhaps by the way in which Maurits took over power in the state during the Truce crisis. On the one hand, the actions he took did resolve the conflict and saved the Republic from the threat of disintegration or civil war, and to this extent he can rightly be seen as having performed a vitally important task, which the existing republican institutions had been unable to perform. Yet, on the other hand, it can be argued that Maurits's opposition to the Truce and his increasingly open support for the contraremonstrants had done much to contribute to the severity of the crisis in the first place. Indeed, it is from this point that we must date the beginning of the rival anti-Orange political myth which became the leitmotiv of States-party propaganda, but this episode also became a major piece of historical evidence for serious republican theorists later in the century as well. From this point of view, Maurits's activities during the Truce and culminating in the judicial murder of Oldenbarnevelt—Vondel's allegorical play on this subject, *Palamedes*, was subtitled *Vermoorde Onschuld* (Murdered Innocence)—were attributed to his inordinate ambition to dominate the Republic. Frederik Hendrik, although more conciliatory and politic, was seen as pursuing the same ambition to undermine republican institutions with more insidious though hardly less effective methods. In this interpretation, the actions of Willem II in 1650 were only an aberration in the sense that his hostility to the States of Holland was open and the personal nature of his ambition undisguised. Willem III could be easily fitted into this picture by stressing not only the *wetsverzettingen* of 1672, but the undoubtedly authoritarian nature of his instincts as a leader, and it is indeed true that his respect for republican freedom was never very evident.

The princes of Orange provided the Dutch Republic with an alternative way of making the political system work. Oldenbarnevelt and later De Witt demonstrated how the leadership of the States of Holland could give the somewhat inchoate institutions of the Republic coherence and purpose; but the princes of Orange could do the same, though in a very different way. The authority of the princes came from their offices in the Generality, their formal powers as stadhouder in the various provinces, and from a patronage system extending throughout the Republic. In particular, their powers of appointment to a wide variety of posts and offices, both in the army and throughout the political and administrative system, enabled the princes to build up an extensive network of dependants, especially in the land provinces. As captains-general, the princes had control over a large number of commissions in the army, particularly places falling vacant during active campaigning; and as stadhouders of most of the provinces, their influence over the appointment to a very large number of posts was extensive. In effect, it would hardly be going too far to suggest that, taken as a whole, the patronage system employed by the princes of Orange at its peak amounted practically to an alternative structure of political authority, underlying and to some extent subverting the formal system.

This alternative system had its beginnings with Maurits, but was built up systematically and most effectively by Frederik Hendrik. While the latter's influence in Holland was far from negligible—the stadhouder had the effective gift of a wide range of attractive posts besides considerable influence over the appointment of *vroedschap-*

pen, schepenen, and burgemeesters in the voting towns—his greatest influence lay in the land provinces, where he was able to gain
almost complete control over the votes of these provinces in the
States General. An important practical, as well as symbolic, expression of this increased power was the granting of the *survivance* of
the stadhouderships of Utrecht, Overijssel (1630), Gelderland,
Holland, and Zeeland (1631) to Frederik Hendrik's infant son, an
important step towards making the position of the house of
Orange in the Republic hereditary. Frederik Hendrik was even able
to muscle in on the position of the cadet branch of the Nassaus in
Friesland and Groningen: on the death of Hendrik Casimir in 1640,
he was able to poach the stadhouderships of Groningen and
Drente, but was unable to prevent that of Friesland from going to
the late stadhouder's son, Willem Frederik. He was able to gain the
survivance of Friesland, however, for his own son in the event of
Willem Frederik dying without issue. Another way in which he
exercised his power was through the development of the *secrete
besognes*, committees of the States General with full powers to
decide and act on the matters delegated to them. For a period in
the 1630s foreign policy was taken almost completely out of the
control of the provinces and put effectively in the hands of the
prince by means of such committees which tended to be very much
under his control.[5] Only after 1643 did the provinces regain much
of their control over foreign affairs.[6] Such secret committees were
also used by Willem III, but seemed to have been less central to his
exercise of power than they were to his grandfather.[7]

The difficulties which this powerful combination of formal powers and patronage could cause in irresponsible hands were demonstrated by Willem II. The essential difference between the young
prince and his father was that Frederik Hendrik had never let his
great authority within the Republic delude him into thinking that
he could ride roughshod over Holland with impunity. The essential
truth that the Republic could only be governed with, not in despite
of, Holland escaped Willem II; in sharp contrast, his father had
always been aware that, if all the means of pressure and patronage

---

[5] Poelhekke, *Frederik Hendrik*, 324–8.
[6] De Bruin, *Geheimhouding en verraad*, 258–9.
[7] De Bruin in ibid. 252–81 gives a stimulating account of the development and
activities of the secret committees of the States General in this period, and is now
the essential starting point for further discussion and research.

at his disposal failed to ensure support from Holland, then the consequences of this failure had to be accepted. Thus in the end Frederik Hendrik went along with Holland's peace policy; Willem II sent in the troops when he could not persuade or bully the province into accepting his *diktat*. Unless the young prince had learnt his lesson from the events of 1650—and it seems unlikely— then his death saved the Republic from serious internal disruption. The situation was that the prince could not win against Holland, but he could do enormous damage.

With Willem III the situation reverted to something similar to the system through which Frederik Hendrik had governed the Republic, though Willem's personal style was harsher and his formal powers were greater. Whereas Frederik Hendrik had adopted a deliberately moderate and conciliatory manner, whatever the realities behind this façade, Willem made little attempt to disguise the authoritarian nature of his political temperament and perhaps as a consequence aroused a great deal more resentment than his grandfather. It could be argued that in fact Willem was little, if at all, more powerful in practice than Frederik Hendrik, but he made the extent of his power all too obvious and so clashed with the ethos of the republican system, while his grandfather, for all the princely allures of his life-style, was much more tender to republican sensitivities. In formal terms, the *regeringsreglementen*, which were imposed on Utrecht, Gelderland, and Overijssel on their deliverance from the French occupation, gave Willem as stadhouder of these provinces extensive powers over the appointment of magistrates in the towns and other politically sensitive offices. Considering the degree of influence which the stadhouder already exercised in these provinces, it may be that this represented a degree of political overkill which only increased the stadhouder's control marginally at the cost of making it all too obvious.

Constitutionally, the fundamental element of the position of the princes of Orange within the political system of the Dutch Republic was their possession of the stadhouderships in a majority of the provinces. Something has already been said about the extent and limitations of the powers of the stadhouder in Holland; here it only needs to be stressed that whatever his influence on political appointments in the province, his control was never complete, and Amsterdam in particular remained largely independent. The stadhouder's power in the other provinces was based on a similar com-

plex of rights and duties as in Holland, but the result was generally a much more complete control of the politics of these
provinces, though how far this stemmed from the formal powers of
the stadhouder and how much from other and less formal sources
of influence varied from province to province. In Zeeland, for
example, the princes were not only stadhouders but also held the
title of First Noble (and thus their nominees represented the nobility in the provincial States) and were marquis of Veere and lord
of Vlissingen, giving them effective control of these two voting
towns as well. However, although Orange influence was thus
understandably great in Zeeland, it was less complete in practice
than in the land provinces, where in some respects the formal powers of the princes were less impressive. The political influence of
the princes in the various provinces of the Republic represented a
typically Dutch mixture of formal and informal powers, leading to
intensely complex situations which, for the purposes of this argument, need not be discussed in detail. Suffice it to say, that outside
Holland the stadhouder was able to act considerably more like the
sovereign he was not than the servant and officer of the provincial
States which he in formal terms remained.

The existence of a cadet branch of the house of Nassau as stadhouders of Friesland, and usually of Groningen and Drente as well,
compromised to a limited extent the lone eminence of the princes
of Orange within the Republic. Although the two branches might
have been expected to co-operate as smoothly as did Maurits and
Willem Lodewijk at the beginning of the century, later on in the
century a latent antagonism became increasingly evident. Willem
Lodewijk played an important military role as Maurits's partner in
the reform of the Dutch army, and he seems also to have acted to
some extent as the latter's political mentor during the Truce crisis.
Frederik Hendrik, however, made it clear that he wished to round
off his family's position in the Republic by taking over the stadhouderships of the Frisian branch, and did indeed manage to get
control of Groningen and Drente. Subsequently, an atmosphere of
distrust generally marred the relations between the two branches of
the Nassaus. After the death of Willem II, Willem Frederik,
although he had encouraged the young prince in his ambitions, was
suspected by those attached to the cause of the young Willem III of
planning to usurp the position of the senior branch of the family.
It was, indeed, partly this deep distrust which weakened the

orangist cause during Willem's childhood. In the end, however, the Frisian Nassaus were vital to the future of the house of Orange in the Republic, as they were able to provide an heir when Willem III died without legitimate issue.[8]

If we restrict ourselves to the seventeenth century, it can be seen that, far from the position of the princes of Orange within the Dutch Republic being stable, there was in fact a constant fluctuation in their real political power. It should not be forgotten that, for something like forty years of the century, the princes were overshadowed by the Advocate or *raadpensionaris* of Holland, and that the power of the princes was never enough to render that of the chief province negligible. From one point of view, there was an overall tendency for the powers of the princes within the Dutch state to increase, not steadily, for there were setbacks, but reaching a higher point each time the pendulum swung in their favour. This is the case when we trace these powers from the relatively modest position of Maurits before about 1609 to the quasi-monarchical position of Willem III just before his death. However, the increase in the princes' power took place largely in the lesser provinces, not in the crucial province of Holland. At the end, as at the beginning, of the century, the ability of the princes to control the politics of the country depended on how far Holland was united in its pursuit of its own vision of internal and external policies.

As has been seen, Maurits's ability to defeat Oldenbarnevelt and his supporters in the States of Holland sprang not so much from his own strength as from the deep divisions within Holland itself between the remonstrants and contraremonstrants and, in particular, between a majority of the voting towns and a minority led by Amsterdam. Similarly, though less dramatically, the continuing, often bitter, divisions between the orthodox calvinists and crypto-remonstrants—perhaps 'erastian' would be a more precise way of referring to this political force, which was no longer remonstrant yet not quite republican—gave Frederik Hendrik the chance to play off one party against the other to the benefit of his own position and policies. Only when the passions of the Truce conflicts had substantially subsided, and Holland became increasingly united in its desire to secure an end to the war with Spain, did the prince begin to lose his grip on foreign policy. The reality of this substan-

[8] Although, of course, Willem IV was not able to succeed to the positions of the elder branch until 1747, after the long interval of the second stadhouderless period.

tial shift in power was signalled not just by the signing of the Treaty of Münster in 1648, but also by the failure of Willem II to achieve his ends in 1650. However the events of that year are assessed, the very fact that Willem found it necessary to attempt a *coup* is a measure of the extent to which the power of the prince of Orange had slipped from its peak under Willem's father.

Although Willem III began his government of the Republic with the substantial advantage, as far as Holland was concerned, of having placed a large number of at least nominally orangist men in the town governments of the province through the *wetsverzettingen* of 1672, his ability to control the States of Holland was relatively short-lived. In contrast to 1618 and the following years, no deep ideological split had existed among the Holland regents in 1672. It proved rather easier for men who had come to power as orangists in that year to move into opposition with regard to the prince's foreign policy than it had been for contraremonstrants to shift to a more secular and pragmatic approach. Already by 1678, the prince had been forced into making peace with France, despite his apparently powerful influence within the town governments of Holland. Subsequently, the States of Holland proved able to hold the prince in check for a number of years, and the final success of Willem's foreign policy, with the invasion of England and the renewal of the war with France, should not be seen as a defeat for Holland. Rather it marks the degree to which substantial and influential elements within the regent oligarchy of the province had been persuaded of the immediacy of the threat presented by France, not by the arguments or political pressure of the prince, but by the actions of Louis XIV himself both in France and outside it. During the government of Willem III, the States of Holland were not uniformly successful in their opposition to his policies, not because they had lost the power to do so or because the political system of the province had been successfully manipulated by the prince, but rather because the issues involved were not clear cut. The prince's policies were neither entirely wrong nor completely against the interests of Holland; genuine differences of opinion existed within Holland as to the right way of dealing with the French threat. Such divisions and uncertainty favoured Willem, whose single-minded conviction seems never to have wavered. It needs to be stressed, however, that Willem could never have achieved what he did without the co-operation of the States of Holland. Specifically, the enterprise of England could not have been embarked upon without substantial support from Holland.

This example of co-operation is a warning that to interpret the seventeenth century as a period of permanent conflict between the princes of Orange and the States of Holland is seriously misleading, as such a view takes into account only part of a complex relationship. Such a struggle did take place, but it was only one aspect of the Republic's political life, for without co-operation between the two poles of authority within the Republic it would have been for long periods impossible to govern the country effectively at all. Even at those times, under Frederik Hendrik and Willem III, when the power of the princes of Orange within the Republic's political system was at its peak, they needed in one way or another to gain the passive acquiescence or active co-operation of the States of Holland. Thus, although there was always perhaps a latent antagonism between the two, there was also a practical awareness of the necessity of compromise to get the business of government done. At its best, this balance between prince and States worked quite well: the States of Holland ensured that the princes' tendency to forget the importance of the economy was kept in check, while the princes forced Holland to keep in mind more than narrowly provincial issues.

It might be argued that the governments of Oldenbarnevelt and De Witt demonstrate that an unadulterated dominance by the States of Holland was at least as effective a way of running the country as this balance between prince and States. In both cases the Advocate or *raadpensionaris* proved a most effective director of the Republic's foreign policy, but it may be that this came at the cost of other areas. De Witt's neglect of the army was not entirely his fault—the impossibility of reaching an agreement in the States General over the reform of the army sprang from deep political divisions between Holland and the other provinces—but it must be admitted that a governing prince of Orange would hardly have been likely to leave the Republic so badly prepared to meet the military threat from France. Oldenbarnevelt, after having practically created the Dutch Republic as a working polity, and having directed its government for nearly thirty years, finally failed to avert the near-disaster of the Truce crisis, and this must partly be explained by his increasingly Hollandocentric view of the nature of the state and its interests. Perhaps he had failed to give sufficient weight to the degree to which the Republic had changed between 1588, when only Holland, Zeeland, Friesland, and Utrecht were effectively free, and 1609, when the Spanish had largely been cleared from the territory of the new state, and thus did not realize that that dominance by Holland, which had been self–evidently right in the former year, needed significant modification now that circumstances had changed so markedly. The princes of Orange were not likely ever to make this sort of mistake, and to the extent that their very presence counterbalanced Holland's natural tendencies to neglect the interests of the other provinces they performed a necessary role in the Dutch political system. If, however, they chose to try to govern the Republic in despite of Holland's fundamental interests, then the survival of the Union was threatened.

5. Religion and the Dutch State

Religion affected the way in which Holland related to the other provinces in the Republic, and to the Union as a whole, during the seventeenth century in both positive and negative ways. On the one hand, the Reformed Church formed an element which all provinces, and especially their ruling groups, held in common, and provided a much-needed force to help bind them together. On the other hand, the need for all the provinces to share the same religion was a potential threat to Holland's autonomy as one province could not change its religious character without putting the Union at apparent risk. Such considerations help to explain why religion continued to play an important role in the Dutch state, despite the high degree of religious diversity which existed, and why the most serious political crisis of the century began as a seemingly esoteric theological dispute within the Reformed Church. As the Republic became more firmly united in other ways in the course of the seventeenth century, the significance of the Reformed Church as a unifying force diminished somewhat perhaps, but it would be unwise to disregard the importance of religion in the politics of the Union even in the more secular atmosphere of the last years of the century.

So, despite the considerable degree of religious heterogeneity in the Dutch Republic, there was an important sense in which it was a calvinist state. The Reformed religion provided the Dutch with a unifying idea and sense of purpose; unfortunately, a rather large proportion of the population could not share this vision of the Dutch state. As has been suggested, the role of the Reformed Church as a significant and perhaps indispensable unifying factor between the disparate provinces needs to be given its proper weight before the religious disputes which played such an important part in the history of the Dutch Republic in the seventeenth century can be understood. Equally, however, these disputes and their political repercussions were profoundly affected by the existence of large numbers of catholics and dissenting protestants.

Protestantism in general, and the Reformed Church in particular, had established itself as a symbol of resistance to Spain in the course of the Revolt, and carried on to be the official religion of the new state. A common religious loyalty was particularly important in the Republic given the widely differing political and economic interests of the various provinces. One aim which they all held in common was the defence of the Reformed faith, which in its turn conferred a universal purpose and significance to the war against Spain. One aspect of the role of religion in Dutch affairs, especially during the Revolt and the early decades of the seventeenth century—though the idea persisted to the end of the century and even later—was the association of Reformed orthodoxy with loyalty to the state. At bottom, perhaps, this idea was simple, even simplistic: the calvinists had to oppose the Spanish for they had no alternative, given the latter's intransigence on the question of religion. So, whatever the vacillations of those who were inspired by political or economic motives, the calvinists were absolutely committed to unremitting opposition to Spain. Such a presumption had a degree of truth, and more than a degree of plausibility, during the first decades of the Revolt, but by the seventeenth century its relevance to both the internal and foreign policies of the Republic was much less evident. Nevertheless, the tendency to confuse and conflate patriotism and Reformed orthodoxy did not fade away entirely, but remained an underlying assumption of Dutch political attitudes, and was liable to surface as a powerful popular force at times of crisis.[1]

Another consideration is that membership of the Reformed Church was one of the few things that the ruling groups of all the provinces had in common. At the beginning of the century, this was perhaps more true in theory than in practice, but as the century wore on the catholics and heterodox protestants were steadily squeezed out of positions of power, and the monopoly of political office by members of the Reformed Church became increasingly a fact. So the rulers of all seven provinces worshipped in the same church and owed allegiance to the same set of theological and ecclesiological principles, and this helped to provide them with a common language and set of ideas, as well as a certain degree of common purpose. The religious diversity of the Dutch Republic

[1] The importance of religion, and specifically the Reformed Church, in the construction of Dutch patriotism in the seventeenth century is stressed from a rather different perspective by De Bruin, *Geheimhouding en verraad*, 589–90.

meant that no single church could satisfactorily act as a binding ideology for all of the population, though the Reformed Church slowly won for itself the majority of the inhabitants of the state, was stronger in the territory of the seven provinces than in the generality lands, in the towns than in the countryside, and in Holland and Zeeland than in many of the other provinces (at least in the early years of the century). However, the monopoly of the Reformed Church over offices of power and profit in town, province, and generality became firmly established in the first decades of the seventeenth century. It may have been unsatisfactory as a national church, but it became the undisputed church of the ruling groups in every province of the Republic.

The catholics, of course, were the most obvious problem as far as religion, Dutch identity, and the nature of the state was concerned. The proportion of the population which was more or less actively catholic was still over 35 per cent at the end of the century, and was probably 50 per cent if not more in its first decade, although all figures on this issue are questionable. Catholics were allowed freedom of conscience and slowly won *de facto* freedom of worship, although their services remained officially banned until the end of the Republican period of Dutch history. However, they were formally, and increasingly also in fact, excluded from political life and all official posts in province or generality. The protestant interpretation of the Revolt and the concept of Dutch national identity as specifically protestant, indeed Reformed, which prevailed in the seventeenth century, left the catholics with what now seems a major problem—if being Dutch meant being protestant, where did the catholics fit in?

This was certainly seen by contemporaries as a practical as well as a theoretical problem—that is, by protestant contemporaries. Throughout the Revolt and the Eighty Years War, the catholics were regarded as a potential fifth column, and even later in the century this general distrust could come to the surface again, as it clearly did in the aftermath of the French invasion of 1672. This was a problem which the protestants brought on themselves; by creating the myth of the protestant nature of the Revolt, and thus of the state which grew out of the Revolt, they conjured up a catholic menace in their own minds. The rival version of history espoused by the erastian regents and republicans played down God and Orange, and stressed the political causes of the Revolt—the defence of age-old Netherlands liberties against a usurping and tyrannical ruler—and in this conception of the Revolt and the nature of the Republic there was a place for catholics, just as individual catholics had played an important part in the Revolt itself. It is hardly surprising that the element of paranoia with regard to the catholics was much greater among the hard-line calvinists than it was among the more latitudinarian of the regents.

In fact, there does not appear to have been any serious case of specifically catholic disloyalty to the Dutch state in the seventeenth century. During the long decades of war with catholic Spain and similarly during the wars later in the century with catholic France, the Dutch catholics showed no signs of sympathizing with or aiding the enemy in any very concrete way. There do not seem to have been significant groups of Dutch catholics at the Spanish court urging the conquest of their country—in sharp contrast, for example, to the very active groups of English catholics agitating against their queen in the late sixteenth century. Perhaps they were not needed, as in all conscience Philip II and his successors were doing the best they could to defeat the Dutch. However, the great mass of Dutch catholics seems to have been much more like the great majority of recusants in Elizabethan and Jacobean England: tenaciously loyal to a state whose political leadership regarded them with abiding distrust. Nevertheless, the catholics were clearly second-class citizens whose full integration into Dutch society would require a redefinition of Dutch identity.

Thus, the fact that over a third of the Dutch population was barred by reason of religion from full participation in the new state was a circumstance which could only exaggerate the problems arising from the lack of obvious unity of interest between the provinces. Nevertheless, this problem of a protestant government faced with a substantial catholic minority was one that Holland shared with all the other provinces of the Republic, and to some extent provided them with a common purpose in ensuring the continued dominance of protestantism in a religiously divided state. Although the presence of so many catholics in the country drove the protestants together for mutual defence, the practical question of how to deal with the catholic question could also deeply divide the ruling groups in the Republic. All the rulers were protestant, but some were more protestant than others. On the whole, the regents, especially in Holland, were inclined to a tolerant policy for a number of reasons. Most importantly, they lacked both the power and the inclination to persecute such a large section of the population. Also, more liberal protestant opinion, especially later in the century, was inclined to view ordinary catholics as already victims of a spiritually oppressive church, and as such rather to be pitied than persecuted. A further practical consideration was that throughout the seventeenth century the Republic had important catholic allies whose sensibilities it needed to bear in mind. In such circumstances, keeping a lid on the catholic problem was a sensible option.

On the other hand, the Reformed Church and the more orthodox of the regents pressed continually and consistently for a more effective set of repressive measures against the catholics, on both moral and practical grounds. For them it was clear that the honour and glory of God required the extirpation of the catholic idolators, and they perceived a section of the population whose essential loyalty was to a foreign power (i.e. the pope) as a threat to national security. In general, the existence of such a considerable catholic population was instrumental in increasing the anxiety level of the protestants. In particular, the general paranoia which marked the Truce crisis was to a significant extent a consequence of the distinctly tenuous hold which the Reformed Church had on Dutch society as a whole. If its following had been greater, if it had not felt so deeply threatened, then it might have been able to tolerate differences of opinion within its own ranks to a greater extent than proved to be the case.[2]

A further, though rather less severe, problem for the religious unity of the Republic in general, and for the harmony between Holland and the other provinces in particular, was presented by the protestants who were not members of the Reformed Church. These dissenters were not the same sort of threat as the catholics appeared to be, and were allowed more or less full freedom of worship, but they too were denied full participation in the political life of the

---

[2] In her comparative study of the contrasting religious history of England, Prussia, and Württemberg in the early modern period, Fulbrook has argued that the extent to which a church was able to tolerate internal dissent was directly related to the strength of its position, i.e. the more secure a church was politically, economically, and socially, the more tolerant it could allow itself to be (M. Fulbrook, *Piety and Politics: Religion and the Rise of Absolutism in England, Württemberg and Prussia* (Cambridge, 1983), ch. 4). It may well be that the Reformed Church became less paranoid as it became more secure of its place within the Dutch Republic.

country. Many of the mennonites in particular would have refused
as a matter of principle to take part in government or administration in any case, but the fact remains that they were not fully integrated into the Dutch state. In so far as the official religion of the
Republic was Reformed, the dissenters could not be totally loyal to
the religious component in the offical ideology of the state.
Certainly, from the point of view of the adherents of the Reformed
Church, the mennonites and other baptist groups were as much a
threat to the religious purity of the national community as were the
catholics, and added to this was the more practical concern at what
were felt to be the socially subversive implications of their doctrines. The reported horrors of the anabaptist Kingdom of God in
Münster in the previous century, when many of the participants
had come from the Netherlands, as well as heavily publicized
excesses nearer home, had given these radical groups the reputation
of being potentially a serious threat to the social order. However, it
would appear that already by the beginning of the century most
Dutch magistrates were convinced that the mennonites at least presented no such threat to society. Moreover, they could be regarded
as natural allies of the official church against the catholics. From
the erastian regents' point of view, they could also be seen as useful
allies against the influence of the Reformed Church, as the dissenters were absolutely dependent on the more liberal-minded of
the regents for protection against the official church, which continued throughout the seventeenth century to press for restrictions on
dissenters in general, as well as for action against particular groups
which it found especially offensive. The dissenters were not very
numerous, but were a palpable presence and, given the relative freedom of the press in the Republic, were able to exert a cultural
influence out of proportion to their numbers. Implicitly at least,
these groups too were an argument for modifying the religious component of Dutch national identity. However, they did not aggravate
in any serious way the relations between Holland and the other
provinces in this period, and so did not prove a problem as far as
the maintenance of the Union was concerned.

In practice, the greatest challenge to the monopoly of the orthodox Reformed Church over the ruling groups of the Dutch
Republic came, not from the catholics or the mennonites, but from
the more liberal movements within the church itself. It was also
religious issues of this nature which were most likely to lead to

serious divisions between Holland and the other provinces. Such doctrinal disputes were endemic in the protestant churches of this period, and indeed of any period, but what made them so serious in the seventeenth-century Republic was the close association which had been established in the course of the Revolt between the Reformed Church and the political leadership of province and Republic. As long as the church pretended to a monopoly of political office for its members, its internal affairs could never remain a purely private matter. The remonstrants represented a particularly dangerous challenge to the established politico-religious system because they were operating within the church, and could rely on the support of a powerful section of the regent oligarchy, in Holland at least, as well as widespread sympathy among the cultural élite throughout the Republic. Moreover, the imbalance in the strength of the remonstrant movement between the provinces threatened to open up a dangerous fault-line in the Dutch polity; the fact that the movement had much greater support in Holland, and on a broader social base, than elsewhere in the Republic helped to make this particular religious dispute especially disruptive of a state that was, or was feared to be, still fragile.

Perhaps the most challenging aspect of the remonstrant movement as far as the orthodox Reformed were concerned was that it represented an alternative to the rather uneasy compromise between church and state which had been established in the Republic by the beginning of the seventeenth century. One of the reasons why the remonstrant movement gained so much political support was that it offered two prospects that were very attractive to the regents of Holland in particular. One was a church on a broader theological base, which might hope to attract a much larger proportion of the population than the existing Reformed Church, and so act as a rather more effective force for national unity. Given contemporary assumptions regarding the incompatibility of religious divisions and political stability, this broad-church solution was attractive to those who were not too concerned about absolute doctrinal purity. Equally attractive to the regent oligarchs in general was the prospect offered by the remonstrants of a national church which was firmly under political control. Where the political theory of the Reformed Church was equivocal[3] and its

---

[3] E. Conring, *Kirche und Staat nach der Lehre der Niederländische Calvinisten in der erste Hälfte des 17. Jahrhunderts* (Neukirchner, 1965), 44–6, 60–6.

practice verged on the theocratic, the remonstrants were willing, out of conviction or expediency, to recognize the right of the civil authority to control over the church—and here the example of the Church of England and also of the Lutheran churches in the Holy Roman Empire and the Scandinavian kingdoms must have been influential in providing the regents with examples of church–state relations which were much more to their taste than the equivocations of the orthodox Reformed with regards to the rights of the magistrate.

Both these prospects, however, were anathema to the orthodox party, who could accept neither what they saw as a watering-down of doctrinal purity, nor any subordination to the civil magistrate in spiritual matters—especially given the dubious religious complexion of the magistrate in question. In the fraught atmosphere of the first two decades of the seventeenth century, any movement away from a distinctly blinkered version of calvinist orthodoxy[4] was seen as the first step on the road to Rome, and subordination to the state would have meant that not only the appointment of ministers but also the ultimate decisions on doctrinal matters would be in the hands of the civil authorities, and this was clearly unacceptable. Such vital matters ensured not only that the conflict between the hard-liners and the liberals would be fierce, but also that after the defeat of the latter they would be persecuted until they were prepared to accept the status of a separate church. As a dissenting religious group the remonstrants would be formally excluded from political office—though this was not always the case in practice— and so would lose the political leverage which had made them so dangerous. When they were no longer perceived as threatening to subvert the church from within, the remonstrants could be tolerated—albeit with the notably bad grace characteristic of the orthodox—in the same way as other protestant dissenters.

Later in the century, there were recurrences of the conflicts between the liberal and the ultra-orthodox wings of the Reformed Church, most notably in the controversy over the ideas of the theologian Cocceius and his supporters (see Part 2, Chapter 6). Yet, however much passion may have been aroused, such dissension

[4] Cf. Van Deursen, *Bavianen en slijkgeuzen*, 227 ff., where it is argued that what was orthodox for the reformed movement had already been clearly established by about 1600. However, it seems premature to date the triumph of one strand of reformed theology to any point before the synod of Dordt.

never again threatened to tear the state apart as the earlier dispute
had seemed to do, and these later problems within the Reformed
Church certainly never endangered the bond between Holland and
the other provinces. Similar issues were involved in these later
quarrels, but the position of the Reformed Church within the
Dutch state was much more secure in the second half of the seventeenth century, the fabric of the state was also much stronger, and
consequently these disputes were not allowed to get out of hand.
Nevertheless, they are a reminder that, given the nature of the relationship between the Reformed Church and the Dutch state, disputes within that church were not and could not be a matter of
indifference to the civil authorities.

The Truce crisis, which grew out of a doctrinal dispute between
liberal and ultra-orthodox tendencies within the Reformed Church,
was the most spectacular example of the importance of the church
to the stability of the Dutch state. At its height the problems which
arose from this seemingly innocuous dispute appeared capable of
giving rise to civil war, if not of bringing about the disintegration
of the Union. Put at its simplest, Arminius and his supporters were
questioning theological positions which were coming to be seen by
many calvinists as the hallmarks of the true faith. The interpretation of predestination, in particular, was a central point at issue,
with the arminians proposing both a greater role for human free
will and a greater stress on God's mercy than on his justice, positions that the rigorists were not prepared to tolerate. The latter
stressed absolute predestination and the utter helplessness of man
in the face of his own sin and God's judgement, and insisted on
treating the Heidelberg catechism and the Netherlands' Confession
as the touchstone of orthodoxy. The arminians were not prepared
to accept the catechism as the standard by which their views were
to be judged—rather they wished the catechism itself to be subjected to a critical examination.[5] The political crisis which arose
out of this dispute within the Reformed Church has already been
discussed in the context of the politics of Holland. What is relevant
at this point is the effect of the controversy on the Republic as a
whole, and in particular on the relationship between Holland and
the other provinces. The basic question is why this religious controversy came so near to tearing the Union apart.

[5] Den Tex, *Oldenbarnevelt*, iii. 69–73.

Of course, one obvious element in the whole question is the timing of the dispute, which was doubly unfortunate in that it took
place at a time when the Republic was still young and consequently somewhat fragile in structure, and also just before the
political divisions over the signing of the Truce with Spain in 1609
began to become acute. In the first two decades of the seventeenth
century, the Dutch Republic had only just taken on its definitive
shape—the significant formative period of the Dutch state still
seems to be the period, 1588–98, singled out by Fruin in the last
century[6]—and its constitutional structure was still open to dispute
and reinterpretation. The very nature of the Union could still be
brought into question, especially because of the importance of
provincial autonomy in Oldenbarnevelt's view of the state. It could
still be asked whether the Union was in fact a new state at all, or
only an alliance of independent polities drawn together by the war
against Spain. The only document which could act as a constitution or founding charter for the Republic, the Union of Utrecht,
was in form at least just such an alliance and no more, and it took
an enormous amount of judicial ingenuity—of which there was,
fortunately or unfortunately, no shortage in the Republic at this
time—to make it appear a more binding and constitutive document. This fundamental uncertainty had apparently been relegated
to the status of a mere theoretical problem by the two decades of
successful operation as a *de facto* new state in the European system, but the approach and signing of the Truce gave a new life to
such old apprehensions. The dilemma was that if the Union was
primarily, or even only, an alliance to prosecute the war with
Spain, what would happen to it when hostilities were suspended?
Would the Union necessarily fall apart with the end of the war
that was its *raison d'être*, or would the separate interests of the
provinces force them apart in the absence of the common military
necessity? In other words, if the war was not there to hold the
Union together, what was? In these circumstances, it is hardly surprising that people who found it difficult to answer the first two
questions in a reassuring way put an extraordinary stress on the
importance of the answer they found to the third question—
religion. If the Union did not have the war to hold it together, then
the binding force of a common religion became all the more

[6] R. Fruin, *Tien jaren uit den Tachtigjarigen oorlog, 1588–1598* (Amsterdam, 1861).

important. Particularly with regard to Holland, the Reformed Church was one of the few things it held in common with its partners in the Union. It was at this juncture that the remonstrant–contraremonstrant dispute threatened to break up the unity of the Reformed Church: thus, the remonstrant movement could, and did, appear as a threat to the very survival of the Union.

Such apprehensions could only be aggravated by the circumstance that the remonstrants were powerful only in Holland, and thus the movement seemed to exacerbate the differences between this province and the rest, which were already a source of serious concern. The remonstrant movement was not confined to Holland—as a theological tendency it spread throughout the Republic—but only in the premier province did it show signs of becoming strong enough to stand up to the forces of entrenched orthodoxy. Remonstrantism outside Holland was dependent for its survival on the success or failure of the movement within the latter province. This dependence on Holland is particularly clear politically. Although there were isolated cases of political support for the remonstrants in the rest of the Republic—Nijmegen and the town of Utrecht are the most obvious examples—there was no mistaking the contraremonstrant character of the states of the lesser provinces. Only in Holland did the remonstrants receive widespread support from the regent oligarchy. Why this should have been the case is far from clear. Perhaps the Reformed groups which governed in the land provinces were even less secure than their counterparts in Holland, as the progress of protestantism in the whole region had been patchy at best up to this point. The real dominance of protestantism in these areas seems to have come in the decades after 1618, so perhaps the embattled church and the protestant rulers of these provinces were not secure enough to allow themselves the luxury of theological subtleties—what they needed was clearly defined and unambiguous doctrine. Moreover, the idea that only a small minority were predestined to salvation might have acted as the theological mirror of their social situation as a minority of true believers in a population of catholics, protestants of indeterminate orthodoxy, and the indifferent.

Thus, the remonstrant movement seemed to represent an especially dangerous threat to Dutch unity, as it seemed possible, even likely, that it would change the character of the Reformed Church in Holland—but only in Holland. The Union of Utrecht had left religious matters to the governments of the separate provinces, but as the rulers of every province opted in practice for the Reformed Church this had not proved the divisive issue it might have been. However, if Holland's definition of what the True Reformed Religion (*Ware Gereformeerde Religie*) was should come to differ significantly from that subscribed to by the rest of the Republic, then the ability of the common religion to bind the provinces together would be weakened if not destroyed. The particular social and political complexion of the province of Holland seemed set to produce a religious situation which would emphasize rather than reduce the internal divisions which were threatening to undermine the Union.

The solution most generally proposed—by the orthodox and most of the provinces outside Holland—for the remonstrant–contraremonstrant controversy was the calling of a national synod of the Reformed Church to settle the issue. This was a logical and apparently reasonable proposal, but suffered from a number of drawbacks which in the end made it totally unacceptable to Oldenbarnevelt and his supporters, as well as to the remonstrants. Quite apart from the important formal question of how the synod was to approach the problem—the orthodox approach meant that the remonstrants would be judged by the compatibility of their doctrines to the Heidelberg catechism and the Netherlands' Confession, while it was precisely these definitions of the faith that the followers of Arminius wanted to challenge—it was clear that the majority in any national synod would be hostile to the remonstrants, and thus if such a meeting were permitted it could only result in the condemnation and expulsion of the latter. This, of course, is precisely what did happen in 1619 when the national synod was finally able to meet. It is understandable that the convinced remonstrants were unwilling to accept this mode of resolving the difficulties. For the more politically motivated supporters of the movement—and here Oldenbarnevelt is the key figure—a national synod in the end proved unacceptable as it would make decisions on religious matters which were prescriptive for the Republic as a whole, and this would have been an invasion of provincial autonomy. As Holland was out of step with the rest of the Republic in religious matters, the synod would be dictating to the premier province on how to run its internal affairs, and this in a matter as important and sensitive as religion. Yet, if there was one thing unambiguous in the Union of Utrecht it was that religious policy was a provincial concern; and if there was one principle that underlay the whole of Oldenbarnevelt's internal policy, it was provincial autonomy, which enabled Holland to dominate the political life of the Republic. The impasse was clear: only a national synod could resolve the religious conflict, but such a synod was unacceptable because it would condemn the remonstrants and infringe the autonomy of Holland. All that was left for Oldenbarnevelt and his supporters to do was to use political and administrative measures, such as a ban by the States of Holland on public preaching or teaching about the controversial issues, to try to damp down the disputes and hope they would eventually fade away. This tactic might have worked, had it not been for the powerful following the contraremonstrants were able to amass within Holland itself, not only among the populace at large, but, perhaps more significantly, among the regents of the voting towns and of Amsterdam in particular.

In the event, the attempts by the civil authorities to defuse the situation in Holland failed. A determined campaign by fanatical contraremonstrant ministers, convinced that they were faced with a mortal threat to the True Reformed Religion, backed by the governments of a number of towns led by Amsterdam, was accompanied by widespread popular violence against the remonstrants in the towns of Holland. It was the inability or unwillingness of the town militias to deal effectively with this protest, together with Maurits's very evident reluctance to use the troops under his command to maintain order in the disturbed towns, which led to the *Scherpe Resolutie* of 1617 empowering the remonstrant towns to engage their own hired troops (*waardgelders*) to deal with the situation. This proved to be one of the precipitants of Maurits's *coup* of the following year, as it could be seen, or be presented, as a prelude to civil war—with the ultimate aim of Oldenbarnevelt being to build up a locally controlled army which could challenge the monopoly of armed force within the state enjoyed by the generality army under Maurits.

A central problem here is why Oldenbarnevelt stuck so intransigently to what was clearly a doomed policy. It was certainly not religious conviction which hardened his resolve against the contraremonstrants, as his own personal beliefs seem to have been 'orthodox'. It may be that his long years of power had made him arrogant and his age inflexible, but his policy is explicable in more rational terms. First, his conviction that the preservation of Holland's autonomy was vital to the survival of the Republic made him see any infringement of that autonomy as a fundamental threat to the state he had done so much to create. From his point of view, a national synod had little short of revolutionary political implications. Moreover, to take the argument a step further, if Holland's autonomy were not respected would it not, sooner rather than later, lead to a break-up of the Union in any case? Closely associated with this standpoint was his deep distrust of what he saw as religious fanaticism, and the danger which he believed it represented to the good of the state. Centrally important here was Oldenbarnevelt's interpretation of key events in the recent past of which he had personal experience. As pensionary of Rotterdam, he had seen the collapse of the fragile unity of the Netherlands after the Pacification of Ghent (1576), leading to the loss of much of the south. He attributed the major share of the blame for this disaster to the activities of the calvinist radicals in Ghent and other towns in Flanders and Brabant, which he believed had driven the nobles and urban patricians into the arms of the Spanish. As the newly appointed *landsadvocaat* from 1587 onwards, he had experienced the problems of the Leicester period in the Republic at close hand, and again in his view much of the difficulty arose from the attempts of religious fanatics to take control of the policies of the state. These experiences had confirmed him in his adherence to *raison d'état* and conditioned him to see the contraremonstrant movement not simply as aimed at restoring strict doctrinal orthodoxy within the Reformed Church, but also as a direct threat to the predominantly secular priorities of the state. Oldenbarnevelt was not entirely wrong-headed in his fears: in the longer perspective the contraremonstrant movement can be seen as part of the Reformed Church's desire to stamp a firmer religious character both on the policies of the Dutch state and on the society of the Dutch Republic. In the event, after the settlement of the immediate problems of the church at the synod of Dordt, secular priorities were reasserted at all levels of society almost immediately, but such a relatively low-key resolution of the crisis could hardly have been anticipated in the fraught years just before 1619.

However, if fundamental issues seemed at stake in the crisis as far as Oldenbarnevelt and his supporters were concerned, the conflict looked no less serious when viewed from the perspective of their opponents. It is perfectly possible to explain the violent hostility of the contraremonstrants to their religious opponents in terms of their differences over the doctrine of predestination and other acknowledged theological positions adopted by the remonstrants. Although superficially the differences between the two sets of beliefs might seem insignificant (and even to insiders the points at issue had until very recently been seen as allowing a variety of interpretations while remaining in the broad Reformed tradition), the history of Christianity is littered with such seemingly esoteric disputes leading to schism and violence. However, in this case there was an extra dimension to the contraremonstrant fear and hatred of their opponents, for it was widely believed that the openly acknowledged doctrines of the remonstrants were only the tip of a heterodox iceberg. It was thought that in private the remonstrant leaders were teaching a much more far-reaching revisionism than they would ever admit in public, the reason for this secrecy being the covert romanizing tendencies of the movement. This last step of imagination sprang from the fixed belief of the hard-liners that the least breach of doctrinal purity was a sign of total theological depravity. So, in the imagination of the contraremonstrants, the followers of Arminius were transformed from calvinist revisionists to crypto-catholics; but the workings of paranoia did not stop at this point, for it was no step at all from this position to regarding them as partisans not just of Rome but of catholic Spain also. Thus the remonstrants came to be seen not only as weakening the Republic indirectly by undermining the unity of the Reformed Church, but also as potential if not actual allies of the Spanish enemy.

It was at this logical point that the suspicions with regard to the beliefs and motives of the remonstrants linked in with unease at the direction of the Republic's foreign policy under the direction of Oldenbarnevelt. From this perspective, the conclusion of a truce with Spain could be seen as designed to give the Spanish a breathing space in which to regain their strength for a renewed assault on the Republic at a later date, and to weaken the Dutch by depriving them of the unifying force of the war. The Truce had taken away one important factor holding the disparate provinces together—the war—but Oldenbarnevelt through his support of the remonstrants was seen as attacking the other main unifier of the Republic, the

Reformed Church. It may seem far-fetched, but in the emotional atmosphere of the time it became widely accepted that Oldenbarnevelt's policies were not just wrong, but were deliberately designed to prepare the ground for a Spanish reconquest.[7] In the light of all that is now known about Oldenbarnevelt, this may seem an absurd charge, but it must be remembered that the vast majority of the Dutch population had little or no reliable information about foreign affairs or any other matters of state. The government and the regents in general regarded such matters as *arcana imperii* and no business at all of anyone outside government circles. In such an atmosphere of deliberate secretiveness about important state matters, those outside the charmed circles of regents easily fell prey to misinformation and perhaps even deliberate disinformation. Excessive government secrecy proved a fertile soil for rumour, insecurity, and paranoia.

It must be added that the international situation in the years after the signing of the Truce only served to aggravate the sense of insecurity in the Dutch population. We know that the Truce lasted its full twelve years, but at the time it cannot have seemed obvious that it would do so. Already in March 1609, the death of the ruler of the Rhineland duchies, Jülich, Kleve, and Berg, was the occasion for a major international dispute over the succession. With one of the opposing candidates converting to catholicism, the contest became confessionally coloured, and Dutch and Spanish troops moved into the region to support the rival claims. A renewal of the war was avoided, but the situation remained unstable, and was part of an international conjuncture in Europe which was becoming increasingly ominous. Confessional tensions were building up within the Holy Roman Empire in these years, giving warnings of the outbreak of the Thirty Years War, which finally came in 1618 just as the problems within the Republic reached their climax. Add to these circumstances the assassination of Henry IV and the succession of a minor in 1610, which left France dominated by a regency government distinctly less keen on good relations with the Dutch Republic than on catholic solidarity with Spain, and the overall international situation looked decidedly threatening for the Dutch throughout the whole period from the signing of the Truce to the outbreak of the Thirty Years War. This situation

[7] J. J. Poelhekke, *Het verraad van de pistoletten?* (Amsterdam and London, 1975).

cannot have helped to keep the anxieties over the internal problems of the Republic within reasonable bounds.

It is also possible that the economic effects of the Truce served to aggravate discontent, not only among proponents of a West India Company intended to attack Spanish and Portuguese possessions in the Americas, but also among the working population of a number of the Holland towns who were affected adversely as a result of changes in the trading environment.[8] While not claiming such economic problems as a major cause of the Truce crisis, a feeling of economic insecurity added to the perceived threats to the Reformed Church and the Union can only have increased the volatility of the Dutch population in general, and not only of the urban *grauw* (mob).

It seems clear that, at this early stage in the seventeenth century at least, a strong Reformed Church was regarded on almost all sides as essential to the preservation of the Union. On the one hand, Oldenbarnevelt and his supporters hoped to broaden the theological basis of the church and thus its popular appeal, while the others saw any dilution of rigid orthodoxy as they understood it as a fundamental weakening of the church. What both had in common was the belief that this was a matter of prime importance for the state, and neither found it possible to back down sufficiently to discover a compromise solution. Indeed, there does not seem to have been such a solution available; acceptance of the remonstrants would have resulted in a drastically changed church, both in its theology and in its greater subordination to the civil authorities; while giving in to the contraremonstrant demands seemed to imply that the secular powers were accepting the dictation of the church, and Holland subjecting itself to a federal decision. What is perhaps the most remarkable aspect of the whole matter is how quickly and effectively Maurits's *coup* was able to defuse the situation. A large number of regents in the towns of Holland were replaced, the remonstrants had to suffer a spasmodically vicious persecution for a few years, and resentment ran so high in some quarters as to lead to conspiracies to assassinate Maurits, but major civil strife was avoided and remarkably few lives were lost. It remains, however, one of the tragic ironies of the period that one of these few lives should have been that of Oldenbarnevelt—not only the great-

---

[8] Israel, *The Dutch Republic*, 59 ff.

est statesman of his time, but the true architect of the Dutch Republic. Yet, to a significant extent, Oldenbarnevelt's system survived him despite the defeat of 1618–19. Holland's defeat did not in the event weaken its power within the Union; as soon as its internal rifts were patched over, the province could resume its dominance in the affairs of the Republic, albeit within a system now directed by a prince of Orange.

What this whole episode seems to demonstrate is that even in the tolerant, almost secular, society of the Dutch Republic in the seventeenth century, a common religion was experienced as being necessary to provide an ideological dimension to the idea of the state. This proved true even in the case of the Reformed Church, which was in many ways unsuited to this role—chiefly because of its limited hold on the population of the Republic. It was, however, all there was, so it had to perform this unifying function despite its unsuitability. In the course of the century the numerical following of the Reformed Church increased and to this extent it gained in credibility, but it was always an imperfect instrument for the task it had to perform, and its ideological leadership may have caused as much division as unity of purpose. Nevertheless, it was the Reformed Church which provided the Dutch state with its official religion: the church in principle embraced all regents and officials, it took responsibility for official prayers and fast days for national disasters, and provided a religious interpretation of the Republic's actions and purpose. To some extent it was thus able to impose on the Republic its own view of the nature and purpose of the Dutch state, though one is driven at times to suspect that this had more effect on later historians than on contemporaries. The Reformed Church also provided a bond linking Holland with the rest of the Republic which may well have been indispensable in the early years of the seventeenth century, although becoming less so as the Dutch state became more securely established. What is clear, but remains difficult to interpret, is that the resulting close association of the Dutch state with the Reformed faith left both protestant dissenters and catholics with a fundamentally ambivalent relationship to the official image of the country in which they lived.

6. Provincial Autonomy and the Survival of the Union

The marked weakness of central government in the Dutch Republic was an apparent anomaly in seventeenth-century Europe, when centralizing, absolutist governments tended to be seen as the *sine qua non* of efficient rule, and provincial and local rights and privileges were regarded as incompatible with a strong state. Yet the Dutch Republic was one of the most successful states in Europe at this time; it may have been a byword in the rest of Europe for the slowness of its decision-making processes, but it can be argued that its government worked at least as well, and probably better in most important respects, than the much-vaunted absolutist systems of the period—though this is admittedly not saying a great deal. Despite its high degree of decentralization, the Dutch political system produced firm and consistent policies that were, if not always successful, sensible responses to the problems facing the Republic.[1] To this extent, the Republic was a living refutation of conventional wisdom regarding the necessity of both strong central direction and monarchical leadership, just as its unusually tolerant religious policies proved, in despite of contemporary assumptions, that religious diversity was compatible with a stable social and political system. Moreover, given the lack of homogeneity between the different provinces of the Republic, it seems clear that not only did the decentralized system work remarkably well, but that such a system was the only way in which the Union could have been made to work at all.

The principal problem which the Dutch state had to deal with was how to construct a stable and workable system despite the enormous imbalance of power and wealth between Holland and the other provinces. The two extreme political solutions to this difficulty were the subordination of Holland to the will of the majority of the provinces or, conversely, subjection of the weaker provinces to the direction of Holland. It is evident that neither

---

[1] See Israel, *Dutch Primacy*, 410–13 for rather similar sentiments.

approach could have been relied upon to provide a satisfactory answer to the problem; indeed, either was likely to lead to the break-up of the Union, or at least to severe domestic unrest. Over-simplifying, it might be suggested that something like the first method was characteristic of the periods when the princes of Orange were the prime movers in the politics of the Republic, while during the supremacy of Oldenbarnevelt and De Witt the balance was tilted towards the second way of providing leadership in the state. However, both extremes were in fact avoided for the greater part of the century, and a reasonable middle ground was found between the interests of Holland and those of the other provinces. The essential argument of this chapter is that the means by which this was achieved was the elevation of provincial auton-omy to the position of the fundamental principle of the Dutch con-stitution; the high degree of provincial independence, so severely criticized by later historians as putting local egoism above national interests, was in fact the cornerstone of the Union.

The reason why provincial sovereignty, or at least a high degree of autonomy, with all its evident and apparent drawbacks, was able in practice to hold the Union together was that it served the interests of both Holland and the lesser provinces. It prevented Holland from being out-voted by the permanent majority which the other provinces enjoyed in the States General—if they could find any issue to agree on—and allowed its financial weight to have an appropriate influence on decision-making. Paradoxically enough, provincial autonomy gave Holland the ability to take the leading role in the affairs of the Union which was the natural corollary of its economic preponderance. Any political system which allowed Holland to be regularly coerced into having to sup-port policies which were against its .perceived interests could not have lasted long. The preservation of Holland's quasi-sovereignty kept the Union together, thus enabling two centuries of common history to prepare the ground for the dissolution of provincial into national identity in the nineteenth century.

Yet the same principle also afforded the weaker provinces an important measure of protection from the danger of being over-whelmed by Holland. They too had a veto in the States General, though their lesser financial weight meant that the refusal of any one of them to agree to a given measure could, at a pinch, be ignored. Their internal affairs were protected from interference by

the other provinces, and in particular Holland was largely prevented from imposing its will on them. Although the opposition of
one of the weaker provinces could be disregarded in a crisis, the
system forced Holland to take the views, needs, and interests of its
fellow members of the Union extremely seriously. In sum, given the
differences in size, population, and wealth of the united provinces,
and especially between Holland and the rest, it is hard to see how
they could have worked together harmoniously without a high
degree of provincial autonomy to protect the weakest, but also to
give greater weight to the most powerful. In the course of the
eighteenth and early nineteenth centuries, the balance in wealth
between Holland and the rest of the country swung significantly in
favour of the latter, and it is arguable that this economic evening-
out was an essential prerequisite for the creation of a centralized
Dutch state.

Looking at the possibility of the establishment of a more centralized government for the Republic in the seventeenth century, this
could only have come from a strengthened position for the princes
of Orange. However, while the house of Orange may have become
a unifying force within the Dutch state in the course of this century, and something of a symbol of national identity, it was also
capable of creating major problems for the Union. In particular,
the ability of first Frederik Hendrik, then Willem II and Willem III
to gain a large degree of control over the votes of three or four
provinces in the States General was a form of usurpation of their
political rights, and badly unbalanced the machinery of government
in the Union. Far from enhancing the harmony between the allied
provinces, it can be argued that this development in fact exacerbated the basic clash of interests between Holland and the rest of
the Republic by adding to the weight of these divisions the fundamental competition between Orange and Holland for leadership of
the state. This substitution of the interests of the princes of Orange
for those of Utrecht, Gelderland, and Overijssel, and to an extent
of Zeeland as well, had already become marked by the middle
years of Frederik Hendrik's period of office, and it became stronger
and more formalized under the *regeringsreglementen* of Willem III.
This corruption of the republican system by the power of the
princes of Orange was in the event not the disaster it might have
been, partly because of the acute sense of political realities which
normally informed the actions of the princes in the seventeenth

century, but also because Holland's quasi-sovereignty protected it from being defeated in the States General by the votes which the princes could manipulate. However, the dangers inherent in this system were suggested by the brief but nearly disastrous career of Willem II. By his blatant abuse of his influence over the votes of the land provinces in the States General, and his refusal to recognize the strength which not only the formal constitution but good sense and precedent gave to Holland's case, he pushed the country to the very brink of civil war, and brought a secession from the Union into the realm of the thinkable, if not quite of practical politics, for the first time. It is no accident that it was precisely in the aftermath of the shock of 1650 that voices were raised suggesting that Holland did not really need the land provinces. If Willem II's attempt to coerce Holland into accepting the military budget for 1650 had succeeded it would have implied that this province's wealth could be used to support policies directly opposed to its perceived interests. It is doubtful whether such a situation could have been sustained for any length of time without serious trouble.

Thus, the influence of the princes of Orange on the actual workings of the political system of the Republic was far from being a simple and straightforward enhancement of the cohesion of the state. The arguments in favour of an *Eminente Hoofd*, particularly at times of internal confusion or external threat, were powerful ones, and have had considerable effect on the judgement of posterity, but the actual ways in which the princes increased their powers tended to corrupt and distort rather than reform the existing system. In the seventeenth century this reached its peak during the period in power of Willem III. His unflinching support for despotic and often corrupt local political bosses did much to undermine the political morality of the regent group in the Holland towns; and the *regeringsreglementen* gave him unprecedented and, in practice, barely challengeable powers in the land provinces. Moreover, all this was to enforce support for a foreign policy which, to say the least, was not always indisputably in the best interests of the country, broadly conceived. In particular, the dynastic entanglements of Orange and Stuart made it peculiarly difficult at times to judge whether Willem's motives were primarily the advancement of the interests of his country or of his family. In such circumstances, only the continued independence of Amsterdam, supported by other of the Holland towns, could keep anything like a healthy

check on the very personal policies of a stubborn but hardly infalli-
ble prince.

On the other hand, it has to be admitted that the Republic's system of government was far from perfect—and one of its most
obvious weaknesses was the inability of its supporters to admit
that it had any flaws—and that its lack of an undisputed central
authority could lead to serious problems. A common contemporary
criticism, particularly from foreigners, was the slow operation of
the process of decision-making, with the necessity of seemingly
endless referrings-back from the States General to provincial, and
even from provincial to town, level. However, in retrospect this
does not seem to have been a serious problem: whether under a
stadhouder or a *raadpensionaris*, ways were found of making quick
decisions when necessary, and the exasperation of foreign ambassadors may stem in part from the tendency of Dutch leaders to use
the system as an excuse for delays which the latter found convenient. More important was the lack of a sovereign power able to
resolve internal disputes and cut through political impasses. The
crises of the Truce period and 1650 show clearly the dangers that
could arise when disagreements between two power-groupings
could find neither a compromise nor a generally accepted authority
capable of imposing a resolution to the issues in question. The perceived need for a final authority within the state to stand above
parties and resolve disputes before they got out of hand led directly
to the Orangist solution of seeing the prince as an *Eminente
Hoofd*. A direct example of such a reaction to the weaknesses of
the Republic's political system is the poet, dramatist, and historian,
P. C. Hooft (son of the archetypal Amsterdam regent, Cornelis
Pietersz. Hooft[2]), who seems to have reacted to the experience of
living through the Truce crisis by looking to an increase in the
power of the princes of Orange to avoid a recurrence of such
difficulties.[3] Unfortunately, although the politic Frederik Hendrik
could present a more than plausible reconciliatory figure, the

    [2] See H. A. Enno van Gelder, *De levensbeschouwing van Cornelis Pietersz. Hooft*
(Amsterdam, 1918), for an account of the attitudes to politics, economic questions,
and religion of this almost ideal-type of the Holland regent.
    [3] E. O. G. Haitsma Mulier, 'Grotius, Hooft and the Writing of History in the
Dutch Republic', in A. C. Duke and C. A. Tamse (eds.), *Clio's Mirror* (Zutphen,
1985), 63–7; S. Groenveld, 'Pieter Cornelisz Hooft en de geschiedenis van zijn eigen
tijd', *Bijdragen en Mededelingen betreffende de Geschiedenis der Nederlanden*, 93
(1978), 51–8, 67.

princes of Orange were not above the divisions which tested the Republic but were in effect party leaders, so that there was always more than a little disingenuousness about this aspect of orangist propaganda. In truth, the princes could not play the part within the Dutch system which Hooft and others envisaged for them— they were part of the problem and could not be the solution.[4]

One of the basic difficulties of the idea of an impartial prince of Orange standing above the conflicting parties and provinces, evaded by the orangist propaganda of the time and largely over-looked by later historians, is that it assumes that there was indeed a set of objective national interests to be discovered and pursued by the patriotic statesman. This ignores the fact that there were genuine, and perhaps inevitable, disagreements over what in prac-tice such interests were. In particular, there were often very great differences between what the political leaders of Holland thought the interests of the Republic were, and what the representatives of the land provinces saw as desirable, and the history of the Republic can be written in terms of the conflicts between Holland and the princes of Orange over such matters. *Raison d'état* was and is a seductive notion, but all too often it involves the elevation of sectional interests into common national ends, and certainly the princes of Orange could be no more relied upon to discover gen-uine national interests than the regents of Holland.

However, in the short term the power of the stadhouder/captain-general could be decisive in bringing internal conflict to an end with something like minimal bloodshed, as was dramatically shown by the events of 1618–19. The way in which matters got out of hand in the build-up to the Truce crisis, and the failure of Oldenbarnevelt or anyone else to find a solution to the conflict within the rules of the existing constitution, are a striking illustra-tion of the potential weakness of a system without a universally accepted sovereign. The only place where something approaching sovereignty in the conventional sense can be said to have been clearly recognizable was at the provincial level—and even here the members of the provincial States can be seen as participating in that sovereignty rather than as subject to it—but it was precisely

---

[4] Cf. Van der Plaat, 'Lieuwe van Aitzema's kijk op het stadhouderschap', where it is convincingly argued that this contemporary historian reacted in a comparable manner to the crisis of 1650, regarding Holland rather than the prince as the cause of the problem.

this commitment to the effective autonomy of the provinces which was preventing a solution to the conflict from being found. Provincial autonomy, indeed, logically excluded any sovereign authority at the level of the Generality. It was precisely this issue that was fudged out of necessity in 1618–19. An entirely spurious but salutary sort of *ad hoc* authority was conjured up for the stadhouders and the States General, which allowed the arrest of Oldenbarnevelt and his closest collaborators, the *wetsverzettingen* in Holland, and the setting-up of a Generality court to try the Advocate and his associates—all of which look very like the acts of a sovereign power. In strict terms, these acts were clearly illegal. In particular, the court which tried Oldenbarnevelt for treason was a legal abomination: he could only legally be tried by one of the courts of Holland, and even then it was the States and not Oldenbarnevelt who held the formal responsibility for their official's deeds. However, driven by the necessity of the times, Maurits's supporters argued that for the Union to survive there had to be some form of central authority in the state, and they found this in a passage of dubious relevance in the Union of Utrecht which empowered the stadhouders to mediate in the case of disputes between any of the allied provinces. Gratefully wrenching this passage out of context, they saw this as implying an emergency authority vested in the stadhouders which was above that of the provinces. Thus, at the last minute a form of sovereignty for the stadhouders was pulled out of the hat to justify Maurits's actions in 1618. A similarly dubious authority was found for the legitimacy of the Generality court which was required to try Oldenbarnevelt.[5]

So, in the emergency of 1618–19, the Republic supplied the need for a final central authority by discovering a sort of residual sovereignty in the States General and the stadhouders. Yet it is a striking fact that this discovery of sovereign authorities in the Generality was discarded as soon as the immediate problem had been dealt with. The Truce crisis left no permanent mark on the Dutch conception of the nature of the Republic; once it was over the idea of provincial sovereignty resurfaced, seemingly as strong as ever and unscarred by what had happened in those years. It is true that these events could not be forgotten, and that the powers

[5] Den Tex, *Oldenbarnevelt*, iii. 636–40; Gerlach, *Het proces tegen Oldenbarnevelt*, 149–52, 389–92.

which had been exercised once with success remained a potent reminder that provincial sovereignty was not unassailable in practice, however powerful it was in theory. However, both Holland and the other provinces had too much to gain from the practice of provincial autonomy not to revert to it as soon as they could, and Maurits and Frederik Hendrik found it convenient to maintain and strengthen their place within the political system by informal rather than formal means. Clearly, all concerned had reasons to step back from the strengthened central authority which had apparently been discovered in 1618–19, and, it must be conceded, this retreat from a more conventional structure of political authority seems to have done little harm. On the contrary, the notably effective government of the Republic in the seventeenth century was dominated by a balance between the princes of Orange and the States of Holland, and the former held back from challenging, while the latter lived by, the principle of provincial sovereignty. Again, it must be stressed that the option in 1618–19 of moving towards some sort of sovereignty for the Generality was only possible because of the deep political and religious divisions within Holland, which led one powerful party to sacrifice temporarily provincial sovereignty for what it saw as a higher cause. As soon as more normal circumstances were restored, the assertion of provincial power and interest would regain its priority and ensure that Holland's autonomy was reasserted.

However, the trial of Oldenbarnevelt and his associates was not the only example of the States General exercising jurisdiction in cases where the whole state was felt to be affected. In 1621, Jacob Mom and four other nobles from Gelderland were tried by a special Generality court, charged with conspiring to betray the town of Tiel to the Spanish. The trials and executions went ahead despite passionate protests from Gelderland at what it regarded as a serious infringement of its autonomy.[6] Other, less spectacular, cases also occurred in the early decades of the century, but the principle of jurisdictional autonomy for the provinces triumphed as the century wore on, championed especially and inevitably by Holland.[7] Such cases are a reminder of the lack of definition in the relationship of the provinces and the Union, especially in the early

---

[6] J. J. Poelhekke, *'t Uytgaen van den Treves* (Groningen, 1960), 139; H. van Heiningen, *Tussen Maas en Waal* (Zutphen, 1972), 122–40.

[7] De Bruin, *Geheimhouding en verraad*, 565–6.

days of the Republic. Perhaps the trial of Oldenbarnevelt and his associates was not so obviously illegal after all, at least at that time.

In normal circumstances, the lack of a central authority with acknowledged superiority over the provinces did not prevent the political system from working with a fair degree of efficiency. Only in 1650 did a crisis centring around the question of the location of final authority in the Republic recur. However, this arose not from the sort of destructive internal divisions which had threatened the survival of the state during the Truce, but from the dissatisfaction and ambition of Willem II. The deadlock over the size of the army which preceded the prince's attempted *coup* was a problem not a crisis, and it was Willem's determination to assert his will at whatever cost which caused the trouble, not the inherent difficulty of the situation itself. Moreover, this deadlock had largely been caused by the prince's manipulation of the votes of the land provinces in the States General so as to set up a head-on confrontation with Holland over the size of the army. Thus, the crisis was not a consequence of provincial autonomy itself, but rather of the usurpation of the political rights of the land provinces by the prince. Without his intervention there is no reason to believe that a solution to both the immediate problem of the *staat van oorlog* of 1650 and to the longer-term question of the foreign policy of the Republic could not have been found quite readily. Admittedly, a constitutional impasse had been reached in 1650, but this became a major problem only because of the uncompromising attitude of Willem II; usually, such difficulties were relatively easily resolved, though sometimes at the cost of considerable bickering and even ill-feeling. For the rest of the century the chief participants in the political system ensured that no similar crisis was allowed to develop, despite the weaknesses in the system which seemed to make such impasses inevitable.

The determination of all concerned to make the existing system work in spite of its flaws is perhaps best exemplified by the calling of the *Grote Vergadering* (Grand Assembly) in 1651. The crisis of 1650, followed by the swift and unexpected death of Willem II, left the Republic in an uneasy and perhaps unstable situation. Willem had left only a posthumous child, and so there was no member of the house of Orange available with an undisputed claim to his offices and power except this infant, who would be incapable of using them for many years. In these circumstances, Holland took the initiative and called a special meeting of all the provinces to discuss the problems with which the prince's sudden death had left the country. This assembly was not to be a normal States General with its need to refer back to its principals, but it was intended that the whole of the separate provincial States would travel to The Hague with the power to make binding decisions there and then. The States of Holland declared their intention of dispensing with the office of stadhouder for their province, and one of the major questions facing the assembly was whether this act was a threat to the Union itself.

Apart from the immediate practical problem of what to do in the absence of an adult prince of Orange—after all, successive princes had played a dominant role in the running of the country for the previous thirty-odd years—the aim of Holland's political leaders was to reassure the other provinces of its loyalty to the Union. The traumatic events of 1650 had again brought the future of the Union in question: Willem II had used his formal and informal powers to turn the majority of the provinces against Holland, and it was to be feared that Holland might reciprocate by breaking the bond with the provinces which had proved such ready tools to be used against it. So the *Grote Vergadering* was symbolically as much as practically important; not a great deal of moment was decided at the assembly but Holland was able to demonstrate its commitment to the Republic in a manner which proved convincing. The slogan of the assembly was in effect *Unie, Religie, Militie*—that is, Holland declared its determination to maintain the coherence of the state, the common religion which helped to hold it together, and the Generality army which defended it. These three terms taken together can be understood as a rough definition of what contemporaries took to be the vital characteristics of the Dutch state. *Unie* stood for the commitment to at least a minimal form of the state, implying that the sovereign provinces surrendered part at least of their independence in effect by agreeing to work with and through the States General and the other Generality institutions; *Religie* is perhaps best understood not just as recognizing the perceived need for a common faith to provide some binding element for an all-too-divided country, but also as standing for commitment to common ideological ends, however imperfectly defined; while *Militie* made concrete the vaguer commitments to the Union by declaring for a centrally controlled and commanded armed force, and not a series of provincial armies. There were also, it is true, less healthy reactions to 1650, especially in the attempts to insure against the recurrence of the attempted *coup* by giving provincial governments control over troop movements within their territories, which show a certain lack of confidence by the regent group as a whole, and a disturbing lack of realism—as if a military commander seriously considering a *coup* would be deterred by legal niceties.

Nevertheless, on the whole the *Grote Vergadering* is an impressive piece of evidence of the extent to which the Republic had become an effective new state by the middle of the century, rather than a wartime alliance of independent provinces. By 1650 the frailty of the state in the early years of the century had been replaced by a matter-of-fact acceptance of the Dutch Republic as an effective and indispensable political vehicle for its inhabitants. Whereas in the first decade or so of the century the argument that the end of the war with Spain might lead to the disintegration of the Union had to be taken seriously, by 1648 such fears were no longer plausible. The Dutch Republic was by then a fact of political life to which there was no realistic alternative. There may not have been a great deal of enthusiasm for, or emotional commitment to, the Republic—in general, people's primary loyalties were probably to their province or even their locality[8]—but its existence and utility were accepted with that cool and realistic pragmatism typical of the seventeenth-century Dutch at their best.

Most of all, perhaps, the *Grote Vergadering* symbolizes the acceptance by Holland of the necessity of the Union. Despite the problems caused by Willem II, and the inordinate influence of the princes of Orange in general over many of the lesser provinces, and despite the continued insistence on provincial sovereignty as a constitutional principle, Holland's leaders accepted that the Republic was the political atmosphere in which they had to live; given that there was no viable alternative, the Union had to be made to work. However, if this assembly marks the definitive assertion of loyalty to the Union as far as Holland was concerned, it also reminds us that this loyalty was absolutely vital to the survival of the Republic. The events of 1650 can be seen as a near-

[8] Cf. Groenveld, *Verlopend getij*, ch. 1.

victory, or at least not a decisive defeat, for Willem II, or they can be seen as a partial defeat for a poorly organized Holland, with the expulsion of the Bickers from the government of Amsterdam and concessions on the army issue being made by the States of Holland. More fundamentally, however, the warning given by the events of the summer of 1650, and to which the Grote Vergadering was one sort of response, was the near-impossibility of governing the Republic unless the peculiar position of Holland was taken fully into account. The economic power of this single province meant that any government of the Dutch Republic had to work with and through the States of Holland. Even the most masterly of the princes of Orange, Frederik Hendrik and Willem III, recognized the need to gain the consent of the States, which they tried to do in their own rather different ways. They knew that there were limits beyond which they could not safely go; coercion such as that attempted by Willem II in 1650 could only succeed with large-scale foreign military aid, which would have effectively destroyed both the Republic and Dutch independence.

It is, on the face of it, a curious circumstance that most Dutch historians concerned with this period have taken a very different view of the question of provincial autonomy in general, and the role of Holland in the political system of the Republic in particular. From the last years of the Republic to the present, a dominant theme in historical writing on the Dutch Republic has been criticism of its lack of political unity, with the stress usually being laid on the inability of the provinces—and particularly and crucially Holland—to transcend their local egotisms in order to conceive and pursue truly national policies. The chief criticisms of the Republican system, and especially of the ruling oligarchy in Holland, were and are that the latter failed to realize the necessity of subordinating the interests, especially economic, of their own province to the greater good of a strong national government, and that the regents failed to recognize the historical task of the house of Orange to transcend local loyalties and provide a symbolic expression of the emergent Dutch nation.

In part, this criticism itself can be explained historically. Severe criticism of the Republic and its institutions was part of a reaction to what was seen as the failure and inertia of the Dutch eighteenth century. The unified kingdom of the Netherlands which emerged in the nineteenth century was seen as the necessary cure for the ills of the *ancien régime*; and the Republic was judged by this standard and was thus regarded as being fundamentally flawed, with more attention being paid to the evident weaknesses of the system according to the criteria of nineteenth-century constitutional thinking than to its practical successes in the seventeenth century. Such attitudes were encouraged by the romantically fired nationalism of the nineteenth century in Europe, which led the Dutch to interpret their history teleologically as the rise to consciousness and nationhood of the Dutch people. It was assumed that the Dutch nation had existed before their state and needed that state to give proper political expression to their pre-existing identity; the apparently more obvious argument that the Dutch nation was a creation of the Dutch state did not have the same emotional appeal. From this nationalist perspective, the intense provincialism of the Republican period was a betrayal of the historical purpose of the Dutch state.

Such preconceptions could produce curious results. The greatest of nineteenth-century Dutch historians, Robert Fruin, was prepared to argue that the whole Republican period was a diversion from the proper course of Dutch history, which would have seen Spanish absolutist rule fulfilling its historical mission of suppressing local and provincial privileges and creating a strong, centralized state which could then have achieved its independence in a more healthy form than the Republic.[9] Possibly the Dutch in the nineteenth, and even twentieth century perhaps, needed to turn their backs to some extent on their period of political, economic, and cultural greatness in the seventeenth century in order to adjust to their new position as a relatively wealthy but minor power in the world. The Republic had been a great power for a brief period, but it had perhaps failed to create what was arguably of more importance to the Dutch people as a whole—a sense of national unity and identity.

Also, the newly created Dutch monarchy of the nineteenth century needed a historical justification to disguise its somewhat artificial nature, and it found it in a refurbished orangist historical vision. In this account of Dutch history, the princes of Orange were always representative of a high-minded awareness of national purpose and needs, and the provincial estates—the States of

[9] J. W. Smit, *Fruin en de partijen tijdens de Republiek* (Groningen, 1958), 155–60.

Holland were again, inevitably, the great anti-heroes—portrayed as blinkered particularists. The princes were both the symbols of Dutch unity and the providential protagonists of the latent Dutch nation. As long as the Dutch monarchy lasts, there will no doubt be powerful cultural forces to support such an interpretation of the national history.

A rival republican tradition survived to compete with the orangist denigration of the Republican system, and in the twentieth century its most influential exponent has been Pieter Geyl. His writings to some extent fit into a republican tradition which relied rather more on moralistic criticism of over-exuberant orangism than on sophisticated analysis. His specific criticisms regarding the dynastic and anti-national elements in the foreign policy of Frederik Hendrik in particular[10] have been effectively challenged recently,[11] and apart from Geyl's iconoclasm the treatment of the seventeenth-century Orange princes has been remarkably respectful, even by recent historians. It is notable that even Willem II has received a markedly lenient treatment from most historians.[12] A more balanced appreciation of the role of the princes of Orange and of provincial autonomy in the Republic has not yet emerged.

An important adjunct to the orange-tinted version of Dutch history, but also a fully fledged myth in its own right, is the calvinist interpretation, which has not entirely lost its force even in the modern Netherlands. This embodies a providential view of history, and sees the Reformed Church and the house of Orange as the instruments for carrying out God's will in the Netherlands. It is hardly surprising that the whole republican tradition is systematically denigrated by this influential school. The point is that Dutch identity is seen from this perspective as essentially calvinist, and that both the Reformed Church and the princes of Orange are seen as the protagonists of this transcendent religious purpose. Inevitably, then, whether during the Leicester period, the Truce

[10] Geyl, *Oranje en Stuart*.

[11] Groenveld, *Verlopend getij*, 108–10. Such criticisms might possibly be applicable to Willem III's foreign policy to some extent, though this national hero was not tackled by Geyl from this perspective, as far as I know, and certainly not in Geyl, *Oranje en Stuart*, which might be considered a curious omission.

[12] G. W. Kernkamp, *Prins Willem II* (Amsterdam, 1943) is the only reputable modern biography, but there are recent discussions of Willem II's actions in Rowen, *The Princes of Orange*, ch. 4, and Groenveld, 'William II en de Stuarts'. All of these studies are notably restrained in their judgements, perhaps too much so.

crisis, or less dramatically throughout the seventeenth century, the regents with their erastian tendencies and emphatically secular priorities are seen as enemies of the true, providential interests of the Dutch nation. Implicit thus in the calvinist interpretation is not only a condemnation of the regents as a force in Dutch history, but also of provincial autonomy, with the centralized Orange monarchy as the appropriate political system for the godly nation.

There have been, of course, dissenting historical movements, but only the rather old-fashioned and threadbare republican tradition has had much to say in favour of regent-rule and the decentralized political system, even with regard to the seventeenth century. The catholics clearly could not accept the calvinist interpretation of the Revolt and Dutch identity, but were primarily concerned to find a historical Dutch identity which could include them, and had no particular quarrel with, for example, the adulation of the house of Orange, as long as it was not exclusively associated with protestantism. Moreover, catholic emancipation's stress on catholic spiritual and cultural values was hardly likely to lead its historians to a sympathetic appreciation of the pragmatic and secular virtues of the seventeenth-century regents. On the other hand, the growth of a left-wing historiography, although capable of recognizing the value of the republican and secular tendencies within the oligarchy, was hardly conducive to a sympathetic understanding of the regent regime, arrogant and absolutist as it was. The socialist movement in particular would have to look elsewhere for its heroes.

Yet, despite this generally unsympathetic treatment of the political system of the Republic in the seventeenth century, it might be asked whether there was really any other way of running the country effectively at the time. It seems obvious that the only possible alternative, before the eighteenth century at least, to regent rule and provincial autonomy was not the introduction of a degree of democracy, but greater power to the house of Orange. So the real question to be asked of the critics of regent rule is whether a more centralized political system could have worked in the seventeenth century, given the disparities between the provinces, and the difficulty of arriving at a common set of values and priorities. This is to argue that the real weakness of the 'unitary' tradition is not its sentimental adulation of the princes of Orange, but rather its anachronistic assumption that a unitary system could have been successfully introduced. The point to stress about the decentralized political system of the Republic is not that it worked pretty well— though it did—but that it was probably the only way in which the heterogeneous amalgamation of territories which comprised the Union could have been run at all at this time.

The basic argument of this chapter is that, in the circumstances of the seventeenth century, provincial autonomy was absolutely essential to hold the Union together. Only a high degree of provincial independence could have satisfied Holland's need to be given proper weight in the politics of the Republic, and at the same time given a sufficient degree of protection to the interests of the weaker provinces. Similarly, the establishment of a more centralized government under the direction of the princes of Orange was simply not on. It is conceivable that some sort of Orange monarchy could have been imposed on the Dutch state, but it would still have had to work within a system which devolved the essentials of power to the provinces. The centralized monarchy of the nineteenth century could not have succeeded at any earlier date, and so judgements on the seventeenth century from this perspective were and are anachronistic. The simple truth is that the political system of the Dutch Republic worked remarkably well in the seventeenth century, and that it did so not despite provincial autonomy and the systematic decentralization of political power, but because of it.

SELECT BIBLIOGRAPHY

AALBERS, J., 'Factieuse tegenstellingen binnen het college van de ridderschap van Holland na de Vrede van Utrecht', *Bijdragen en Mededelingen betreffende de Geschiedenis der Nederlanden*, 93 (1978), 412–45.
—— *De Republiek en de vrede van Europa*, i (Groningen, 1980).
AITZEMA, L. VAN, *Saken van Staet en Oorlogh, in ende omtrent de Vereenigde Nederlanden, 1621–69*, 7 vols. (The Hague, 1669–72).
BAELDE, M., *De collaterale raden onder Karel V en Filips II (1531–1578)* (Brussels, 1965).
BANGS, C., *Arminius: A Study in the Dutch Reformation* (Nashville, 1971).
BARENDRECHT, S., *François van Aerssen, diplomaat aan het Franse hof (1598–1613)* (Leiden, 1965).
BAXTER, S. B., *William III and the Defense of European Liberty 1650–1702* (New York and London, 1966).
BIELEMAN, J., *Boeren op het Drentse zand 1600–1910* (Wageningen, 1987).
BIJL, M. VAN DER, 'Familie en factie in de Alkmaarse stedelijke politiek', in *Van Spaans beleg tot Bataafse tijd* (Zutphen, 1980), 13–32.
—— *Idee en Interest: Voorgeschiedenis, verloop en achtergronden van de politieke twisten in Zeeland en vooral in Middelburg tussen 1702 en 1715* (Groningen, 1981).
—— 'Pieter de la Court en de politieke werkelijkheid', in Blom and Wildenberg, *Pieter de la Court*, 65–91.
BLÉCOURT, A. S. DE, *Ambacht en gemeente* (Zutphen, 1912).
BLOK, D. P. *et al.*, *Algemene Geschiedenis der Nederlanden*, v (Haarlem, 1980).
BLOK, P. J., *Geschiedenis eener Hollandsche stad onder de Republiek* (The Hague, 1916).
—— *Frederik Hendrik, prins van Oranje* (Amsterdam, 1926).
—— 'Nederlandsche vlugschriften over de vredeshandelingen te Munster 1643–1648', *Verslagen en Mededelingen der Koninklijke Nederlandsche Akademie van Wetenschappen*, afd. Letterkunde, 4e reeks, i (1897), 292–336.
BLOM, H. W., 'Political Science in the Golden Age: Criticism, History and Theory in Dutch Seventeenth Century Political Thought', *The Netherlands Journal of Sociology*, 15 (1979), 47–71.
—— and WILDENBERG, I. W., *Pieter de la Court in zijn tijd (1618–1685)* (Amsterdam and Maarssen, 1986).
BOER, M. G. DE, *De woelingen in Stad en Lande in het midden der zeventiende eeuw* (Groningen, 1893).

——— 'Merkwaardige notulen van de Staten van Holland', *Tijdschrift voor Geschiedenis*, 59 (1946), 52–64.

BONTEMANTEL, H., *De regeeringe van Amsterdam, soo in 't civiele als crimineel en militaire (1653–1672)*, ed. G. W. Kernkamp (The Hague, 1897).

BOOGMAN, J. C., 'De raison d'état-politicus Johan de Witt', *Bijdragen en Mededelingen betreffende de Geschiedenis der Nederlanden*, 90 (1975), 379–407.

——— 'The Union of Utrecht, its Genesis and Consequences', *Bijdragen en Mededelingen betreffende de Geschiedenis der Nederlanden*, 94 (1979), 377–407.

BRANDT, G., *Historie der Reformatie en andere kerkelijke geschiedenissen in en omtrent de Nederlanden*, 4 vols. (Amsterdam and Rotterdam, 1671–1704).

BRUIJN, J. R., *De admiraliteit van Amsterdam in rustige jaren, 1713–51* (Amsterdam, 1970).

BRUIN, G. DE, 'De soevereiniteit in de Republiek: een machtsprobleem', *Bijdragen en Mededelingen betreffende de Geschiedenis der Nederlanden*, 94 (1979), 27–40.

——— *Geheimhouding en verraad: De geheimhouding van staatszaken ten tijde van de Republiek (1600–1750)* (The Hague, 1991).

BRUIN, C. C. DE, *Joachim Oudaan in de lijst van zijn tijd* (Groningen, 1955).

BUNT, A. VAN DER, 'Kerk en staat tijdens de Republiek', *Historia*, 15 (1950), 29–31.

BUSSEMAKER, TH., 'Lijst van ambten ter beschikking staande van Burgemeesteren van Amsterdam', *Bijdragen en Mededelingen van het Historisch Genootschap*, 28 (1907), 474–518.

CAPELLEN, A. VAN DER, *Gedenkschriften*, ed. R. J. van der Capellen (Utrecht, 1777–8).

CHRIST, M. P., *De Brabantsche Saeck: Het vergeefse streven naar een gewestelijke status voor Staats-Brabant 1585–1675* (Tilburg, 1984).

COLLEY, L., *In Defiance of Oligarchy: The Tory Party 1714–60* (Cambridge, 1982).

CONRING, E., *Kirche und Staat nach der Lehre der Niederländische Calvinisten in der ersten Hälfte des 17. Jahrhunderts* (Neukirchner, 1965).

CORNELISSEN, J. D. M., *Johan de Witt en de Vrijheid* (Nijmegen and Utrecht, 1945).

COURT, P. DE LA, *Aanwysing der heilsame politieke gronden en maximen van de Republike van Holland en West-Vriesland* (Amsterdam, 1669).

——— *Het welvaren van Leiden* (The Hague, 1911).

DALEN, J. L. VAN, *Mr. Cornelis de Witt* (Dordrecht, 1918).

DAVIS, N. Z., *Society and Culture in Early Modern France* (London, 1975).

DEKKER, R. M., 'De rol van vrouwen in oproeren in de Republiek in de 17e en 18e eeuw', *Tijdschrift voor Sociale Geschiedenis*, 12 (1978), 305–16.

DEKKER, R. M., *Oproeren in Holland gezien door tijdgenoten: Ooggetuigenverslagen van oproeren in de provincie Holland ten tijde van de Republiek (1690–1750)* (Assen, 1979).

—— 'Het Kostermanoproer in 1690, complot of spontane beweging?', *Rotterdams Jaarboekje* 1981: 192–207.

—— *Holland in beroering: Oproeren in de 17de en 18de eeuw* (Baarn, 1982).

—— '"Politiek geweld" en het process van staatsvorming in de geschiedenis van de Nederlanden', *Sociologisch Tijdschrift*, 10 (1983), 335–53.

—— 'Women in Revolt: Popular Protest and its Social Basis in Holland in the Seventeenth and Eighteenth Centuries', *Theory and Society*, 16 (1987), 337–62.

DEURSEN, A. TH. VAN, 'De Raad van State en de Generaliteit, 1590–1606', *Bijdragen voor de Geschiedenis der Nederlanden*, 19 (1964), 1–48.

—— *Honi soit qui mal y pense? De Republiek tussen de mogendheden (1610–1612)* (Amsterdam, 1965).

—— *Bavianen en slijkgeuzen: Kerk en kerkvolk ten tijde van Maurits en Oldenbarnevelt* (Assen, 1974).

—— 'Staat van oorlog en generale petitie in de jonge Republiek', *Bijdragen en Mededelingen betreffende de Geschiedenis der Nederlanden*, 91 (1976), 44–55.

—— 'De raadpensionaris Jacob Cats', *Tijdschrift voor Geschiedenis*, 92 (1979), 149–61.

—— *Het kopergeld van de gouden eeuw*, 4 vols. (Assen, 1978–80); trans., *Plain Lives in a Golden Age* (Cambridge 1991).

DILLEN, J. G. VAN, 'De West-Indische Compagnie, het Calvinisme en de politiek', *Tijdschrift voor Geschiedenis*, 74 (1961), 145–71.

DIJK, H. VAN and ROORDA, D. J., 'Sociale mobiliteit onder regenten van de Republiek', *Tijdschrift voor Geschiedenis*, 84 (1971), 306–29.

—— —— 'Het patriciaat van Zierikzee tijdens de Republiek', *Archief. Mededelingen van het Koninklijk Zeeuwsch Genootschap der Wetenschappen* (1979), 1–126.

DUKE, A. C., 'The Ambivalent Face of Calvinism in the Netherlands 1561–1618', in M. Prestwich (ed.), *International Calvinism 1541–1715* (Oxford, 1985).

ELIAS, J. E., *De vroedschap van Amsterdam*, 2 vols. (Haarlem, 1903–5).

ENGELBRECHT, E. A., *De vroedschap van Rotterdam, 1572–1795* (Rotterdam, 1973).

ENNO VAN GELDER, H. A. *De levensbeschouwing van Cornelis Pietersz. Hooft* (Amsterdam, 1918).

—— *Vrijheid en onvrijheid in de Republiek* (Haarlem, 1947).

—— *Getemperde vrijheid* (Groningen, 1972).

EVENHUIS, R. B., *Ook dat was Amsterdam*, 3 vols. (Amsterdam, 1965–71).

EYSINGA, W. J. M. VAN, *De wording van het Twaalfjarig Bestand van 9 april 1609* (Amsterdam, 1959).

FABER, J. A., 'De oligarchisering van Friesland in de tweede helft van de zeventiende eeuw', *Afdeling Agrarische Geschiedenis Bijdragen*, 15 (1970), 39–65.

—— *Drie eeuwen Friesland: Economische en sociale ontwikkelingen van 1500 tot 1800*, 2 vols. (Wageningen, 1972).

—— *et al.*, 'Population Changes and Economic Development in the Netherlands', *Afdeling Agrarische Geschiedenis Bijdragen*, 12 (1965), 47–113.

FEENSTRA, H., *De bloeitijd en het verval van de Ommelandse adel, 1600–1800* (Groningen, 1981).

FOCKEMA ANDREAE, S. J., 'Het Rotterdamse oproer van 1690', *Rotterdams Jaarboekje* 1949: 202–22.

—— *De Nederlandse staat onder de Republiek* (Amsterdam, 1961).

FOUW, A. DE, *Onbekende raadpensionarissen* (The Hague, 1946).

FRANKEN, M. A. M., *Coenraad van Beuningens politieke en diplomatieke aktiviteiten in de jaren 1667–84* (Groningen, 1966).

FRUIN, R., *Tien jaren uit den Tachtigjarigen oorlog, 1588–1598* (Amsterdam, 1861).

—— *Geschiedenis der staatsinstellingen in Nederland*, ed. H. T. Colenbrander (The Hague, 1901).

—— 'Het proces van Buat', in *Verspreide Geschriften* (The Hague, 1901), iv. 261–304.

—— 'Bijdrage tot de geschiedenis van het burgemeesterschap van Amsterdam tijdens de Republiek', in *Verspreide Geschriften* (The Hague, 1901), iv. 305–37.

—— and JAPIKSE, N. , 'De Dordtsche regeringsoligarchie', *Bijdragen voor Vaderlandsche Geschiedenis en Oudheidkunde*, vi (1924).

FULBROOK, M., *Piety and Politics: Religion and the Rise of Absolutism in England, Württemberg and Prussia* (Cambridge, 1983).

GAASTRA, F., *Bewind en beleid bij de VOC 1672-1702* (Zutphen, 1989).

GABRIELS, A. J. C. M., 'De Edel Mogende Heren Gecommitteerde Raden van de Staaten van Holland en Westvriesland, 1747–1795: Aspecten van een buitencommissie op gewestelijke niveau', *Tijdschrift voor Geschiedenis*, 94 (1981), 527–64.

GELDEREN, M. VAN, *Op zoek naar de Republiek: Politiek denken tijdens de Nederlandse Opstand (1555–1590)* (Hilversum, 1991).

GERLACH, H., *Het proces tegen Oldenbarnevelt en de 'Maximen in den Staat'* (Haarlem, 1965).

GEYL, P., *Oranje en Stuart 1641–1672* (Utrecht, 1939); transl. *Orange and Stuart* (New York, 1969).

—— *Het stadhouderschap in de partij-literatuur onder De Witt* (The Hague, 1947).

GEYL, P., *Democratische tendenties in 1672* (The Hague, 1950).

—— 'Historische appreciaties van het zeventiende eeuwse Hollands regentenregiem', in *Studies en strijdschriften* (Groningen, 1958), 180–200.

—— 'Aitzema de kroniekschrijver en nieuwsleverancier', in *Figuren en Problemen*, i (Amsterdam and Antwerp, 1964), 38–45.

GONNET, C. J. (ed.), *Briefwisseling tusschen de gebroeders van der Goes 1659–1673*, 2 vols. (Amsterdam, 1899).

GOODISON, R. R., 'England and the Orangist Party 1665–72', *Bulletin of the Institute of Historical Research*, 13 (1936), 173–6.

GRASWINCKEL, D. P. M., *Graswinckel: Geschiedenis van een Delfts brouwers- en regentengeslacht* (The Hague, 1956).

GRAYSON, J. C., 'The Civic Militia in the County of Holland, 1560–81: Politics and Public Order in the Dutch Revolt', *Bijdragen en Mededelingen betreffende de Geschiedenis der Nederlanden*, 95 (1980), 35–63.

GREVER, J. H., 'Committees and Deputations in the Assemblies of the Dutch Republic 1660–68', *Parliaments, Estates and Representation*, 1 (1981), 13–33.

—— 'The Structure of Decision-Making in the States-General of the Dutch Republic 1660–68', *Parliaments, Estates and Representation*, 2 (1982), 125–53.

—— 'The States of Friesland: Politics and Society during the 1660s', *Parliaments, Estates and Representation*, 9 (1989), 1–25.

GROENHUIS, G., *De predikanten: De sociale positie van de gereformeerde predikanten in de Republiek der Verenigde Nederlanden voor ± 1700* (Groningen, 1977).

GROENVELD, S., *De prins voor Amsterdam* (Bussum, 1967).

—— 'Pieter Cornelisz Hooft en de geschiedenis van zijn eigen tijd', *Bijdragen en Mededelingen betreffende de Geschiedenis der Nederlanden*, 93 (1978), 43–68.

—— *Verlopend getij: De Nederlandse Republiek en de Engelse Burgeroorlog 1640–1646* (Dieren, 1984).

—— 'The Mecca of Authors? States Assemblies and Censorship in the Seventeenth-Century Dutch Republic', in A. C. Duke and C. A. Tamse (eds.), *Too Mighty to be Free* (Zutphen, 1987), 63–86.

—— 'Willem II en de Stuarts', *Bijdragen en Mededelingen betreffende de Geschiedenis der Nederlanden*, 103 (1988), 157–81.

—— 'Holland, das Haus Oranien und die ander nordniederländischen Provinzen in 17. Jahrhundert: Neue Wege zur Faktionsforschung', *Rheinische Vierteljahrsblätter*, 53 (1989), 92–116.

—— *Evidente factiën in den staet: Sociaal-politieke verhoudingen in de 17e-eeuwse Republiek der Vereenigde Nederlanden* (Hilversum, 1990).

—— '"J'équippe une flotte très considerable": The Dutch side of the

Glorious Revolution', in R. A. Beddard (ed.), *The Revolutions of 1688* (Oxford, 1991).

—— and LEEUWENBERG, H. L. PH., *De bruid in de schuit: De consolidatie van de Republiek 1609–1650* (Zutphen, 1985).

—— —— (eds.), *De Unie van Utrecht* (The Hague, 1979).

GUIBAL, C. J., *Democratie en oligarchie in Friesland tijdens de Republiek* (Groningen, 1934).

GIJSWIJT-HOFSTRA, M. and FRIJHOFF, W. (eds.), *Nederland betoverd: Toverij en hekserij van de veertiende tot in de twintigste eeuw* (Amsterdam, 1987).

HAAK, S. P., 'De wording van het conflict tusschen Maurits en Oldenbarnevelt', *Bijdragen voor de Geschiedenis en Oudheidkunde*, 6 (1919) and 10 (1923).

HAITSMA MULIER, E. O. G., *The Myth of Venice and Dutch Republican Thought* (Assen, 1980).

—— 'Willem van Oranje in de historiografie van de zeventiende eeuw', in Haitsma Mulier and Janssen, *Willem van Oranje*, 32–62.

—— 'Grotius, Hooft and the Writing of History in the Dutch Republic', in A. C. Duke and C. A. Tamse (eds.), *Clio's Mirror* (Zutphen, 1985).

—— 'The Language of Seventeenth Century Republicanism in the United Provinces: Dutch or European', in A. Pagden (ed.), *The Languages of Political Theory in Early Modern Europe* (Cambridge, 1987).

—— and JANSSEN, A. E. M., *Willem van Oranje in de historie 1584–1984* (Utrecht, 1984).

HAKS, D., *Huwelijk en gezin in Holland in de 17de en 18de eeuw* (Assen, 1982).

HARLINE, C. E., *Pamphlets, Printing and Political Culture in the Early Dutch Republic* (Dordrecht, 1987).

HART, M. 'T, 'Cities and Statemaking in the Dutch Republic 1580–1680', *Theory and Society*, 18 (1989), 663–87.

HAZEWINKEL, H. C., *Geschiedenis van Rotterdam* (Rotterdam, 1940).

HEIJKOOP, H. L., 'Het turfoproer aan de Zaan in 1678', *Economisch- en Sociaal-Historisch Jaarboek*, 42 (1979), 1–14.

HEININGEN, H. VAN, *Tussen Maas en Waal* (Zutphen, 1972).

HERINGA, J., *De eer en hoogheid van de Staat* (Groningen, 1961).

HOFMAN, H. A., *Constantijn Huygens (1596–1687)* (Utrecht, 1983).

HOLMES, G., *British Politics in the Age of Anne* (London, 1967).

HURSTFIELD, J., *Freedom, Corruption and Government in Elizabethan England* (London, 1973).

ISRAEL, J. I., 'The Holland Towns and the Dutch–Spanish Conflict, 1621–48', *Bijdragen en Mededelingen betreffende de Geschiedenis der Nederlanden*, 94 (1979), 41–9.

ISRAEL, J. I., 'The States General and the Strategic Regulation of the Dutch River Trade, 1621–36', *Bijdragen en Mededelingen betreffende de Geschiedenis der Nederlanden*, 95 (1980), 461–91.

—— *The Dutch Republic and the Hispanic World 1606–1661* (Oxford, 1982).

—— 'Frederick Henry and the Dutch Political Factions, 1625–1642', *English Historical Review*, 98 (1983), 1–27.

—— *Dutch Primacy in World Trade 1585–1740* (Oxford, 1989).

JAPIKSE, N., (ed.), *Notulen gehouden ter Staten-vergadering van Holland (1671–1675) door Cornelis Hop and Nicolaas Vivien* (Amsterdam, 1903).

—— *Johan de Witt* (Amsterdam, 1915).

—— *Prins Willem III: de stadhouder-koning*, 2 vols. (Amsterdam, 1930–3).

JONG, J. J. DE, *Met goed fatsoen: De elite in een Hollandse stad, Gouda 1700–1780* (Dieren, 1985).

—— *Een deftig bestaan: Het dagelijks leven van regenten in de 17de en 18de eeuw* (Utrecht and Antwerp, 1987).

JONGSTE, J. A. F. DE, *Onrust aan het Spaarne: Haarlem in de jaren 1747–1751* (Dieren, 1984).

KALMA, J. J., SPAHR VAN DER HOEK, J. J., and VRIES, K. DE (eds.), *Geschiedenis van Friesland* (Drachten, 1968).

KERNKAMP, G. W. (ed.), 'Twee memoriën van Mr. Gerrit Schaep Pietersz. over de regering van Amsterdam', *Bijdragen en Mededelingen van het Historisch Genootschap*, 16 (1895), 333–71.

—— *Prins Willem II* (Amsterdam, 1943).

KERNKAMP, J. H., 'Brieven uit de correspondentie van Pieter de la Court en zijn verwanten (1661–1666)', *Bijdragen en Mededelingen van het Historisch Genootschap*, 70 (1956), 82–165.

—— 'Brieven uit de correspondentie van Pieter de la Court en zijn verwanten (1667–1683)', *Bijdragen en Mededelingen van het Historisch Genootschap*, 72 (1958), 3–195.

KLEIN, P. W., 'De heffing van de 100e en 200e penning van het vermogen te Gouda, 1599–1722', *Economisch-Historisch Jaarboek*, 31 (1967), 41–62.

KLOEK, E., *Wie hij zij, man of wijf: Vrouwengeschiedenis en de vroegmoderne tijd* (Hilversum, 1990).

KLUIVER, J. H., 'Zeeuwse reacties op de Acte van Seclusie', *Bijdragen en Mededelingen betreffende de Geschiedenis der Nederlanden*, 91 (1976), 406–28.

KNEVEL, P., 'Onrust onder de schutters: De politieke invloed van de Hollandse schutterijen in de eerste helft van de zeventiende eeuw', *Holland*, 20 (1988), 158–74.

KOOPMANS, J. W., *De Staten van Holland en de Opstand* (The Hague, 1990).

KOOIJMANS, L., *Onder regenten: De elite in een Hollandse stad, Hoorn 1700–1780* (Dieren, 1985).

KOSSMANN, E. H., *Politieke theorie in het zeventiende-eeuwse Nederland* (Amsterdam, 1960).

—— *Politieke theorie en geschiedenis* (Amsterdam, 1987).

KRÄMER, F. J. L. (ed.), *Lettres de Pierre de Groot à Abraham de Wicquefort* (The Hague, 1894).

KURTZ, G. H., *Willem III en Amsterdam* (Utrecht, 1928).

—— *Haarlem in het rampjaar 1672* (Haarlem, 1946).

LAMET, S. A., 'The Vroedschap of Leiden 1550–1600: The Impact of Tradition and Change on the Governing Elite of a Dutch City', *Sixteenth Century Journal*, 12 (1981), 15–42.

LANGE, P. W. DE , 'De ontwikkeling van een oligarchische regeringsvorm in een Westfriese stad: Medemblik 1289–1699', *Hollandse Studiën*, 3 (1972), 119–46.

LEEUWEN, M. VAN, *Het leven van Pieter de Groot* (Utrecht, 1917).

LEFÈVRE-PONTALIS, A., *Vingt années de république parlementaire au dix-septième siècle: Jean de Witt, grand-pensionnaire de Hollande*, 2 vols. (Paris, 1884).

MCSHEA, R. J., *The Political Philosophy of Spinoza* (New York and London, 1968)

MEES AZN., G., *Het Rotterdamsche oproer van 1690* (Amsterdam, 1869).

MELLES, J., *Joost van den Vondel* (Utrecht, 1957).

—— *Joachim Oudaan* (Utrecht, 1958).

—— *Ministers aan de Maas: Geschiedenis van de Rotterdamse pensionaris-sen met een inleiding over het stedelijk pensionariaat 1508–1795* (Rotterdam and The Hague, 1962).

MENTINK, G. J. and WOUDE, A. M. VAN DER, *De demografische ontwikkeling te Rotterdam en Cool in de 17e en 18e eeuw* (Rotterdam, 1965).

MERENS, A., *De geschiedenis van een Westfries regentengeslacht, het geslacht Merens* (The Hague, 1957).

MOQUETTE, H. C. H., 'Een miniatuur oorlog in de 17e eeuw', *Rotterdams Jaarboekje* 1927.

MOUT, M. E. H. N., 'Van arm vaderland tot eendrachtige republiek: De rol van politieke theorieën in de Nederlandse Opstand', *Bijdragen en Mededelingen betreffende de Geschiedenis der Nederlanden*, 101 (1986), 345–65.

MUINCK, B. E. DE, *Een regentenhuishouding omstreeks 1700: Gegevens uit de privé-boekhouding van mr. Cornelis de Jonge van Ellemeet, Ontvanger-Generaal der Verenigde Nederlanden (1646–1721)* (The Hague, 1965).

MULLER, P. L., *De Unie van Utrecht (1579)* (Utrecht, 1878).

NABER, J. C., *De staatkunde van Johan de Witt* (Utrecht, 1882).

—— *Calvinist of Libertijnsch?* (Utrecht, 1884).

NAMIER, L. B., *The Structure of Politics at the Accession of George III* (London, 1929).

—— *England in the Age of the American Revolution* (London, 1930).

NIEROP, H. F. K. VAN, *Van ridders tot regenten: De Hollandse adel in de zestiende en de eerste helft van de zeventiende eeuw* (Dieren, 1984).

NOBBS, D., *Theocracy and Toleration: A Study of the Disputes in Dutch Calvinism from 1600–1650* (Cambridge, 1938).

NOORDEGRAAF, L. and VALK, G., *De Gave Gods: De pest in Holland vanaf de late middeleeuwen* (Bergen, NH, 1988).

NUSTELING, H., *Welvaart en werkgelegenheid in Amsterdam 1540–1860* (Amsterdam and Dieren, 1985).

NIJENHUIS, W., 'Varianten binnen het Nederlands calvinisme in de 16e eeuw', *Tijdschrift voor Geschiedenis*, 89 (1976), 358–72.

PATER, J. C. H. DE, *Maurits en Oldenbarnevelt in den strijd om het Twaalfjarige Bestand* (Amsterdam, 1940).

PLAAT, G. N. VAN DER, 'Lieuwe van Aitzema's kijk op het stadhouderschap in de Republiek', *Bijdragen en Mededelingen betreffende de Geschiedenis der Nederlanden*, 103 (1988), 341–72.

POELGEEST, L., 'De raadsheren in de Hoge Raad van Holland, Zeeland en West-Friesland in de achttiende eeuw', *Bijdragen en Mededelingen betreffende de Geschiedenis der Nederlanden*, 103 (1988), 20–51.

POELHEKKE, J., *De vrede van Munster* (The Hague, 1948).

—— *'t Uytgaen van den Treves* (Groningen, 1960).

—— *Geen blijder maer in tachtig jaer: Verspreide studiën over de crisis-periode 1648–1651* (Zutphen, 1973).

—— *Het verraad van de pistoletten?* (Amsterdam and London, 1975).

—— *Frederik Hendrik, Prins van Oranje* (Zutphen, 1978).

PORTA, A., *Joan en Gerrit Corver: De politieke macht van Amsterdam 1702–1748* (Assen and Amsterdam, 1975).

PRAK, M., *Gezeten burgers: De elite in een Hollandse stad, Leiden 1700–1780* (Dieren, 1985).

—— 'Civil Disturbances and Urban Middle Class in the Dutch Republic', *Tijdschrift voor Sociale Geschiedenis*, 15 (1989), 165–73.

PRICE, J. L., 'The Rotterdam Patriciate, 1650–1672', Ph.D. thesis (University of London, 1969).

—— 'William III, England and the Balance of Power in Europe', *Groniek*, 101 (1988), 67–78.

REINTGES, TH., *Ursprung und Wesen der spätmittelalterlichen Schützengilden* (Bonn, 1963).

ROLDANUS, C. W., *Coenraad van Beuningen: Staatsman en libertijn* (The Hague, 1931).

—— 'Adriaen Paets, een republikein uit de nadagen', *Tijdschrift voor Geschiedenis*, 50 (1935), 134–66.

—— *Zeventiende-eeuwse geestesbloei* (Utrecht and Antwerp, 1961).

ROODENBURG, H., '"Een soorte van duivelsche afgoderije": De bestrijding van toverij door de gereformeerde kerkeraad te Amsterdam, 1580–1700', in Gijswijt-Hofstra and Frijhoff (eds.), *Nederland betoverd*.

ROORDA, D. J., *Partij en factie* (Groningen, 1961).

—— 'Een zwakke stee in de Hollandse regentenaristocratie: De Hoornse vroedschap in opspraak, 1670–5', *Bijdragen voor de Geschiedenis der Nederlanden*, 16 (1961), 89–116.

—— *Het rampjaar* (Bussum, 1971).

—— *Een eigenaardige bureaucratie* (Leiden, 1972).

—— 'Het onderzoek naar het stedelijk patriciaat in Nederland', in W. W. Mijnhardt (ed.), *Kantelend geschiedbeeld* (Utrecht and Antwerp, 1983), 118–42.

—— *Rond prins en patriciaat* (Weesp, 1984).

ROWEN, H. H., *The Ambassador Prepares for War* (The Hague, 1957).

—— 'The Revolution that Wasn't': The Coup d'Etat of 1650 in Holland', *European Studies Review*, 4 (1974), 99–117.

—— *John de Witt, Grand Pensionary of Holland, 1625–1672* (Princeton, NJ, 1978).

—— *John de Witt: Statesman of the 'True Freedom'* (Cambridge, 1986).

—— *The Princes of Orange: The Stadholders in the Dutch Republic* (Cambridge, 1988).

—— and LOSSKY, A.(eds.), *Political Ideas and Institutions in the Dutch Republic* (Los Angeles, 1985).

RIJPPERDA WIERDSMA, J. V., *Politie en justitie: een studie over Hollandsche staatsbouw tijdens de Republiek* (Zwolle, 1937).

SCHAMA, S., *The Embarrassment of Riches* (New York, 1987).

SCHMIDT, C., *Om de eer van de familie: Het geslacht Teding van Berkhout 1500–1950* (Amsterdam, 1986).

SCHÖFFER, I., 'La Stratification sociale de la République des Provinces Unies au XVIIe siècle', in R. Mousnier (ed.), *Problèmes de stratification sociales* (Paris, 1968).

—— 'The Batavian Myth during the Sixteenth and Seventeenth Centuries', in J. S. Bromley and E. H. Kossmann (eds.), *Britain and the Netherlands*, v (The Hague, 1975), 78–101.

SCHULTE VAN KESSEL, E., *Geest en vlees in godsdienst en wetenschap* (The Hague, 1980).

SCHUTTE, G. J., *Een Hollandse dorpssamenleving in de late achttiende eeuw: De banne Graft 1770–1810* (Franeker, 1989).

SHARLIN, A., 'Natural Decrease in Early Modern Cities: A Reconsideration', *Past and Present*, 79 (1978), 126–38.

SHRIVER, F., 'Orthodoxy and Diplomacy: James I and the Vorstius Affair', *English Historical Review*, 85 (1970), 449–74.

Sickesz, C. J., *De schutterijen in Nederland* (Utrecht, 1864).

Slee, J. C. van, *De Rijnsburger collegianten* (Haarlem, 1895).

Slicher van Bath, B. H., *Samenleving onder spanning* (Assen, 1957).

Smit, C. G. (ed.), *Notulen gehouden ter vergadering der Staten van Holland in 1670 door Hans Bontemantel* (Utrecht, 1937).

—— 'De introductie van den Prins van Oranje in de Raad van State, 1670', *Historia*, 8 (1942), 286–93.

Smit, J., *De grootmeester van woord- en snarenspel: Het leven van Constantijn Huygens* (The Hague, 1980).

Smit, J. G. (ed.), 'Prins Maurits en de goede zaak: Brieven van Maurits uit de jaren 1617–1619', in *Nederlandsche Historische Bronnen*, 1 (The Hague, 1979), 43–173.

Smit, J. W., *Fruin en de partijen tijdens de Republiek* (Groningen, 1958).

Spaans, J., *Haarlem na de Reformatie: Stedelijke cultuur en kerkelijk leven, 1577–1620* (The Hague, 1989).

Spierenburg, P., *Elites and Etiquette: Mentality and Social Structure in the Early Modern Northern Netherlands* (Rotterdam, 1981).

Stone, L. and Fawtier Stone, J. C., *An Open Elite? England 1540–1880* (Oxford, 1984).

Temple, Sir W., *Observations upon the United Provinces of the Netherlands*, ed. G. N. Clark (Cambridge, 1932).

Tex, J. den, 'Le Procès d'Oldenbarnevelt (1618–1619): fut-il un meurtre judiciaire?', *Tijdschrift voor Rechtgeschiedenis*, 22 (1954), 137–68.

—— *Oldenbarnevelt*, 5 vols. (Haarlem and Groningen, 1960–72).

—— 'Oldenbarnevelts geschil met de hoven van justitie', *Bijdragen en Mededelingen betreffende de Geschiedenis der Nederlanden*, 84 (1969), 5–23.

—— 'Maurits en Oldenbarnevelt vóór en na Nieuwpoort', *Bijdragen en Mededelingen betreffende de Geschiedenis der Nederlanden*, 85 (1970), 63–72.

Tracy, J. D., *A Financial Revolution in the Habsburg Netherlands: 'Renten' and 'Renteniers' in the County of Holland, 1515–1566* (Berkeley, Calif., 1985).

—— *Holland under Habsburg Rule, 1506–1566: The Formation of a Body Politic* (Berkeley, Calif., 1990).

Tijn, Th. van, 'Pieter de la Court: Zijn leven en economische denkbeelden', *Tijdschrift voor Geschiedenis*, 59 (1956), 304–70.

Ubachs, P. J. H., *Twee heren, Twee Confessies: De verhouding van Staat en Kerk te Maastricht, 1632–1673* (Assen, 1975).

Uit den Bogaard, M. Th., *De Gereformeerde en Oranje tijdens het eerste stadhouderloze tijdperk* (Groningen, 1954).

Unger, J. H. W., *De regeering van Rotterdam 1328–1892* (Rotterdam, 1892).

VANDENBOSSCHE, H., *Adriaen Koerbagh and Spinoza* (Leiden, 1978).

VET, J. J. V. M. DE, *Pieter Rabus (1660–1702)* (Amsterdam, 1980).

VIJLBRIEF, I., *Van anti-aristocratie tot democratie: Een bijdrage tot de politieke en sociale geschiedenis der stad Utrecht* (Amsterdam, 1950).

VOORST VAN BEEST, C. W. VAN, *De Katholieke armenzorg te Rotterdam in de 17e en 18e eeuw* (The Hague, n.d.).

VRANKRIJKER, A. C. J. DE, *De staatsleer van Hugo de Groot en zijn Nederlandsche tijdgenooten* (Nijmegen, 1937).

VRIES, J. DE, *The Dutch Rural Economy in the Golden Age 1500–1700* (New Haven, Conn., 1974).

—— *Barges and Capitalism: Passenger Transportation in the Dutch Economy (1632–1839)* (Wageningen, 1978).

[VROESEN, W.], *Waaragtig verhaal van de muiterij binnen de stad Rotterdam* ... (n.p., 1785).

WAARDT, H. DE, 'Vervolging of verweer: Mogelijke procedures na een beschuldiging van toverij in het gewest Holland voor het jaar 1800', in Gijswijt-Hofstra and Frijhoff (eds.), *Nederland betoverd.*

WAGENAAR, J., *Vaderlandsche Historie*, 21 vols. (1st edn. Amsterdam, 1749–59; Amsterdam, 1790–6).

—— *Amsterdam in zijne opkomst, aanwas, geschiedenissen, voorregten, koophandel, gebouwen, kerkenstaat, schoolen, schutterije, gilden en regeeringe*, 4 vols. (Amsterdam, 1760–88).

WANSINK, H., *Politieke wetenschappen aan de Leidse Universiteit, 1575–±1650* (Utrecht, 1975).

WATERBOLK, E. H. (ed.), *Proeven van Lieuwe van Aitzema 1600–1669* (Leeuwarden, 1970).

WERTHEIM, W. F. and WERTHEIM-GIJSE WEENINK, A. H., *Burgers in verzet tegen regentenheerschappij: Onrust in Sticht en Oversticht (1703–1706)* (Amsterdam, 1976).

WERTHEIM-GIJSE WEENINK, A. H., *Democratische bewegingen in Gelderland 1672–1795* (Amsterdam, 1973).

WICQUEFORT, A. DE, *Histoire des Provinces-Unies, depuis le parfait établissement de cet état par la paix de Munster*, 4 vols. (Amsterdam, 1861–74).

WIJNNE, J. A., *De geschillen over de afdanking van 't krijgsvolk in de Vereenigde Nederlanden in de jaren 1649 en 1650* (Utrecht, 1885).

WILLEMSEN, R., *Enkhuizen tijdens de Republiek* (Hilversum, 1988).

WITT, J. DE, *Brieven van De Witt*, ed. G. W. Kernkamp and N. Japikse, 4 vols. (Amsterdam, 1906–13).

—— *Brieven aan Johan de Witt*, ed. N. Japikse, 2 vols. (Amsterdam, 1919–22).

WITTE VAN CITTERS, J. DE, *Contracten van correspondentie* (The Hague, 1873).

WOLTJER, J. J., 'Dutch Privileges, Real and Imaginary', in J. S. Bromley and E. H. Kossmann (eds.), *Britain and the Netherlands*, v (The Hague, 1975), 19–35.

WOUDE, A. M. VAN DER, *Het Noorderkwartier*, 3 vols. (Wageningen, 1972).

—— FABER, J. A. and ROESSINGH, H. K., 'Numerieke aspecten van de protestantisering in Noord-Nederland tussen 1656 en 1726', *Afdeling Agrarische Geschiedenis Bijdragen*, 13 (1965), 149–80.

ZUMTHOR, P., *La Vie quotidienne en Hollande au temps de Rembrandt* (Paris, 1959).

INDEX

Vecht, river 55
Veere 226, 255
veertigraad 20
Visch family 44
Vliet 181
Vlissingen 226, 255
VOC (East India Company) 31, 69, 76
Voet, Jacob (Voetius) 197
voetians 197
Vondel, Joost van den 105, 251
Vries, Jan de 224
vroedschap 8, 20, 21, 22, 23, 24, 26, 27,
    28, 30, 31, 32, 33, 34, 37, 40, 43,
    44, 46, 48, 51, 52, 53, 54, 56, 62,
    69, 73, 75, 86, 102, 133, 140, 175,
    252
Vroesen, Willebord 95 n. 11

waardgelders 146, 163, 272
Walloon church 71
waterschappen 150
weesmeesters 24
West India Company 176, 276
Westergo 227
wetsverzettingen 39, 40, 42, 43, 44, 52,
    59, 64, 103, 116, 118, 120, 121, 135,
    136, 138, 143, 157, 159, 160, 171,
    240, 244, 252, 257, 284
Willem Frederik, stadhouder of
    Friesland 168
Willem I, prince of Orange 7, 9, 10,
    114, 115, 135, 138, 160, 186, 216,
    238, 247, 248, 249
Willem II, prince of Orange 41, 114,
    142, 165, 166, 168, 170, 171, 174,
    187, 212, 215, 241, 242, 250 n. 2,
    252, 257, 289, 291
    attempted coup in 1650: 39, 60 n. 5,
    117–18, 137, 145, 147, 159, 163–4,
    173, 213, 237–8, 253–4

and land provinces 280–1, 287
Willem III, prince of Orange 4, 103,
    124, 145, 164, 166, 168, 171, 231,
    233, 250 n. 4, 252, 289
    foreign policy 158–9, 174, 175, 241,
    245, 291 n. 11
    and land provinces 212, 254, 280–1
    power 25, 29, 43, 51, 61, 102, 138,
    141–2, 144, 240, 253, 254, 256,
    257–8, 281
    prestige 119, 251
    and religion 187, 188, 198, 199
Willem IV, prince of Orange 147, 256
Willem Lodewijk, stadhouder of
    Friesland etc. 255
witchcraft prosecutions 201, 202
Witt, Cornelis de 143, 167
Witt, Johan de 30, 42, 48, 50, 60, 66,
    67, 97, 129, 143, 167, 244
Woerden 123
women 36, 104–8
Württemberg 264

Zaanstreek 17
Zeeland 2, 13, 14, 31, 58, 63, 112, 114,
    118, 149, 151, 197, 202, 211, 212,
    213, 216, 218, 222, 223, 226, 227,
    228, 229, 232, 235, 236, 244, 247,
    253, 255, 259, 262, 280
Zevenwolden 227
Zijdewind 88
Zutphen 224
Zuylen van Nievelt, Jacob van 29, 101,
    102, 142, 144
Zwolle 226

Compiled with the help of Kevin Hall